Tuesday Tales

Rina Ríos

Royal Rivers
Press

These stories are for entertainment purposes.
Any advice or recipes contained herein
will be followed at the reader's own risk.
This book is sold with the understanding that the author
is not engaged to render any kind of professional advice.

Copyright © 2023 Rina Ríos.

ISBN 979-8-9887821-9-3 (Paperback)
ISBN 979-8-9887821-0-0 (Hardcover)
ISBN 979-8-9887821-1-7 (Ebook)

Library of Congress Control Number:
2023913902

Brothers lyrics printed with permission of the
Carl M. Steubing Memorial Music Fund, Inc.
Music available for purchase at www.ArrangeMe.com.

This book is dedicated to my grandparents,
Felix Ríos and Alicia Palacio,
to those who came before them, and to those who
have come since, My Family.

Introduction

3 November, 2014

Today is my mother's 73rd birthday. I celebrate her every day. She is a remarkable woman and it is truly a gift for us all that she lives downstairs and my children are able to see her daily.

This morning, among congratulatory calls, she got the news that my grandfather had just died. For years, I said that my grandfather was in better shape than I was. That was probably true until recently. At 98, he took a quick turn and left us before many of us even saw him sick.

My grandfather was the first of the family singers. He always had a good story and lots of wit. He seemed to be a historian when he was just talking about his life. In his honor, I'm going to try to post a little story every Tuesday.

In 2014, I was still posting updates on FaceBook, usually about my children. After making the above announcement, I went on to post a short story every Tuesday, but for five, through August of 2018.

I've removed the dates, but you'll notice that my stories are often about the holidays we were celebrating and the things we were doing. I also sometimes refer to the original platform on which my Tuesday Tales appeared. I know you will understand, dear reader.

I wrote my Tales hurriedly and sloppily and was often surprised by the positive reactions and the encouragement to publish. Thank you. This collection is for all of you original readers, and hopefully for new ones.

Putting this book together, brought me much joy through both tears and laughter. I'm so happy you made me do it. It turns out, though, that I still have many more tales to tell...

My grandfather worked as an upholsterer for many years after arriving in NYC. The workshop was technically in another town from where he lived, though not too far away. He took the bus there and back every day. He was a good upholsterer, likely because creativity is often multiply-manifested within individuals who possess it, and he was a very good employee. In 1996, he was 80 and still working. That year, there was a blizzard in New York.

I remember waking up the morning after the clouds had been emptied of their billowy precipitation. The sky was clear and the sun, reflecting off of the snow-covered everything, blinded anyone who dared to go out. I had, in fact, been out with my mother and a friend, wading through the white gusts the night before, but now it was morning and I awoke in balmy heat, under downy covers that were tucked in all around my body and covered my face. I was surprised to find the comforter tucked under my head because I hadn't covered my face in sleep for many years. It was cozy, but stifling, so I uncovered myself and discovered my nocturnal genius. The room was COLD outside of the covers. There was no heat and the windows were framed with ice. That day, my mother and I hosted several neighbors who envisioned us as people who could eradicate the situation by complaining to the landlord, and perhaps just as friendly people who might be able to offer warmth of one kind or another. I think we did a little bit of the latter.

Before anyone knocked on our door, my mother got the great idea to call my grandfather to check in on him. She was relieved when he answered the phone. She told him how happy she was that he hadn't followed a misguided notion and dared to go outside. He responded with silence. "Felix Colina?" She retorted. Some of my family members quirkily call him by his stage name. While there are others in the family with his first name (seven at the time of this writing) I don't think they do it to distinguish him from them. I mean, he was the original Felix and this is how they address him, so it is a mystery to me. Well, my mother said his name, maybe like a parent scolding a child, maybe acknowledging her bewilderment as she figured things out.

It so happened that he had indeed left his house to go to work that day. He had left his warm apartment all bundled up and had trekked through the waist-deep snow to the bus stop. He waited for the bus and, since New York City was basically shut down that day, no bus arrived, so he had started walking.

He got a ride for part of the trip because he was likely the only person stumbling through the snow by foot. It is perfectly fine to accept rides from strangers in these instances, despite the decades-late protestations of my friend's husband when he heard that that's just what we had done the night before. My grandfather arrived at his workplace to find it closed, of course. The owners were home, warm and SAFE, along with most everyone else for miles and miles. Behind the door of the shop, couch frames would remain bare and chairs uncushioned for at least a couple of days more. By the time my mother had called him, early that morning, my grandfather had already trekked to his job and back home.

✝✝✝✝✝✝

My parents met in Panama and I narrowly escaped being born there. When I was eleven, I spent a large part of the summer visiting my cousins in my almost homeland. I remember taking a road trip with them one day and stopping to take photos by a bridge. Back then, I looked good in photos, so it seemed like a fine idea, although to me there was nothing particularly noteworthy about the location. Clearly, though, I took note of it back then and even now, literally. Once home, I told my mother about this pit stop. She laughed and said that we had stopped that day because that bridge was the only real bridge in the country. It was supposed to be a big deal.

When I was three, my mother, sister and I went to Panamá to bring my grandmother back with us to live in New York. I have a few vivid memories of that trip, but I was very young so this story is one I only recall hearing about, even though I was there. I wish I had a real picture of it in my mind. I wish I could see my grandmother's childlike expression as she looked out of the airplane window as it approached its destination.

It was nighttime and my grandmother had never been to New York City. She looked in awe as her brain tried to attach meaning to what she was seeing. I can imagine the face my grandmother was making as she asked my mother if it was some sort of holiday and if that's why the mountains were decorated with lights. Our plane was in NYC airspace after all. She was looking at our illuminated bridges. We have more than one, more than a few.

‡‡‡‡‡‡‡

After having a delicious and nutritious meal, I would like to post a story about an avocado. About twenty years ago I was dating a man. He was a body-building hunk and very health conscious. He was also a high school teacher with an extensive vocabulary. His sesquipedalian ways were accompanied by the assumption that his listeners needed interpretations of his words and, of course, the requisite lengthy explanations. I imagine that his students found him nice on the eyes and not on the ears. It was true for me most of the time too.

One afternoon, he called me while I was preparing lunch. He was horrified when I told him I was having an avocado with olive oil, balsamic vinegar, salt, and pepper. This was a yummy and perfectly acceptable meal, I thought. He disagreed. A decade later he would probably find himself buying avocados by the bag, but at this point, he wanted to teach me how fatty they were and that I shouldn't have too much and that a whole avocado was definitely too much. I didn't argue with him. I just listened with my mouth full of avocado. It was delicious. That relationship lasted about three months and I still love avocados.

‡‡‡‡‡‡‡

Once upon a time I used to do an exercise class in a studio in Carnegie Hall. That's just where the classes were held. There's a whole tower with offices and rehearsal spaces and such attached to the performance space. Even just on the other side of the curtain on the stage, beyond where the audience sitting in the beautifully ornate house can see, it's pretty ordinary and even kind of dumpy. At this time in my life, I was rarely on the great gilded stage there, but I could regularly be found upstairs in a nondescript studio with up to a dozen other exercisers.

4

Most of us had regular times when we went. It was a small class and people were usually pretty friendly, often sharing conversation before class started, but mostly we didn't know one another well enough to say we were friends. One day, I walked in during a conversation between a woman who was in her fifties and another who was in her twenties. The older woman was telling the younger one how painful "it" was and she sort of grabbed her crotch. It didn't seem to be a private discussion, but I immediately regretted sticking my nose in when the woman told me she was talking about "the first time she had had a Brazilian". I couldn't believe it! First, I had no idea that Brazilian men had such a crotch-pain-inducing reputation. Why had I not heard of this and why now from people with whom I shared very little, yet apparently so much? I was shocked that these two women were talking about it so casually. I had nothing to add to the conversation and just kept listening because, well how could I not listen? It's a good thing we had all gotten there so early. There was enough time before class for me to quietly put things together and figure out that they were talking about a waxing procedure and not a man. The woman had had her first Brazilian. She had hair from her nether regions removed painfully. It's a common term now, but it wasn't back then, ok? We all laughed about it and me. I still do.

‡‡‡‡‡‡‡

One Christmas Eve, a couple of decades ago, my family gathered in my mother's house to celebrate. Christmas Day was always for cleaning up and recovering, but Christmas Eve was our real holiday. That's the day when we would come together to share good food and conversation and the company of several generations. It wasn't about gifts. It was about being together. On this year, aunts and uncles and countless cousins were there and even some family members who weren't actually related because, as my grandmother would say, "What does the tiger care about one more stripe if he has no one to count them."

My grandmother had many business ventures and could bring partners into her schemes easily by selling them a tapestry of "butterfly farts," according to my great-grandmother, in mere moments. During these years, she was, as always, a great entrepreneur, selling fine jewelry. In the living room that evening, while my cousins and I talked to her, we noticed a new cluster of sparkles on her finger. She was wearing a ring I had never seen before. I knew this because I would've remembered it's several large diamonds. I commented on it and we all marveled at its beauty.

My grandmother did not humbly take the attention. She proudly displayed her ring, outstretching her arm and then resting her hand daintily on her clavicle. I wondered to whom she might try to sell it and for how much of a profit, and then she surprised me. She looked at the ring and agreed with us. It was beautiful. Then she said that she only wore it for special occasions. That made sense, of course, especially when she added, "Because I don't want it to turn black!" I guess that wasn't one of her finest pieces.

‡‡‡‡‡‡‡

I am thinking a great deal about my beloved aunt Magaly, the first-born child of my grandparents. She is in South Carolina with her own grandchildren now, but I have many delightful memories of growing up with her as another mother.

She did not escape the familial trend of having five children. Her two daughters are older than I, just a bit. The summer before I turned four, she had twin boys, and on their second birthday, she had another boy. I remember her twin belly protruding impossibly from her body before we knew she was carrying two babies. It was the seventies, so no one found out they were twins until the week they were born, each fully-grown, one weighing 7lbs 8oz and the other 7lbs 12oz. Seeing that she was so accommodating, their brother grew to 9lbs 15oz before he made his way out into the world.

It was the birth of the boys that afforded me special time with my aunt. She was spending time at home and I was not yet school-aged, so I kept her company. We took care of each other. Probably, she was taking more care of me than I of her, but I know I at least gave her the opportunity to laugh sometimes, as evidenced in this tale.

It was a funny episode about which I couldn't get upset. It was Tia Magaly, though, so I wouldn't have wanted to be angry

6

anyway. On this day, in her house in Queens, I was eating soup, while her monster triplets likely napped in the living room under the stippled ceiling. After eating what I deemed to be enough, I told her I was done. Our family didn't have a rule about eating all of our food. Except for that one asparagus incident I should like to forget, I can't remember ever being told I had to finish something off of my plate. My family's food is really good, so the children were all in there with the eating, as I recall. With this soup, though, my aunt sweetly requested that I take only three more spoonfuls. "Tres cucharadas más." That was fine. I didn't have a problem with the soup and it wasn't an unreasonable request. I agreed and my aunt promptly went to the adjacent kitchen and emerged with the humongous-to-my-eyes serving spoon in hand. I was little and the spoon was big, so she helped me eat my three spoonfuls, which was the rest of the soup, of course, while we both laughed.

‡‡‡‡‡‡‡

When the movie *A Beautiful Mind* was in theatres, I went to see it with my mother and our friend. Sometimes I go to a movie without knowing what it's about and this was one of those times. Now I know that it's about Nobel Laureate, John Nash.

Well into the movie, we find the genius seeing patterns and words in newspapers. I could totally relate! I turned to my friend and excitedly said, "I do that too!" How often have I walked down the street memorizing license plate numbers, repeating them over and over in my head? Whenever I look at a digital clock, I make things out of the numbers—they always have hidden meanings. I'm not a mastermind, but this smarty on the big screen in front of me was doing some of the wacky things I do too. Wow! Vindication. The secret codes I see all around might just be hidden for the gifted to discover. Yes, thank you very much.

Did you see the movie, though? Well, let me tell you. A few scenes after my confession to my friend, we learn that he wasn't only prodigious. John Nash, it turns out, suffered from mental illness, including schizophrenia. That thing he was doing with the newspapers—not genius as much as mental instability. I don't go around telling too many people about my special powers since then, so my friends, let's keep it hush hush.

‡‡‡‡‡‡‡

I know that many of you look forward to laughing at my posts on Tuesdays, so I want to warn you that this is not a funny one. I'm not being sarcastic either—I know many of you expect that as well.

Years ago, in one of my incarnations, I was a personal shopper at Macy's in Herald Square. We had an annual client who would have us choose thousands of dollars' worth of gifts and deliver them to a children's hospital where his daughter had spent her last days, years before. This was a challenging assignment since Macy's had closed its toy department, but those of us who worked on this project started way before the holiday season and loved gathering appropriate gifts from different corners of the store. Of course, it was also touching and fulfilling.

The day the gifts were delivered was the best of all. I'll never forget it. We didn't use a mail service or even a courier. A truck brought the gifts to the hospital, but they weren't just delivered to the children by a truck driver or a nurse. The children didn't even get them from their doctors or parents. No. This was a very special production, so while the gifts were en route, my boss and I went up to the eighth floor to pick up Santa Claus himself along with one of his gnomes.

It was a really magical car ride to the hospital. Santa was amazing and witty and all of the wonderful things you would imagine him to be. On the way back to the store, I told him that I wanted to visit him in Santaland with a friend. Christmas was fast approaching and I was planning to see him the following week. I asked him how I could make sure to see him personally as I knew he had helpers who dressed up like him in order to satisfy the demand. He told me not to worry and gave me his special password.

The following week, a couple of days before Christmas, I went up to Santaland with my friend and excitedly told him that he was in for a treat. We were about to see the real Santa if ever there was one. When we got to the elf greeters, after waiting on line, I told them my password. I remember them vividly as they looked at each other and then turned to me and told me that he had just died of a heart attack. I started to cry. I couldn't believe it. Santa Claus was dead. I was crushed then, but as I write this with tears in my eyes, I am grateful that I got to meet him and that we spent a few enchanted hours together.

‡‡‡‡‡‡‡

In honor of the 36 and a half year and a few weeks and some days anniversary of the US premier of the movie *Grease*, I will tell you the tale of how I was almost whisked away by Olivia and John themselves to be a child star on the road with them.

When I was about five, my mother, sister, and I moved out of the apartment where we had lived, at times with up to fourteen family members (It was a really big apartment.), into our own place. My mother had had her own business and was doing very well before coming to New York, but having to start over again was kind of tough, so there we were in our own apartment, with very little furniture. What we did have was a grey, plastic record player—much more important than a couch because the *Frosty the Snowman* LP wasn't going to play year-round all by itself, after all.

When I wasn't listening to *Frosty*, I was listening to *Grease*. "Listening" isn't really the right word, though. I had the whole thing memorized and I also had an unfurnished living room. I would pull my skirt up above my chest so that it was a mini dress and I would sing and dance. I was really good too. I had to be. I was being scouted.

At some point in my life, I learned that when someone is photographed while looking into the camera lens, their eyes appear to move and follow the viewer. At the age of five, though, I hadn't yet learned this. What I had learned, or at least started believing, is that the world is a magical place. At other points in my life, I would be unrealistically optimistic and wonderful things would happen. At five, my magical thinking was a beautiful pastime that kept me hopeful for what my tomorrows could bring.

So there I was, in my makeshift dress on an empty dance floor in front of none other than Olivia Newton John and John Travolta. I would stand the album cover up on the floor against the wall and they would watch me. Their eyes would follow me as I twirled and leapt across the floor, singing every word of all of the songs. They were watching and they were pleased. I knew that they would be knocking on my door any day to ask me to join them on their tour. Were they even on tour? I don't know, but back then I knew. They were and they wanted me to go with them.

‡‡‡‡‡‡‡

Although it is rare, there are times when you would be able to eat off of my floors. You know, due to the abundance of crumbs that haven't been cleaned up. More often, though, they are fairly clean, despite the fact that, as homeschoolers, we don't actually spend that much time at home and, when we do, my energy is usually spent on other things, not of the cleaning variety. I definitely like to have a clean home more than I like to be the cleaner of the home. Nonetheless, I have been known to get on hands and knees with a small brush to scrub my floors. While my daughter calls this "the toothbrush story", the brushes I use are somewhat larger than the size of a toothbrush, but sometimes the small spaces do require an actual toothbrush, so let's go ahead and agree that this is indeed *The Toothbrush Story*.

It was a rainy day. Let's call it Wednesday. It wasn't just a rainy Wednesday. It was, in fact, stormy. I remember that my children were eagerly getting dressed to go out for a walk in the storm with their father. On this day, I had decided to scrub the living room floor with a small brush. I didn't decide it on this day, of course. I had planned it at some point because I am an extreme planner. The living room floor is vast for a woman on her hands and knees with only a small brush, after all. These things must be planned.

My living room floor is in an apartment on the top floor of a building, at the top of a hill. We can see storms rolling in from New Jersey and view great lightning displays from our windows. On this floor-scrubbing Wednesday, little more light came in from the dark outside than from the flashes of electricity made by the heavy clouds.

There I was scrubbidy-scrubbing when a bolt of lightning hit our window only a couple of meters away. Now, I can't be absolutely sure that it actually hit our window, but it sure is more interesting to say that it did, and wherever it hit, it was close enough to kill our computer across the room. Dead computer. Alive floor-scrubber. Alive and startled. I stopped scrubbing and jokingly declared that that had been a sign that I shouldn't be cleaning the floor with a small brush.

It was definitely a joke because there I was, on another rainy day (uh, do I only clean when it rains?), on my hands and knees, scrubbing the kitchen floor with a small brush. It wasn't a stormy day, just rainy, and there was no lightning, but it had been raining for a long time.

We have a fairly large kitchen, but it isn't as big as the living room, of course. Being a kitchen, though, it is particularly tough work for a small brush to tackle. It took a long time, but I did a great job. I felt like I should close off the kitchen, lest we lodge dirt back into the now spotless crevices.

I rested in the living room, satisfied and exhausted. As I rested, it rained. It rained and rained and, apparently, the rain was pooling on the roof. We're on the top floor, remember? Pooling water is heavy. Too heavy, it seems, for the roof on the other side of my kitchen ceiling, above my spotless floor. With a great crash, the ceiling, roof, and water came down onto my floor. My just-scrubbed-with-a-small-brush floor.

This time I wasn't joking when I said it was a sign, and I haven't gotten on my hands and knees to scrub the floor with a brush since.

‡‡‡‡‡‡‡

Tomorrow, my little baby boy will be eight years old. Even though he was technically born eight years ago already, he is still only seven today, and for several months I will be saying that "he just turned eight", probably until June. That's the kind of parent I am—hanging on to the past. Luckily, he's the kind of son who hangs on too. He hangs on to his babyness and he hangs on to my legs. He has invited me to be the doula at his children's births, which should be pretty easy since he also told me that I'll be living with him when he grows up. My bags are practically packed.

I'm a planner and, when I got pregnant with my son, I had planned to have another girl. The first girl had been planned for almost twenty years and that was working out well. I figured the boy would be baby number three and then the fourth and beyond, I'd just leave to chance. At some point early on in the pregnancy, however, I got an overwhelming desire to have a boy. It wasn't rational and it wasn't that I thought I was having a boy. I knew it, and I was very pleased. My husband, being much more fact-oriented and rational, tried to counteract my conviction and prepare me for a possible surprise by referring to my baby in the feminine while I kept saying "he", "him" and "his". The habit lasted him for several months after our son's birth!

At the time of this pregnancy, Mark was working an evening shift, so I would put our daughter to bed five nights a week. Until pretty recently, this was a fairly long ritual, involving reading and singing. When I did it, I'd sing four or five songs, always ending with the same two. One of the two was *Los Pollitos* because it was *Los Pollitos*. I know I don't have to explain that because it's *Los Pollitos*. The other was *I Will* by the Beatles. Mark and I danced to this song at our wedding and he sang it to our daughter right after he kissed her all over moments after she was born.

These were the two wind-down songs. I'd sing them while standing by my daughter's bed, swaying and rubbing my belly. For months, my son heard them too. He heard them and he loved them. This is probably when he started making plans for us to live together for the rest of his life. One day, hours after hearing me sing, he started knocking on my uterine door, causing a torrent of amniotic fluid to gush onto my living room floor. As soon as the sun came up, my husband and I did the only logical thing—we went for a walk to the bakery and had cheese danishes and hot chocolate. Later, while eating eggplant parmigiana and a vanilla milk shake (what a delicious labor I had!), I felt that my little boy was ready to see the world and he was born within the hour. As soon as he was born, he started crying. What was going on? He had been so comfortable. So I started to sing "I Will" and he looked at me. Remembering his plan to be with me forever, he stopped crying.

12

I think that one day he'll forget about those plans. I wonder if singing his song will help him remember. If so, I'll sing it every day.

‡‡‡‡‡‡‡

I live in New York City, where I was born and raised. I'm up in the Bronx, the only borough that's attached to the mainland. From my window I can see New Jersey. I also see lots of birds, mostly gulls, pigeons, sparrows, starlings, hawks, and mourning doves. We also have a good number of blue jays in the neighborhood. I like to take credit for bringing them slightly south, into the area. I'm probably wrong, but if I did, in fact, introduce them to the area, that wouldn't be so brag-worthy as they are raiders. I even witnessed them take over a tree one morning.

The blue jays weren't far from the area (we'd occasionally see one or two) and bringing them south was initially unintentional and fairly easy. When my daughter was about three, we made a bird feeder out of an empty milk carton. It was great watching the birds come to our window every day. The starlings and the mourning doves were my favorites, until one day when I saw a blue jay. It was beautiful and I wanted to see more so I did some research and found out that blue jays most like to eat peanuts and they prefer to find them in their shells. Easy! Eventually, we had lots of blue jays. There were nests nearby and the funny-looking chicks surprised me with their crestless heads one spring.

Soon we needed a sturdier bird feeder and a new location. We got a wooden specialty blue jay feeder and put it in our other window, keeping it full of peanuts all of the time. Blue jays are very loud, but I'm a morning person and they never bothered me. One morning, though, a blue jay seemed to be lingering on the windowsill, crackling open his peanuts for a long time. This happened on several consecutive mornings, so one day, I peeked through the slats of the blinds, careful not to be noticed. I was indeed noticed, however, by the squirrel who had discovered the blue jays' stash. He looked up at me boldly and kept munching. It turns out that this tale isn't really about blue jays after all.

I didn't mind the squirrel. It climbed up the side of the building to get food, and it was good food. The squirrel didn't seem to be scaring the blue jays away, so we were all living in harmony. Sometimes when people, or rodents, are comfortable, they spread out. They take a little more and get a little more comfy, they overstep their boundaries. Sometimes the boundaries are even windows! My mother came into my empty apartment one day to find Squirrely the Squirrel feasting in the middle of the living room floor. My husband came home to a similar sight once too. How had Squirrely gotten the impression that ours was more than a take-out establishment!?! That's not where it ends, though. During those dining visits, our furry friend had been looking around and making plans. Winter was coming, you know, and Squirrely had big food-stashing plans.

One day, we came home to find peanuts tucked into slippers and in between couch cushions. It was surprising and entertaining, and it had to stop. We ended up putting up a window screen that remains there year-round. I felt a little bad once, thinking that the poor squirrel would have a hard time finding food in the winter, but then I remembered that the bird feeder would still be there as full of peanuts as my guests would allow it to be. And then there was the day I saw him digging up the soil around the flowers I had planted to retrieve a buried peanut. Freaking Squirrely.

‡‡‡‡‡‡‡

I lived with my mother until I got married. Even for college I just took the train downtown to NYU. I applied only to New York University, with no second choice, and was happy to remain a city girl for college. My advisor in high school thought I should go to the University of Southern California to nurture the theatre and music that was in my blood. I had no desire to go to California at all, I didn't want to leave home, and I wasn't planning to have a career on the stage. My advisor seemed to be focused on someone else's dreams, maybe his own.

So off I went, downtown, to study Early Childhood and Elementary Education. My schedule didn't reflect that major as I mostly took music classes, both of the appreciation and performance variety. I got credit for taking classical voice lessons and singing in a jazz ensemble. I think it's safe to say that the partying I did in school was less than typical. I even took Professor Chusid's "Music and Drama in Opera" for two consecutive semesters.

Once, I took a class in which we would study different works including operas and orchestral pieces. What a great way to spend my college days! This was a spring semester. The city was lovely. I remember I would walk around the Village alone, enjoying the weather and watching people in Washington Square Park. I didn't really have college friends, probably due to my aforementioned "party" habits.

This was the year that brought us the cinematic pleasure of *Like Water for Chocolate* to delight our senses, a movie brimming with the magical realism found in García Márquez novels and much of my everyday life alike. Of course, I had to see it. I went on a sunny afternoon to the Angelika Film Center and sat with a handful of other women, experiencing the ins and outs, ups and downs of the de la Garza-Muzquiz romance. It was thrilling!

I am a cryer. When a movie makes me cry, it gets a bonus point. To say that Like Water for Chocolate made me cry would be an understatement. I felt like stopping by the box office on my way out and throwing cash at them. It was so satisfying.

The very next day, I was in class. We met in a different room that day. The lights were dim and there was a turntable up front. We were discussing *Tristan und Isolde*, another epic story of lovers destined to doom, and on this day, we would listen to an orchestral arrangement of Isolde's *Liebestod* "love death." With the first chord I felt as if the violin bow had punctured my heart and soon, I was sobbing. It was a little baffling, but I embraced it because, hey free tears.

It took a while for my drowning brain to realize that I was reliving the emotions of the previous day because the *Liebestod* was reminiscent of the music in the last scene of *Like Water for Chocolate*, when that thing happens to the people and there's all that light and heat, which I'm not going to elaborate on in case you'd like to see the movie yourself sometime. Really, the composer would have been foolish to make his theme any less similar to this, one of Wagner's great works. The undeniable resemblance was either intentional, a product of great musical education, or just romantic magic.

I know it seems crazy for me to say that this is one of my favorite college experiences, but it is!

‡‡‡‡‡‡‡

As a doula trainer in New York City, I have the pleasure of training people from all parts of the world. Usually, they live in the area, though, having come from somewhere else to make their homes here. I've had people come from California, Pennsylvania, Connecticut, the United Arab Emirates, Japan, the Dominican Republic, and the Cayman Islands specifically to attend my workshop. Many of them make the trek in order to have a trip to New York. That makes sense, but a few have been lured by me, somehow, and feel that they have to cross borders to get to me. Luckily, that has worked out for them so far.

During one workshop, among the sixteen participants, we had native speakers of six different languages. During our introductions, as we closely listened through various accents, we heard one person say that she likes to "sue" and another say that she was a "liar" back home. We all had a good laugh as we figured out that the liar was a lawyer and that the woman who liked to sue used needle and thread rather than a court room. I love that, even when no one travels from afar to get to my workshops, I can still meet people there from around the world.

‡‡‡‡‡‡‡

On August 21st of last year, I started working out, 11 months late for that get-fit-by-forty goal I never had. I was supposed to start on Tuesday the 19th, but I woke up at 6:05 that morning and noticed that my alarm had been set for 5:30 PM rather than AM. Darn those meridians! I e-mailed my would-be trainer and told him what had happened, inquiring if I should show up that Thursday or, since I missed the first class, if I should go ahead and wait four weeks for the next session to start. He told me to, "Come on Thursday, if you'd like." Uh, no, I wouldn't like! That's why I suggested I sit this session out. You know, sit being the operative word there.

That first class was disgusting. Really, they're all pretty bad, but on day one I felt nauseated just after the warmup. On the third day of class, the trainer had me sprinting up a hill repeatedly. Well, he tried to have me sprint, but even on the way down, I was pretty unsprinty, sometimes walking and, eventually, just stumbling. I tried to contain my sensations, both physical and emotional, but during the cool-down stretches, they spilled out of my eyes in salty streams. It was terrible. It still is. Nonetheless, I've been going twice a week since I started and I haven't missed a day.

I also started doing Yoga semi-regularly. Unlike the fitness classes with the trainer, I've never felt like Yoga was going to kill me, but once I did feel like I was going to be killed on my way to the class. Even though I live in the Bronx, I do almost everything in Manhattan and, if it's close enough, I walk there. I like to count my brisk walk as a warmup to my workouts. My unsympathetic trainer agrees, but refuses to lighten my load, ever fueling the flames of our hate-hate relationship.

On this particular Sunday evening, I was on my way to a nice calming Yoga class. The weather was mild and the sun was low in the sky. I was quite pleased with my efforts and had a spring in my steppidy steps. I wound down "suicide hill" and began to cross the small bridge that would take me to the northern-most part of Manhattan. This tale could very well be about how this bridge almost killed me. Despite the fact that it supports four lanes of vehicular traffic, along with elevated tracks on which run 400-ton trains every few minutes, the pedestrian walkway looks like it's going to crumble beneath my feet. There are steel patches in several places and I can see the water through the seams. Maybe I'm picky, but I don't like to see water between my feet when I'm walking on a bridge. Still, I cross this bridge and survive on a regular basis along with many others. Some of the others have bicycles and, as instructed by signage on either side, they dismount and walk across. Others of the others with bicycles do not dismount, riding across instead. It was one of these who whisked by me in what seemed to be an attempt to trim my ear hair. The walkway is narrow and I managed to start communicating with the rider before he passed me. I told him he's supposed to dismount and walk. He said, "Ah?" Not "ah," like "oh, I understand." Not "ah," like, "the weather is lovely," but "Ah?" A sound equivalent to "Huh?" in English. Kind of rude, but I understood it to mean, "Pardon me, young lady, I do not understand English. How might I better comprehend what you've just told me?" So, I went ahead and told him in Spanish, to which he responded, "¡Vieja estupida!" Literally, this translates to "stupid old lady", but surely that's not what he meant!

A little frazzled, I proceeded to my destination. It was still a fine day and I was going to have a great Yoga class. I walked past the car wash and, just before the bus depot, I saw a group of children throwing glass bottles on the ground. They were children, all boys, but because there were about six of them together, they had the courage of foolish men. I asked if they live in the neighborhood with the intention of helping them see the importance of taking care of the place where they live. Silly me. They responded harshly and angrily. I kept walking and they kind of followed, dispersing and yelling. Amidst the cursing and insults, they threw two bottles at me, shattering one in front and one behind me. These are kids who I'm sure would not have acted like this individually, but individuals often forget who they are when in groups. I started to sob and continued my walk. I arrived at the Yoga studio and cried, half explaining what the matter was. The receptionist got me some water and agreed that perhaps I was meant to stay home on this day. I dried my face and went on my way. I took the train. I had had enough of walking.

Six months later, I am still working out. It always feels a little life-threatening, but never quite like that walk.

✝✝✝✝✝✝✝

At this time fifteen years ago, I was on the Caribbean coast of Colombia. My father lives in Barranquilla, my mother's hometown. He went back to Colombia soon after I was born. That's a tale for another day. As a child, I always wanted to meet him. I wanted to see my Italian nose on his face. In my mind, he was among the tallest of men and I wanted to see him in person.

I met him when I was eight. My mother and I flew to Bogotá, where he lived at the time. I have vivid memories of that trip, like the cream of broccoli they served at his office. I have some foggy memories too, like did we leave without saying goodbye to my father? I really can't remember, but I do know that once I had met him and we came home, I was done with that longing I had had. I don't think I heard from him again and it would be almost a decade until he heard from me.

I remember sitting on my bed calling international directory assistance and then connecting with his office, the one with the broccoli soup. He was no longer there, but they told me where I could find him. He had moved years before to a more tropical clime with more oxygenated air, where the sandstorms of April are the only break from the consistently hot, sunny weather.

When I was finally able to get a hold of my father, we just chatted. I know he expected a deep conversation, but that was an inconceivable notion to me. How could I respond to a question like, "How've ya been?" when my height had doubled and I had gone through teenhood since the last time we had spoken? I never had any abandonment issues or felt resentment for my father, but he was pretty much a stranger to me—not in a sad way, just matter-of-factly. Out of our talk came an invigorating hope and a drive to contact and eventually meet the siblings of which he spoke.

One of my sisters was equally excited to know that I was walking on the earth as I was to learn of her. We sent letters back and forth and I got photos of her and four other siblings: an older sister in Panamá and the three children that my father had had with his wife, the oldest of which I had met momentarily when I was in Bogotá as a child. I remember being in his house, seeing him standing next to his mother as she prepared to leave town with him while my father's ex and Gringa daughter were around. Those details I learned when I was a little older.

Just as my father had asked, my sister wanted to know when I was going to visit. I think that people in other parts of the world think that it's easy for us to just pack up and go. Perhaps it's because we've got all that money lying around. Don't they know that we're also tethered to our jobs with only very short vacation times? Of course, I wanted to go and meet them too. It took some years, but I finally boarded the plane in the winter of 2000.

I was met at the airport by my three sisters and a brother and lots of hugs and tears. My father was there too. As my father was catching up on different family members, asking questions, I mentioned that one of my uncles had gotten his wife and mistress pregnant at the same time and how awkward that was. They all laughed, sort of at me, and I realized that two of my siblings right there with me were born only months apart to two different women.

One day, I sat with my father on a lonely pier which jutted out into the Caribbean Sea, eating delicious fried fish eggs with lime juice, thinly sliced fried green plantains and local beer. I knew at the time I would always remember this day. My father was surprised that I had ever eaten fried fish eggs before. We all make foolish assumptions. The sister in Panamá whose photo I had at home had been killed by her husband a few years before this trip. I leaned in closer to him and asked, "So, is it five of us now?" Referring to my four local siblings and myself. With a slow shake of his head and a solemn response, he broke my heart. He shattered my illusions of meeting all of my siblings when he told me that there are, in fact, eighteen of us, some of whom don't speak to him. I understand why they wouldn't want to reach out to him, but I sure wish they would just so they could learn about me and want to meet me some day too.

‡‡‡‡‡‡‡‡

For this week's tale, I'll start by sharing a little more about a sibling. This time, though, I'm talking about my real sister, the one with whom I was raised. Growing up, my sister was the readingest reader I knew and she was super smart. She was also an athlete! She ran and she biked. She ran track in school, she jogged for exercise and fun (!?!), she biked interstate for causes. She was the amazing one who did all of these things and I was, well, not. The only sign that I might also be smart was that I got good grades even though I did my homework in front of the television. The only sign that I too had muscles in my body was that I was able to get off the couch during commercials to get myself snacks.

When I was in junior high school, we'd have Field Day at the end of each school year. We'd compete in organized "games" like races and broad jumps and other forms of torture. It was terrible. I had perfect attendance most years, but the thought of Field Day was enough to make me sick for a whole month. I always participated in the broad jump. My long legs should have guaranteed me a good show, but I didn't move them with much power, apparently, because my ribbons were always for "participation." The shoe scramble was my other event. Everyone's sneakers were put in a pile. We had to find them, put them on and run to the finish line. I didn't even try. How quickly could I be expected to tie my sneaker laces with so little practice? They only came on for gym class, in which I tried to spend my time socializing with the teacher, Mr. Ocupinti.

Because I have loose ligaments, in my youth, my ankles were often twisted and sprained from merely walking. Perhaps the reason has something to do with the amount of time they spent propped on couch cushions while I watched TV. I don't know. By junior high school this was no longer a problem really, but the memory lingered. When I was in 7th grade, as the end of the school year approached and with it the horrid tradition of sun-drenched boredom and humiliation awarded by satin strips of blue, red, and gold with no apparent benefit but a day off from schoolwork, which I never longed for myself and didn't understand those who did, I decided it was a good time for a sprained ankle. Could they possibly force me to participate if I showed up with an ace bandage and smelling of Chinese menthol? I thought not.

I could've probably gotten out of it by simply asking. These people liked me. I was the student who made friends of all the teachers. I'm the one who sat in the office and played secretary when there were staff meetings and such. I was in charge by myself at times. I answered the phones and even made announcements over the PA system. They loved me and I'm sure they wouldn't have forced me if I had just asked. Instead of asking, I jumped on my twisted foot a few times. I wasn't dumb enough to do it so hard that it actually hurt me, though, so I went into the corner of the closet where my mother's hammer was kept and retrieved it. Don't freak out. I wasn't as smart as my sister perhaps, but I wasn't stupid. I only tapped around the ankle in order to make it a little swollen, a little bruised. That, combined with a limp would surely get me out of Field Day. It did. That was a good Field Day. I think I even got a ribbon.

The following year was my last year in the school. On the morning of Field Day, they needed my help in the office. Then, they needed me to run an errand. I loved doing things for the office! While I was busy adulting, my class had gone off to start Field Day. Don't get too excited. I knew I wasn't going to miss it. I'd just have to get there on my own. The field was about three quarters of a mile away. At first, I started walking in the wrong direction, though. I was anxious to catch up to my class, not because I was eager to get to the activities, of course. I was just nervous and feeling a little lost. I was a bit disoriented for a couple of minutes, but then I recognized the correct path—the unshaded path. It was a hot summer day. I was speed walking (as much as lazy me could speed walk. Just humor me here.) I don't like the heat. The heat gets to me. It was hot.

When I got to the field, I was out of breath. One of my friends, I mean teachers, one of my teachers looked at me with wide eyes and asked if I was OK. He told me to sit in the shade and said I must have heat stroke. I followed his instructions because the poor guy was so concerned. Another friend/teacher confirmed the findings. I was not well. I couldn't possibly run around in the sun with the other children. I didn't want to upset anyone, so I allowed them to shower me with attention and cold drinks. Why, yes, we should put that cold towel on my forehead. Such a little people-pleaser I am, and this time, one of the people was me!

Maybe it was heat stroke. Maybe I was just a lazy adolescent who had walked swiftly on a summer day. I can't remember, but you better believe I was taking the excuse. I spent the day relaxing in the shade and even took a ride in the English teacher's car to do some task. That was the best Field Day ever, heat stroke and all.

‡‡‡‡‡‡‡

My grandmother was born in the popular tourist town of Cartagena, Colombia. It is a beautiful, historic city, but I'm sure the part of the city she knew well wasn't quite built with tourist riches as much as by slave sweat. I could write a plethora of tales about her alone. Her entrepreneurial spirit led her to travel for many years. Eventually, it had her lead others to travel. That's how much of my family ended up in the US. That's why I am a New Yorker. I will always be grateful to her for that!

When I was a young child, my grandmother joined us in New York. Someone should have warned the wholesalers in the fashion district, the jewelers, realtors and many other business folk, about her. She could sell anything to anyone and she bought only at prices she set.

She was here, dealing and wheeling for more than three decades, but in Her late 80s, it turned out that she had become intolerant of our cold winters. She decided, at some point, to spend half the year in Central America, where people would come running to get a whiff of the dollars she was waving. She was a New Yorker by then, reigning in a small town on an isthmus. She had lots of demands. Today's tale will demonstrate that her intolerance wasn't only of cold winters.

When she returned from one of her trips to the outskirts of the equator, she told me this story. I remember she laughed, not quite recalling what the disagreement was about, but it seemed that, upon her arrival, she had gotten into a dispute with a neighbor's dog. I can picture it. Being the antithesis of cuddly to me and several others, she was not one to inspire warmth in children or animals. She told me that words had been exchanged with the dog and the neighbors and I imagine many of them were in what some might call French.

That night she settled into her bed, probably laughing at the snow she had left behind and, as she noticed dark darkness of not New York City, she found herself under attack. The neighbors "malparidos" (this word, literally "wrongly birthed", means "birth defect", but it is much more to those who use it or have it used about them) were throwing rocks at her house. It was terrible. She hardly slept that night, and in her wakefulness, she likely composed a mental letter. She had written many letters in her life with poison ink, her words carefully chosen to do much damage, and I can imagine that she had planned such a letter for these people, these dog people. How could they do such a thing to her!?!

The next morning, the neighbors were seemingly well-rested and cordial, friendly even. The dog fight was in the past. They understood that my grandmother was crotchety. Why then, she demanded, had they mistreated her so on her first night there? Who throws rocks at a house all night long? She didn't understand it.

That morning she learned, over breakfast, which the dog-owning neighbors had prepared for her, that they had been able to rest well because they, unlike herself, were accustomed to sleeping through the sound of ripe mangoes falling from the trees onto the zinc roof.

✝✝✝✝✝✝✝

A little while ago I noticed that I was catching the eye of a certain type of man. I'd like to say older men, but really, they're just old men. I mean old men who are old, really old. It's doing wonders for my self-esteem to know that the only people who are attracted to me in public are those who can hardly see. I know! It's because I'm old too.

There was a man next to me on the train one day who looked like he was fresh off a boat from some Caribbean Island. He was very polite so it surprised me when he very seriously insisted that it didn't matter that I was married, we could still be friends and go out to dinner. He was well dressed and all, but I'm too young to be helping my date down the street and with his spoonfuls of mush or something.

There was a time, though, when I attracted a type that was a little less centenarian. Like so many of us, there are some scary stories I can tell, but for today, I'll share some of the funny ones.

I live in New York City and, as you may guess, I have lots of colorful tales to tell about riding the subway. We have all sorts of preachers trying to save us from ourselves, so I wasn't surprised when someone came up to me and loudly declared, "Jesus loves you." He said it again and, as he squeezed himself into the half spot between me and my neighbor, he asked me if I knew that Jesus loved me. I was thinking that maybe I looked particularly sinful that day until he said more quietly, "My name is Jesus." He definitely got a laugh out of me, but he didn't get my number.

Another time I was on the train that has the longest route in the city. I embarked on the northernmost stop and would be going through three boroughs before I got off. About four minutes into my ride, I found myself sharing personal space with a very chatty character. He was homeless and he was on his way to visit his mother, who was in the hospital. He told me all about her and, since his conversation was rather loud and disorganized, I got rescue offers from a couple of other passengers. I was tolerant, though, and definitely not fearful. He seemed to need someone to listen to him and a shoulder to lean on, sometimes literally. It was a little weird, but never weirder than when, as I was getting off the train, he yelled out his phone number loudly and repeatedly, urging me to call him.

Once I was stopped by a police officer for jaywalking. What? Didn't he know I was a New Yorker? Was there even a law? Before I started crying, though, he said that he needed my name and number. I'm still a fugitive, I suppose.

Another time, about a million years ago, I was walking aimlessly with a friend, feeling sassy as I was often prone to feel. A young man asked my name and I said, "Guess." I acted shocked in response to his first attempt, telling him he had gotten it right. He had probably said something like "Maria". He was so pleased with himself as his friends cheered him on. Emboldened by his apparent powers of divination (you know, obviously this was meant to be), he asked me for my phone number. I simply responded, "Guess." He never called.

‡‡‡‡‡‡‡

Being old fashioned, my husband wanted to honeymoon in Niagara Falls. It's nice there. I've been there a few times. We could walk there if we had the time, though. I wasn't interested. He had never been abroad and I had been to more than a dozen countries. I won. Off we went to Ireland, from whence his people hail.

It was dreamy. I mean it actually seemed like a dream at times. We went during the off season and apparently had the run of the land. We climbed castle ruins (Well, really, he climbed while I cried into the video camera that I would be widowed on my honeymoon. I'm sure you can detect the tremble of my hand in the recordings.), approached grazing sheep (Never quite reaching them because of that third eye they apparently have.), befriended dogs (Everyone's dog is just roaming around, friendly as can be.), got stuck in traffic jams behind herds of cattle (They mooove slowly.), saw rainbows almost daily (really, almost every day), and marveled at the two-way roads that seemed only big enough for one car (exciting, terrifying—same thing).

Another thing we noticed is that a common mode of transport is hitch hiking. I had never done this before nor was I interested in trying it, but we had a car anyway, so it didn't matter. One day, on our way to a wool shop (Those sheep aren't there just for decoration and blocking the roadways, you know.), we stopped to check our map. I'm smiling just thinking about what happened next. Smile with me as you imagine that, as we pulled over a bit, just before a small stone overpass, to check our map for directions, the back door of the car opened. Before we had time to figure out what was happening, there was already comfortably situated in the back seat an older man wearing a blazer and tweed cap, ready for us to take him to his destination or at least part of the way. Would you believe that this had never happened to me in New York? Not once.

Of course, we gave the man a ride. It was charming and we felt like we had gotten a full Ireland experience. Happy St. Patrick's Day!

‡‡‡‡‡‡‡‡

The summer of 1982 was huge. I met my father that summer, but better than that, millions of people met E.T., the Extra-Terrestrial. My earthly meeting happened before I met E.T., but really it could've gone either way. If I had tried a little harder, I could have met E.T. in person that summer too. I was possibly distracted by the introduction to my father. Maybe I was too scared or not ready. I'll never know the reason for sure.

You see, I am a magical thinker. I'm sort of superstitious, but I only believe in the good things. Let's say I'm somewhat-stitious rather than super-stitious. It's really quite convenient. I even say that Friday the thirteenth is a day of good luck for me. Good luck has to go to someone if so many people think they'll have the opposite!

The house I stayed in during my trip to Colombia, where I met my father, was fertile ground for my imagination, but at the time it wasn't my imagination at all. It was a very strong desire that I felt I could just will into reality. The house had a large garden at the entrance. You had to walk through lush plants to enter or exit the living quarters. Was it really as grand and verdant as I remember? Let's say yes.

I don't recall if it was that marketing was less aggressive at the time or if the E.T. Movie posters didn't contain his image. Either way, before I saw the movie later that year, I didn't know what the little alien looked like. I sort of had a picture in my mind, but I was also kind of scared to explore the possibilities too much. Equipped with this ignorance, I decided that on this trip I would see E.T., I would meet him and he would be my pet and guardian angel. I actually thought that I would meet the actual creature, actually. I knew I was special and figured that the universe had chosen me for this. I was scared, but it was important to me. I was ready to let this magical being be a part of my life. We were to meet in my host's indoor rainforest. If I imagined him enough, I was sure he would come. I would peek out into the garden fearfully and expectantly.

Day after day, there were just plants. At some point I realized that the universe wasn't going to send me my own magical being to accompany me through life quite yet. Maybe I didn't get to meet E.T. because I was afraid of him. I'm pretty sure I cried, but I also figured that my magic would come in other ways. Just as some real things are magical, I know that some magic is real. I will never stop looking for the wondrous secrets of the world. If I don't believe that magic exists, I'll be much less likely to find it.

‡‡‡‡‡‡‡

When I was little, my family used to go to the Easter Parade on Fifth Avenue annually. Even though it was explained to me every time, it took me years to figure out that we were, in fact, the parade and that we hadn't gotten there too late to see the floats. I remember an old man who used to sell little plastic birds that we'd fill with water so that they'd chirp when we blew into them. I remember seeing all of the fancy people. In those days, we would get dressed up to go to the movies, to a restaurant, or on a plane ride. When Easter came around the dressing up was taken to a new level, always involving a slip, pantyhose, a handkerchief, and other fine accessories. It's no wonder we were in a parade!

It had been a while since we had left the parade tradition behind and one day, in my teens, someone decided that we should meet at the parade and then go out to eat. My grandparents were there, my mother and my sister, a few cousins and a couple of aunts. We were going to watch the beautiful strangers walk by and then go eat with the beautiful familiars.

We went to a Brazilian restaurant. We arrived and sat down and my grandmother promptly asked the waiter for some bread as she did e v e r y t i m e she went out to eat. She even asked for bread or complained of its absence in Chinese restaurants where, um, they don't have bread. We were all aware of this custom and we took turns making fun of her. I can't remember who was at it this time, the time that would be pretty much the end of that strain of mocking.

On this Easter Sunday, in response to our laughter, my grandmother asked, "Do you know why I always ask for bread? Do you know why I love bread so much?" Her tone and expression made it clear that, not only were these rhetorical questions, but they were only the beginning of an important lesson and the end of a long-running joke.

My grandmother went on to tell us about how, as a child, she and her siblings would go to bed hungry. Their mother would return from work while they were asleep and would gently wake them just enough to put pieces of bread in their mouths. They chewed, only half-awake, on the morsels and likely dreamt that they were at a feast.

While awake, my grandmother would later dream of feasting with the generations that were yet to come. It was those dreams that fueled the success and prosperity her family was to have.

We all cried. The bread was extra delicious that day.

‡‡‡‡‡‡‡‡

One of the things I like about baking yeast breads is that I always think of my aunt. I don't remember eating her breads, but I remember watching her make them. I'm sure I had my share. I always thought that her bread-making was a special, special thing, just like her.

She's the only person in my family I ever saw make bread, but here's the story of my uncle's father who once worked for a famous baker in a small town.

This bakery was known for its egg bread. Every morning the smell of this bread would fill the town and every morning, before the bakery opened, the line of people, waiting to get their loaves, would form in the street.

When my uncle's father got his job in the bakery, he knew that, even if he didn't make the bread himself, he would be part of the magic. Imagine his surprise when, on his first day of work, in those predawn hours, he was told he would be making the egg bread. What an honor. The smell that would waft through the streets on this day would emanate from his own labor.

He wondered if he would be made privy to the mystery that held the town captive with its aroma and delectable taste. He was told to mix the ingredients just so and call the owner, the master baker, when it was time for the special ingredient. How many eggs did this delightful bread call for? It was time to find out. The baker came into the room and nonchalantly took a bottle off of a dusty shelf. He tilted it until a yellow stream of chemical, non-egg product poured into the dough, and returned it to its shelf until the next day.

That day, the loaves of bread each had a measure of disillusionment in them. Today, we're hardly surprised to find out that our food isn't as much actual food as we'd like. I still make my bread with identifiable ingredients like my aunt did. I even feel like I'm cheating a little when I use a dough hook, but I know she'd still approve.

‡‡‡‡‡‡‡‡

My sister is eight years older than I am. Growing up, there were times when we definitely weren't friends. Other times, I admired her so much. She did such amazing things. She was an athlete, she was smart—she seemed to have it all.

I remember, one day when I was ten, sitting in the living room with her, looking at her beautiful penmanship on sheets and sheets of college ruled paper (that was the cool kind). She had written a bunch of poems. I read one and it was genius. It was to me the best poem ever written.

I can't recall what it said, but I still remember the image that the words formed in my mind. I can see her hanging out with friends in her high school cafeteria. She went to a specialized school for smarties, of course, so the scene was pure perfection.

Sometime after reading my sister's masterpiece, my fifth-grade class was assigned the task of writing a poem. My fifth-grade teacher was a fairy lady. She looked like a 50's pinup come to life. I remember her face and her hair. I remember her four names and her little car. I loved her. I remember being crushed when I found out she was getting married.

She told us to write a poem and said it had to rhyme. I felt at the time that this requirement was a little restrictive, but I had my sister's recent inspiration, so I put smudgy erasable pen to paper and got to work. It was really challenging, but I got it done. I felt like she and my sister might even be proud of me.

The poems were collected and Miss Fabula Perfectio read them to herself while her students worked on something else. Sometimes she read the best examples out loud.

As luck would have it, she did indeed read my poem to the class. She read something about "rain through the roof of my stable" and something about a "cafeteria table". The class laughed at my poem. The teacher laughed at my poem. The teacher laughed at me. She didn't identify me as she humiliated me, but that didn't make it any better.

She had required me to write six rhyming lines in fifteen minutes. To her, the outcome was nonsensical. I tried to tell her that it had hidden meaning. It was, after all, inspired by my sister's great works, so it must be good. It wasn't to her, though, and thus were my hopes for a poetic life all wet, like rain through the roof of my stable.

‡‡‡‡‡‡‡

My husband usually makes the pancakes in my house. He uses whole wheat flour and various fruits, depending on the season and his mood. Mine are multigrain and plain. Either way, my mother, who lives two floors away, usually ends up at our pancake breakfasts.

Yesterday, while we ate ours, my mother said she remembers the first time she ever had pancakes. She was about eight years old and, from Colombia, she had to visit her mother who worked and lived in Panamá.

She remembers how good these pancakes tasted and how beautiful they were. They were small and golden, just as pictured on the Aunt Jemima package.

When I was little and slept with my mother, I would stir from my sleep as she rustled to get out of bed in the morning. I would wrap my long-for-my-age leg around her body and try to persuade her to stay home from work, saying, "You no like trabajar hoy." I wouldn't want her to leave for work, but I knew she would be back that evening, that very day.

I have no memory of eating pancakes for the first time. Nor can I remember being a child and having a reunion with my mother after a separation of more than hours. If those two memories were intermingled for me, I would cry every time I had pancakes. My mother is a big ol' pain in my butt sometimes for reasons I will share in a carefully worded story sometime in the future, but she is always welcome to have pancakes at my house.

‡‡‡‡‡‡‡

Years ago, I got my daughter a book for a dime. It looked interesting and I figured she could read it sometime in the future. I didn't know she could already read so well at the time and she got through the whole book that night. It was one of the books in the Magic Treehouse series and, that spring, my daughter read all of them. These are not big books, but they have chapters and at about 150 pages, they are big for new readers.

Soon my children knew all about the author and her husband and about the research they did and where they live and the names of their horses and such. Imagine their excitement when they found out that the author was going to be signing books at the Cloisters. We could see the Cloisters from our window! We were totally going. It was a two-day engagement and, since my daughter had dance classes on Saturday, we decided to go on Sunday.

This happened in early May. As I write this, it is late April. The sky is clear with only the wispiest clouds smiling coyly at the bright sun and the temperature is in the sixties, fluctuating only as the breeze kisses us goodbye on her way north. We happen to be at the Cloisters today and I'm on the grass with my shoes off.

This day in early May, when we went to meet the author, was not such a day. Skies were grey and threatening and we were not dressed for the breeze that wanted to penetrate our bones. Still, we went. We got there early because that's what I do, and I was surprised to find that we were so early that there was no sign of this event, no other families waiting for a glimpse of this famous writer.

I paid my dollar or so, not taking the suggestion of a $25 admission fee, and turned to the nearest guard to inquire where the event was taking place. Where, it turned out, wasn't the right question because the event had happened the day before. I know that it will sound like an exaggeration if I use the word devastated, but really, that is how we felt. My daughter, son, and I sat on the nearest bench and cried. We couldn't even bear to go into the museum. We went out onto the lawn to have lunch and the day's disappointment made the cool, damp air bitter.

Luckily, we had a chance, a few months later, to meet the same author at the zoo. We were there early, of course, and all signs pointed to a successful meeting. When it was our turn, we shared our whole story. She was gracious and patient and we took lots of photos. My children have moved on to other books and other authors, but every visit to the Cloisters reminds us of the time we cried on the bench.

‡‡‡‡‡‡‡

Several months ago, I was considering donating a kidney. Initially, it was an easy decision, but as time went on, thinking about it took away some of the ease. Still, I was on board until I was disqualified.

My cousin's son and I had a special connection. I remember staring at the ceiling having chats with him when he was a little boy. When my son was born, I was so happy to see such a strong resemblance to him. Others didn't quite see it. Maybe I was looking at their hearts.

When he was four, I took my cousin's son to see the movie Space Jam. It opens with a short cartoon. At the end of the animation, he turned to me and told me he wanted to leave. Smart kid, I should've listened. He had seen the best part of the movie, albeit brief, and was ready to go.

On Sunday, he did the same thing. At the age of twenty-two he had seen the best parts of his life, touched so many people with his warmth and humor, and he left us.

At the transplant center, the receptionist asked who my kidney recipient was to be, and the whole room melted when I told them his name because they knew him well. He was too sweet to be so sick. He had to go.

╫╫╫╫╫╫╫

When I was in college, I used to go to the opera often. This was when the Metropolitan Opera House had no titles anywhere. One was expected to follow the story or just be lost and admire all of the other things that were going on—the singing, orchestra, scenery, costumes, acting, dance. There is so much to an opera production. I was among those who were against the addition of titles. I thought they would be intrusive and detract from the experience. It turns out that they did a great job and even I have used them more than once. Luckily, my neighbors can't tell when I do because they are so discreet. What would people say if I was caught reading subtitles? Heavens!

Once, I got myself a ticket to see *Die Zauberflöte*. I was very familiar with this opera's music and story—one of my favorites. Nonetheless, I spent a few hours that day next door at the Library for the Performing Arts. I did that a lot too back then. That day, I read the libretto for *The Magic Flute* (again) in preparation for my journey into Mozart's magical world of love, lies and masonry.

Because I had just read the libretto, as I watched the performance, I found myself laughing at a particular joke even though it was in German. I don't know German, but I understood the joke and appreciated the delivery. To my surprise, I found that only myself and the man next to me were laughing. We looked at each other and laughed again.

During the intermission, he started to speak to me in German. Luckily, he spoke English too. I found out that my seat mate was visiting from Germany. He understood more of the words during the performance, but I understood more of everything else. After the opera, we went out for dessert. That's another thing I love, so it was a great day of music and laughter and sweets!

‡‡‡‡‡‡‡

I walked through Times Square the other day, not because I'm crazy, but because it was between my start and end points. It's always interesting to be in that area. The most entertaining part for me is watching the people, mostly the tourists.

On this particular day, I saw something new—a female version of the naked cowboy. She was wearing eighteen inch tall red, white, and blue feathers on her head, a little something on the bottom and patriotic paint on top. Before I left the area, I saw three other similarly clad (or unclad) young women. One was covered in a loose dress as she walked away from the bustle with a look of exhaustion on her sweaty, heavily made-up face.

Today, Times Square is a hub for touring families who want to buy the latest theme gear from Disney, WWF, M&M's and many more. I remember a different Times Square, one I would walk through with my head down, afraid to be caught looking at the XXX signs or the pictures or the stores. Everything was dirty and, instead of the crowds of people, there were just a few of the scariest people in the world hanging around. When I was growing up, one of the worst things another child could say to you was that your mother worked on 42nd Street. What!?! Insult of insults.

Now the streets are cleaner and the lights are brighter. Things are much safer in that part of town. Rather than having to wear a disguise to sneak into a seedy club to see the topless women, you can just pay a couple of dollars and take a photo with them. Just be careful with their body paint.

‡‡‡‡‡‡‡

We are a homeschooling family. Sometimes I joke that the children educate me. Sometimes I joke that I'm only in charge of recess. Both of those are a little bit funny. Both are a lot true.

I'm super organized and envisioned at first that our homeschooling would follow a timeline, at least for Yoga, baking and snack time, if not for Maths, English, and Science. No such timeline has ever been followed for more than a couple of weeks, yet miraculously, my children still learn, and off go my cerebral dendrites expanding along with theirs.

Part of the miracle formula is their love of reading. They can and do spend hours lost in a book. They get this from their father. Another thing they get from their father is detailed explanations about everything. He doesn't usually do this in an attempt to homeschool, it's just the way he is. As a matter of fact, he does this with adults too. He will go on ad nauseam whether you'd like him to or not. Luckily, I'd usually like him to. I've learned a great deal from him. I'm sure he would say that he has learned a great deal while explaining things too. You see, the children are educating us and, because we are open to letting conversations go in any direction, the end point is often a wondrous surprise.

While many of the families I know are opting out of standardized tests, we are doing them in our kitchen. We aren't required to do them this year, but it's nice to get a sense of what's going on in those little brains and also, my daughter loves them. I was just like that!

She eagerly looks forward to the tests and finishes each section way before the allotted time expires. Once she's done, she doesn't check over her answers as she should, because, hello, that's just boring. Totally like her mother! I used to sit there waiting for everyone else to finish instead of checking over my work. I don't know why, but I do know I passed that gene along. We both test well and get a small number of answers wrong due to careless mistakes. Life is full of imperfections, though. We'll be OK.

My son started testing for the first time this year. He works very slowly. Just like his mother. He has fantabulous words in his brain and they are spoken with the finest eloquence and wit, but getting them on paper (or a computer) is a different matter. He's a math whiz too, but only given time. I was nervous about his test taking because it is a timed exam. I assigned him Math, Part I and came back with a few minutes left on the clock. He had finished Part I and was partway through Part II, so I worried for nothing. He ignored the instructions to stop, as he often does when he's reading.

It's a good thing they get so much from their father because I'd just screw them up on my own!

‡‡‡‡‡‡‡

My mother grew up on the Caribbean coast of Colombia and, because there are so many Native Americans there and descendants of African slaves, it was very important for there to also be lots of missionaries to save their souls. This is a tale of the missionaries in its two versions.

My mother is a great cook. Somehow, while being a single mother and working full-time, she managed to always make a delicious dinner every night. We didn't eat canned goods, instant meals, fast food, or junk food. She made great meals, but she couldn't bake and she didn't fry. I heard her many a time talking about how she couldn't fry and how the missionaries had taught her to cook a perfect egg.

The missionaries must have had a tough time with my mother, always the skeptic. She watched religious goings-on all around her, all the time. She wouldn't have any of it. All they gave her was a couple of fun outings, a few catchy tunes, and the skill of "frying" an egg.

When my mother tells the story, she says that they taught her to sprinkle a few drops of water on the pan and heat it just so before cracking the egg onto it and covering it. Her story includes the hand gestures that go along with her sprinkling technique and I'm pretty sure that her mouth waters as she describes the crispy edges and gently runny center of sunny-side-up perfection.

Now, that's a good enough story as-is, but after years of not hearing it, I was shocked to experience its retelling as an adult. Maybe it's because I knew that so many houses in my mother's hometown had their daily kitchens outdoors and used firewood. Maybe it's because I knew that my mother's homeland was the womb of so many magical things. No matter the reason, for many years the picture in my mind which went along with my mother's story was a little different.

With my inventive eye I see women wearing long skirts teaching the young heathens how to cook out in the rainforest. There's a big rock in this forest, which someone wipes off with her hand and a little bit of water before letting a few drops fall from her fingertips to "grease" the surface. Then, of course, the egg is cracked and it somehow cooks perfectly. Now, since my brain has cooked up this scenario so far, it also has to cook up this egg. Why not go ahead and imagine that the egg is cooked by the sun? The equator goes right through Colombia, so I'm thinking this isn't entirely impossible, and that is just how I remember this story.

There you have it. The missionaries taught my mother how to fry an egg using a few drops of water, a rock, and the heat of the sun—very useful in case you ever get lost in the rainforest with an egg! This is the story that will be passed along to my children jokingly, but eventually the humor will be lost, I imagine, and it will just be the story. It won't be the first time a tale evolves this way and it won't be the last.

‡‡‡‡‡‡‡

I attended one of New York City's specialized high schools. At the time, there were only a handful of them and prospective students had to be tested or auditioned for admittance. They were called specialized because they specialized in something— math & science or music & art. In order to gain admittance, one had to prove one's intelligence or talent. I, probably lacking enough measure of either of these, actually proved to have a combination, evidenced by my talent for test-taking.

I should have auditioned for Fiorello H. LaGuardia High School of Music & Art and Performing Arts. My whole life my mother had complained, with a roll of her eyes and twist of her mouth, that I was always on stage. Instead, I took the entrance exam for The Bronx High School of Science, despite Mrs. Lynch telling me that it was only for nerds and Mikey telling me that it was like Chinatown there. Such darling neighbor people, just lovely balls of wonderfulness they were, who I was always so happy to see hanging out on the street when I turned the corner, especially after I got into Bronx Science!

Apparently, I acted as if my test-taking skills were amply sufficient and scored highly enough on the entrance exam to gain admittance to the nerd school, but many of my friends were at LaGuardia—on the real stage. I spent my high school days performing and just merely acting like a student when I was in the school building. It was yet another stage for me, I couldn't be bothered to transform myself into a good student when things didn't interest me. Really, how gauche. I mean, I know it was a math and science school, but those two subjects in particular were, at times, lacking in a certain glittery panache I craved for, the type of glitter called logic and panache called sense.

I loved physics and all of its physical physicality. It made sense. It was real. It was jazzy, baby. The teacher was new to the school and ended up being the principal a couple of years later. He was great. I elected to take an additional physics class the year my classmates elected to take calculus. For those of you who didn't attend a specialized high school, I shall explain that electing to take a class means that you choose it, presumably because you want to. They weren't forced to take calculus, they embraced it because, apparently, nerds aren't so bright. Anyhowsers, I was rocking my physics classes with full participation, astute questions, and cogent observations. I didn't do any of the homework assignments or reading, but it all came to me in my zeal. My time in those classes was fabulous and deserving of some type of award, similar to an Oscar, but less shiny and three-dimensional, perhaps more like a letter on paper. Yes, let's say an A. I deserved an A and the teacher knew it even though he also knew that I wasn't doing any of the work. I was just getting it. What's not to get? Physics, man.

The previous year, I had taken Chemistry. Chemistry was much less physical and much more Chemical. Perhaps, being a drug prude had something to do with it. I mean, I never even put a cigarette to my mouth. Or maybe it was the teacher. I remember him well. Do you know the teacher in the movie *Ferris Bueller's Day Off?* The one who drones on in a monotone that can make a vacuum cleaner jealous? I think this chemistry teacher took lessons with him and failed the class due to his lack of enthusiasm. Nonetheless, we were friendly, as I was with many of my teachers, and I'd stay after class to chat with him. We talked about something that we had in common. I can't recall nor imagine what it could have been. Perhaps the fact that we both occasionally had gas. Although, I didn't keep the gas stifled in my neck as this teacher seemingly did. He knew I didn't like his class, that I wasn't understanding anything, and that I wasn't planning to memorize his little letter codes for elements or whatever they were. I have memorized many a soliloquy and recognize the beauty of language. Don't truncate it and stuff your abbreviations down my throat and into my eyeballs, man! Even as a chemist, he didn't have the right solutions for me. (Get it? Solutions as a chemist. That was a pun. It was hilarious, but you ruined it by making me explain it. Thanks a lot.) The worst part is that my final grade was dependent on how well I did on the statewide Regents exam. It's funny that I wrote "how well" because well really was going to have nothing to do with it. I wasn't going to do well at all. It was going to be like another language to me, a language without words or meaning, involving torture and bad smells. My plan for taking this exam was for me to be like an atom and make up everything. (I am going to control myself here and forego an explanation because I'm sure you're already laughing.)

Sho' 'nuff, on the morning of the exam, I wasn't even nervous. It's not like I had to cram and recall valuable information that was stored in my brain. It wasn't there at all. Some words on the page would surely be familiar to me, but I had no intention of giving them any weight. Really, in order to graduate from this school, I had to take approximately five thousand, three hundred twenty-four Regents, so there I was, just planning to show up. As I was getting dressed, I had the radio on and heard that someone had stolen the answers to the exam and that they had been published on the front page of the Daily News.

Later that morning, I sat on the front steps of the school and there were several reporters interviewing students, because this was Bronx Science. Have you heard of it? Look it up, dude. One of them stuck her microphone and her question in my face. Was I going to cheat by looking at the answers? Of course not. How dare she insinuate that I might dredge in the moral mud of cheating or worse, that I might actually need to see the answers? I mean, she couldn't be proposing that any one of us from this fine institution might actually benefit from seeing the answers in advance. Could she see in my head?

The exam was cancelled that year, less than an hour before it was scheduled to start. Students throughout the land rejoiced, but at Bronx Science, more than a couple were very disappointed, including that Wong kid—such a nerd. How could they flaunt a perfect score when everyone was granted a mere passing grade? Even I, wearing my mask of indifference, passed my Chemistry Regents. I also passed the class that year, the teacher likely recognizing that he was partly at fault for not instilling in me a love for his chosen field. I never even bothered to act as if I understood or enjoyed it. I saved my vim and my vigor for after class conversation. Whatever we talked about was enough for him to see that I did not need to take that class again the following year and that decision was oxygen potassium by me! (I wish I could have just been able to write OK, but that isn't a thing, really, on the periodic table thingy. You see, oxygenated potassium is actually K2O or potassium oxide, sometimes known as potash, which is used as a fertilizer, and you know what else is commonly used as a fertilizer, so let's just leave it there.)

╫╫╫╫╫╫╫

Recently, I was smacked in the face with the heart-wrenching proof of my failure as a parent. It has taken me a few weeks to be able to write it down because I am so disappointed and I know that my people, way back to Colombia, Martinique, Angola, Italy, and Spain (yeah, I think even the Europeans in my ancestry could recognize my great failure) would be heartily dismayed as well.

On this day, my dear, darling son made an unusual request. He is basically normal except for being exceptionally, bright, charming, and handsome, very patient, artistic, generally amazing, and a really good eater. It is this last point that made his request of several weeks ago particularly difficult to understand and accept. We only had green bananas in the house. They looked green and they smelled green and they were hard. My son, he knew they were green. Still, he asked me to cut one into his oatmeal. I declined, reprimanding him for making such a request. He insisted so I, holding back tears, started to cut banana slices into his bowl. It was quite a challenge between the pain the resistance caused in my wrist and the unripe smell that emanated from that poor excuse for a fruit, but I did it for my little boy, confident that he would surely reject it in disgust once he tasted it. Who eats green bananas like that? Oh, that's right, he's his father's son too and his father is a Gringo, unfamiliar with the FACT that green bananas give you a stomachache and they're just plain yucky.

This whole pathetic situation reminds me of a story my grandmother once told me. Living in Colombia with some siblings and in-laws perhaps, she went out and got a bunch of bananas. This wasn't a bunch like you see in the store. Those are actually hands—at least that's what we call them. This was a bunch of hands. Think Harry Belafonte, think plantations of upside-down bananas. She came home with a bunch of bananas and, although they weren't green, because that whole buying green bananas thing is just a crazy idea in which my grandmother would never partake (until she got to this land of wonders, at least), they were not quite at the perfect speckled ripe stage yet. She took her big bunch of beautiful bananas, put them in a corner and covered them with a sheet to wait for them to reach their perfect peak.

While she waited, her stash was discovered and uncovered by many a housemate. One by one, two by two, the bananas began to disappear. They began to disappear and they finished to disappear and, by the time my grandmother approached her delicious fruit, all that was left was a thick, woody stalk. My grandmother laughed as she told me the story, but the day it happened, she was furious. She would never eat the stalk that hands of bananas grow on, just as she would never eat a green banana. They taste terrible and they give you a stomachache. These are facts known to my people and here I generously share them with you. You're welcome.

‡‡‡‡‡‡‡

I'm going to go ahead and say it: I do not identify as black and I never have. I also don't say that I am a person of color or a person of culture. We all have color and culture. On forms that don't include "other" as an option, I choose Native American. I don't necessarily identify as an Indian, but I do more so than black and certainly more than white. Most of the time, I prefer "other". That term suits more and more of us as time passes. Maybe one day the question will be eliminated.

Luckily, my race never played an obvious role in my life when I was growing up. My neighborhood has been changing for decades, but it has always been fairly diverse and I've never had to think about fitting in or being different. Last month, a friend told me I'm ethnically ambiguous. In my neighborhood, people assume they can speak to me in Spanish, down the hill the store owner thinks I speak Arabic, downtown they think I'm East Indian.

When I was twelve or thirteen, I slept over at a friend's house. They were Irish and Catholic. When morning came, it was Sunday and, in an effort to extend the friendly fun, I agreed to go to church with them. In case you don't already know, I will tell you that this is not a good idea. Catholic masses serve their purpose, I suppose, but they are not a good way to end a sleepover, date, or any other type of fun event in my opinion. Just don't do it.

After the mass, as we were exiting the church, there was some All in the Family type congestion in the doorway. When we were outside, my friend's mother apologized to me somehow. In the confusion I searched my mind to figure out what she was talking about and remembered hearing the words "stupid spic." I hadn't even realized I should've been offended. I had nothing to do with the woman to whom this had been directed. We weren't even from the same country. I just didn't understand it. I didn't even know at the time that I was a spic.

In the end, I was only embarrassed for her and embarrassed for my friend, and clearly, I never forgot it.

‡‡‡‡‡‡‡

Once I flew in a mosquito. Officially, it was a Piper Archer aircraft, but really the two are practically the same. We had to drive a while to get to an airport that would accommodate us, maybe because the regular airport only allowed real airplanes.

The story starts at a friend's house where a group of us were discussing our plans for traveling to an event in Virginia. One of the young men among us offered to fly my mother for $50 in a rental plane. Eventually, I decided to join them. I had been on many plane trips in my life and this guy was probably a pilot, so shaving travel time and cost from my trip sounded like a good idea.

The airport from which we were to depart was about an hour away from my house. When we got there, the pilot dude pointed out our plane and my mother said, "That one? It's so cute." Dude responded, "No, the one behind it," pointing at a plane that looked like the small plane's grand baby, about a third of its size. There was some talk about weight and, suffice it to say that, today my mother and I probably would not be allowed to fly together on this toy plane.

Soon enough we had crammed ourselves into the aluminum can, and I would like to tell you that the inside of the plane was smaller than the inside of a car, but you will probably think I am exaggerating or joking as I have been known to do, so I will not tell you that the inside of this plane was smaller than the inside of a car even though that is the truth.

Small and loud. You know how you hear muffled noise when you're on a plane? You know how, when you're on the ground, you can hear loud planes far away in the distance? Well, in this piece of flying furniture, you are in the noise and the noise is in you. Clunky headphones do very little to keep the sound out and you can only hear the voices of the pilot and the front seat passenger. Also, cold. It's just cold and loud up there, and cramped.

It was beautiful, though. The sky was clear with only wispy clouds. We flew between the pillars of the George Washington bridge and passed the Statue of Liberty. We also heard control tower conversations and learned interesting stuff. The trip was fast and the landing was smooth. We had fun in Virginia over the weekend and then it was time to come home.

The trip home was on a Sunday night. We flew over the heavily-trafficked highway and appreciated not being in one of the cars that contributed to the wonderful site of ribbons of red light.

This time around I was up front next to the pilot. I, of course had no intention of touching anything, but at one point, in the midst of some frantic actions and words I could hardly make out, I managed to get the message that the pilot needed my help immediately. There was some problem with the plane and he needed me to fly it while he fixed it. I really don't know the extent of the issue, but we were either about to die or we weren't and, since I'm telling this tale and it's about me, let's just say that we were about to go down. Spoiler alert: we survived. I didn't even have a driver's license at the time, but I somehow managed to keep us in the air. Now, don't let anyone tell you that once you're in the air there's really nothing to flying a plane because, even though that's true, it will really just ruin the feel of my story at this point.

Soon after the trouble started, it was over and we continued our beautiful nighttime journey passing the illuminated skyline of my fine city, almost home. Almost home we were, but not before I got another opportunity to dip my toes into the sea of deathful fear.

It turns out that just as boats make wakes in the water, planes make wakes in the air. These wakes cause turbulence for anything else that is trying to glide through the sky. Even though we were landing in a mosquitoport, we had to pass New York City's two major airports and make our way through the bumpy air that the five hundred, eighty-seven million jumbo jets that were buzzing around that night made. Not only that, but we were flying just above the water to avoid the traffic. Just above the water was our default and then the turbulence would sometimes dip us lower.

When I teach, I talk about fear and excitement being exactly the same in our bodies and that the only difference is in the label we use for the sensations we experience. Let's just say that I was so excited I thought the excitement would kill me! KILL ME!

To my surprise, we survived again. We even remained dry. My pilot friend never charged me nor my mother the $50 in the end. Maybe I paid my way by being instrumental in saving us the first time. Maybe he felt bad that he and the "excitement" almost killed me the second time.

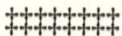

My husband is really good at explaining things. He loves it. He has information about lots of different things and enjoys sharing his knowledge. Sometimes he also just puts things together and makes up explanations. Recently, I heard him tell my children why people like to shop. His explanation sounded really good. It might even be factual.

It doesn't explain, though, why I do not like to shop. Why I do not like to shop so much that, if I was one who used the word "hate," I would say I hate to shop. You know what? I'm going to go ahead and say that I hate to shop. It is like the punishment I get for using stuff up. Cruel and too frequent punishment.

According to my husband, and possibly some super smart anthropologists or something too, humans are programmed to shop because we are programmed to look at our surroundings and choose the things that will benefit us, to look at a group of plants and "shop" for the ones that wouldn't harm us.

That sounds great, but I suppose I would've poisoned myself or starved. It's even more likely though that I would have stayed behind, everyone recognizing that my talent was for either cooking or for helping the child-bearers. Yeah, I think I would've just had others do the shopping for me and then come deliver the goods to my door. That's the way to do it!

One summer day (maybe spring (maybe even autumn. I don't know. It doesn't really matter. Just keep reading.) at least a dozen years ago, my husband, stepchildren, brother-in-law and his wife and son decided to go downtown semi-aimlessly.

It was hot. I think that I might prefer shopping to uncomfortable heat. We walked around casually and, as we approached an outdoor flea market, it looked like we were all going to go through and check things out. If I have to shop, the best scenario is to be in an establishment that organizes things neatly by type, color, or size, preferably all of these. Also, clean things are a plus. And not in the sun. This flea market had none of these preferences. Furthermore, there was a $1 fee for admittance. $1 is very little, but if one does not want to be there, it is too much.

Before long, my husband and I were a little disgruntled with each other and I ended up insulting all of the happy shoppers there asking (probably at the top of my voice) why I would want to pay a dollar to look at old junk.

I walked away and cried and ended up back home with a terrible migraine. Years later, we still go to flea markets, and I have managed to survive. I do not disrelish them any less and I do not like shopping anymore, but almost always there is no need for me to yell about it among happy shoppers.

╫╫╫╫╫╫╫

I shared recently about my ethnic ambiguity and how I've never felt discrimination or aggression that I thought was related to my race, whatever it might be—I'm not going to be the one to assign myself a particular race.

There was one time, however, just after a deadly Palestinian-Israeli scuffle, when I was definitely targeted, albeit falsely, and watched as a possible threat to a whole theatre full of people.

I remember how surprised I was and that it was fairly amusing. I do like attention, after all. My husband and I had decided to have an impromptu date and headed to Broadway to see The Tale of the Allergist's Wife.

This show was not billed as a Jewish show, it wasn't advertised as a Jewish show, and people didn't generally call it a Jewish show, but anyone who knew it would say this was a Jewish show. Valerie Harper was in it. That's Rhoda Morgenstern to my generation and the one before. Need I say more?

The show was very entertaining and laugh-out-loud funny at times. Before we went up to our seats (and I'm sure we went up, way up), though, I noticed in the lobby that I had caught the eye of a man. Now I'm sure you're thinking, "Of course you did! Do you own a mirror? This surely happens to you all of the time!" Well, I'll leave that for another tale and just say that this eye I caught was scrutinizing me differently than usual.

I have on several occasions been thought to be Israeli. My horticulture teacher in high school was actually obsessed with the disbelief of my non-Israeliness. In a crowded theatre, among hundreds of NYC Jews, the owner of the attracted eye saw me as different, very different and a possible threat.

I was never approached, but I was followed and I was definitely watched. It was so obvious that, had I been planning some violent act, I would've probably backed down. I can't be sure about that, though, because I don't know how a violent actor thinks. Still, they would have noticed that they had been busted.

I said it was fairly amusing, but I know that there are people to whom this type of thing happens regularly and they are surely not amused.

✝✝✝✝✝✝✝

Communication is very important. When I teach, I devote an hour and a half to this topic. I could spend a day and a half on it, though, and still only scratch the surface.

I am, as I write this, recovering from the effects of a little breakdown in communication myself.

I have an injury, which I've been hoping just heals itself for many months now. Sometimes it seems to be getting better and then it's not and then, my favorite part, it gets worse. I started going to an acupuncturist for general well-being and he chose to focus on my injury, because in his mind, unlike the mind of the useless western medicine doctor I went to before, the injury should not be ignored. Wacky Chinese ideas, I know.

Today, after placing the needles in all of the right places, he told me, in his heavy accent, that he was going to use the steam machine. He said "stim machine", similarly to how my heavily-accented mother would say it. Usually, he uses a heat lamp and today he was going to use steam instead. Groovy. Let's go.

I was face-down on the table and heard him wheel over a little cart. It took him a few minutes to get everything adjusted, and then he told me to tell him when I feel something and to let him know if it's too strong. Sure. No problem. It's steam. I don't really like moist heat, but this was going to be fine. Except that it wasn't exactly. When he turned on the machine, I felt an electric pulse and my leg started twitching uncontrollably. I gasped (or something. Maybe I screamed. I'm trying to forget), and exclaimed, "I thought you said 'steam machine'." I laughed at myself as he said, "No, stim machine, for stimulation." Yeah, I got that part. No need for explanation, thanks very much. He had actually pronounced it perfectly and I resisted believing him.

I should have known too. This "healing" place is all about the torture, leaving my back with multiple bruises every time, from cupping, a technique that has been used for thousands of years just because people are scared to decline it, knowing that the practitioners are capable of much worse. Oh, sure, go ahead and suction me with your glass orbs and open flames. I'll just stay here motionless hoping I come out alive.

The first time I went, the acupuncturist said he would ask "the lady" to come in and massage me. Oooh, I like massage. I really like massage. This was going to be great. She would smooth away the tension caused by the performance artist who had turned me into a porcupine. Nice!

When I was on my belly, someone walked in. No words were spoken and I couldn't turn to see who was there because needles. Needles everywhere. The mystery person quickly removed the needles and, as she reached for a bottle of oil, I could see polished toenails peeping out of some comfort sandals. Then, as she dotted my body with the bottle, I got the familiar smell of childhood injuries. We called it Chinese menthol. The massage was about to begin. Calm and relaxation would soon ensue. Too bad no one told the lady about this plan!

She proceeded to try to kill me. I didn't scream because I thought, if I let one sound out, I won't be able to stop, or worse, I would encourage her to do more and do it harder (not that harder could even be possible!). I am a lover of deep tissue massage, but this woman's forearm was trying to become one with my back. Her elbow tried to touch the table through my butt. I know this sounds like an exaggeration, but it is so true that I'm laughing right now even though thinking about it also makes me want to cry.

When she was satisfied that I would never be able to peel myself off of the table, she spoke for the first time, saying only, "O.K." I didn't quite agree with that assessment.

I got myself dressed and walked out of the torture chamber and into the reception area where I saw her looking at me with a grin on her face. I'm sure she was pleased. I smiled back, and boldly showed her my resilience. I felt like punching her in the face, but never having punched anyone in the anything before, I refrained, lest I injure myself and have to go through more torture for another body part. I keep going back, though. Is one of us trying to prove something? Are we both?

How are there so many people in China? How is it that they survive this stuff!?!

‡‡‡‡‡‡‡

I remember some of my early beach days, when I didn't want to be apart from my mother, sometimes only touching the water if she was face down in the sand and I was on top of her. We didn't go in very far. I remember fearing sharks and other unseen things that might possibly be lurking in the algae-tinted waters. I also remember a general displeasure for having sandy bits and pokey things and the fact that, right after washing stuff off in the ocean, stuff got stuck back on. Oh, and the handfuls of sand that were always left in my bathing suit no matter how well I tried to swish it out in the water.

Later, I remember having a marvelous time in the water with my cousins. A day at the beach meant I would spend the whole time in the water. It still does. I don't understand why people enjoy sitting in the sun or tanning on purpose. I would be very happy if all beaches had a roof, and fewer icky things, also no sand would be good. "Pool" is probably the word I would use to describe my ideal beach. Still, I love spending hours being crashed by waves. That end-of-the-day exhaustion is like no other to me. Especially when it includes the smell of rice with "chipi chipi" or the little clams that my uncles dug up in the afternoon for my aunt, grandmother, and mother to cook.

For a couple of years, the family would spend the day at the beach, all the girls donning the same bathing suit, and then enjoy the evening in my aunt's pool in the backyard. The pool and a hose-down was easier than waiting for your turn in the shower. I remember being in that pool when my grandmother taught me that, even though "agua" is feminine, you need to say "el" and not "la" because it starts with an "a". She didn't explain it to me then. She just corrected me brusquely and I will never forget it.

I remember Far Rockaway beach and my grandmother bringing conch salad to the lifeguards and swimming at night with the whole family. There's nothing like night swimming. My grandmother bought a house two blocks from the beach, planning to sell it to the casino developers who never came. We enjoyed it for a few years while we waited for them. Our waters always had sea jellies in August and horseshoe crabs, which we called manta rays and seriously thought they would insert their foot-long tails in us if we stepped on them. Fear did not keep us, though, from spending full days in the water from sunrise to moonrise.

Soon I'll be going to spend the whole week at a beach, making memories with my own small family. We'll have a good time and the memories will be beautiful, but they will be totally different because so many of the key players have scattered away to distant shores. Yes, I am on the verge of tears.

‡‡‡‡‡‡‡

Almost half a century ago, my mother settled in a small town in Panamá, where my grandmother had a business and where other relatives were living as well. She had a thriving hair salon and a beautiful toddler. She even remembers her furniture from these days with fondness. Life was good.

At some point, a couple of my relatives came to New York, pioneered by my uncle whose father was Puerto Rican. That father did nothing much for my uncle nor the rest of our family other than, by virtue of his nationality, making it possible for many of us to end up in the U.S.

When my aunt came to New York to try to find a better way for her family, she left her two young daughters in my mother's care. A couple of years later it was time for them to join her, but now my mother was pregnant. This was not a problem for my grandmother, spinner of webs, schemer extraordinaire.

My mother did not want to move to New York, but the girls needed to be here and my grandmother had already planned for her belly to hatch on U.S. soil. She was also trying to escape from the man who gave her the belly, so she went along with the plans as the plot thickened.

My mother would travel with her own eight-year-old daughter and her nieces, aged five and three. Somehow, the man from whom she was trying to get away, ended up joining in on the adventure too. Armed with tour packages for Disney World, my grandmother managed to get visas for everyone's

innocent child could possibly be accused of. Was she trying too much to kiss her stone-hard butt? Well, sorry!

The teacher came up close to me and said, "Your daughter needs a real dance school. We have nothing to offer her here." I felt like I was being scolded yet somehow, I found a compliment hidden in her words. For the rest of the year, I had to apologize for not pulling her out of the school early. Then I had to apologize for not matriculating her at the Alvin Ailey school, the teacher's top suggestion. She managed to smile sometimes as we discussed her vision of my daughter's stardom.

Seven years later, my daughter has proven her smart parent wrong. She is joyously still dancing and has received a full three-year scholarship to a great pre-professional program into which she was recruited in a similar fashion as described above. She has also proven to be a smart child, staying grounded even if only on her toes. She loves dance, but that love hasn't blinded her to her other myriad interests.

✠✠✠✠✠✠✠

In the second week of September of 1973, my mother walked over to the hospital for her first prenatal visit in the U.S. I was due to be born that month, so good timing, Ma. My sister had been born via cesarean eight years earlier and my mother's new doctor confirmed that I would be born the same way. He also told her that it would need to be soon because "the baby was too big." These communications were mostly made through hand gestures and with little help from the Puerto Rican interpreter.

On September 20th, my mother went to her second visit and was told that she would have her surgery that day. She explained to her doctor that that would be impossible. She had too many things to do and other children to care for. She penciled it in for the next day. Good thing too because I love my birthday. Of course, I'm sure I'd love it no matter what day it was.

For various reasons, my mother thought she was having a boy this time around. Sure enough, when she said to the doctor "boy?" He winked and responded "girl". The wink of course, meant that he was joking because that's really something to joke about at that time. After the surgery they showed my mother her baby and in her narcotic stupor she indeed saw some version of male genitalia. Later she thought it strange that in this country they wrapped the boys in pink blankets.

When relatives came to visit and talked about her daughter's big nose, she thought they were joking—not about the nose, about the daughter. Eventually, my mother figured things out. No one thought I was a boy. Everyone still thinks I have a big nose, though.

‡‡‡‡‡‡‡‡

There is a certain neighborhood in Manhattan that makes me feel like a celebrity. Among these thirty or so blocks I am never surprised to hear someone calling my name.

Last week, at the library, I heard "Rina!?!" I looked over to see an unfamiliar face with the corners of her lips pinned to each ear. I responded with a simple smile which surely revealed to this woman that I needed a little help. Of course, she offered, "You were my doula," and generously added, "Five years ago." After only one blink, my brain worked it out and I said her last name and then her first. She was impressed. So was I.

I would never totally forget a client, but after supporting hundreds of laboring families, sometimes it takes me a few seconds or thirty. I've chatted, reminisced, viewed photos, and heard expectations of future pregnancies on street corners, grocery stores and coffee shops.

In one week alone, I saw three former clients and one woman who had interviewed me and had chosen someone else. She called me after her baby was born, asking if I was available to be her nanny since she had missed out on having me as her doula. That was a little odd, but when I saw her in the grocery store, while I was comparing peanut butter labels, it was nice to hear her talk about her birth story and to have her know that I got it.

At the end of that week, I was leading a birth doula training workshop. During the lunch break, I was, as I often am, speaking to a stranger. I was somewhat surprised to find that he knew just what I was talking about when I told him I am a doula. At a time when so many people of childbearing age have never heard of a doula, it was lovely to find that this single, forty-something-year-old man who spoke a certain way and definitely looked a certain way, seemed to know about my profession, my vocation.

He not only seemed to know what a doula is, he actually proved himself, describing his sister-in-law's experience with her great doula. He continued to share how she was due to birth her second child any day and how she had the same doula again. He continued continuing, shattering my bias, and told me about the difficulties of the first birth and went as far as mentioning his young nephew by name. The name he called him was one I had only ever heard once before. It was the name of a baby who had been born a year and a half earlier. His mother was pregnant and due around that time and I was her doula. That's right. This man was my client's brother-in-law. Crazy coincidence.

It's always great seeing former clients. We have shared a momentous experience so it makes sense that I will remember them even if it takes my brain a few seconds to connect the non-pregnant figures with the people I worked with in the past.

Once, I was at the theatre, in the bathroom after the show. The woman washing her hands at the sink next to me saw my reflection in the mirror and turned to me with her jaw nearing the floor and exclaimed, "You were at my birth!" My friend had been her doula and, although this isn't the appropriate place to share the details, let's just say that I went to this birth to assist my friend and ended up taking over. It was a beautiful birth which proved her triumphant over her previous traumatic experience. I spent about four amazing, dimly lit hours with her, mostly in her bathroom, and now we were in a bathroom on Broadway and she was hugging me and crying.

She introduced me to her family and told them that I had changed her life. I know I did not. I know that I was just a witness and facilitator to the amazing work that she did that night. I guess this goes along with my kind of celebrity!

‡‡‡‡‡‡‡‡

I didn't grow up eating lots of red meat or pork. We ate seafood frequently and poultry. I now eat it even less. I cook mammal, as we call it, once a year on St. Patrick's Day. That's it.

I certainly don't consider myself a vegetarian and, if you invite me over, I'll eat whatever you give me. I'll also bring a delicious dessert, so go ahead and invite me over. (Really, I'm a lovely guest and I like to plan ahead, so PM me or something. I'm serious.)

I would eat more meat if it wasn't for the fact that I don't particularly enjoy the flavor or the texture or the idea of eating meat—just those small things, you know. If you make it on the grill like my Tia Magaly used to with some magical from-the-ground seasoning, I will probably like it. Animals get stuck in my teeth, though, and I will be reminded that I don't like to eat meat as I am picking the pieces out.

I don't know if I would like meat more if I had eaten it as a child. Maybe there was an incident that turned me away from meat. If there was, it was probably this one. It might seem strange to you, but that's only because it is strange. (It's very, very strange and I know by sharing this tale I am decreasing my chances of being invited over for dinner (even though I could bring dessert and even an appetizer or two)).

On this day, when I was eight or nine (I'd like to say I was younger to decrease my shame, but I was definitely at least eight), I was home maybe by myself, maybe my sister was in the room sleeping. I'm thinking I was by myself and that my mother was working at the beauty parlor a five-minute walk away. I called my mother at work and asked her what I should make for lunch and she must have told me to make myself a hamburger.

We never had hamburgers. Never, except for this one time when my mother had prepared some meat and made patties to freeze in this fancy Tupperware hamburger-freezing-keep-them-apart tower. The Tupperware lady really scored with that sale because this was a very unnecessary purchase for my mother. Nonetheless, there it was, in my freezer, full of frozen dead cow patties.

Of course, I had never made a hamburger before, so I followed my mother's instructions. After waiting a few minutes of letting my future meal cook over a low flame, I lifted the lid of the pan for a peek. I couldn't believe what I saw. My innocent chunk of chopped flesh had metamorphosed into a grey, oozing monster. I'm not just describing it as a monster today. I actually called my mother crying and told her it was a monster. She told me to turn off the stove and go to her job.

I seemed so brave when I went into the kitchen to turn off the stove, but I was really scared. I remember, as I was locking the door to the apartment, I imagined that the monster burger thing had grown and was approaching the door. I got out of there so quickly. The fear was real. Are you laughing at me? I'm laughing at me.

(Feel free to invite me over, but if you are making meat, please make sure it's cooked before I get there because I clearly cannot handle that nonsense.)

‡‡‡‡‡‡‡‡

In September I attended a conference for childbirth educators. One of the sessions I chose was Cultural Competence, Hidden Bias, and Maternal Child Health. Being in New York City, working with people of diverse backgrounds who are serving a multifarious community, and often even an under-resourced group very different from their own, I always strive to find tools that will help me understand, impart understanding, and do the right thing by the incommensurable individuals that make up my town.

I've said it already in several tales and I still have a couple of tales to go in which I will repeat that I have never felt like a minority in my city. So there I was in this conference session, straddling the conversation with one foot planted in a place blossoming with privilege and the other planted in the soil of minority inequities.

The speaker, a former clown, was charismatic and engaging, leading the discussion with great enthusiasm. The group was larger than she anticipated, so she took us into the corridor and demonstrated how we could not guess one another's secrets based on our looks alone and how our biases might lead us to make mistaken assumptions. This was entertaining enough, but I wasn't learning anything new. In the end, I can't say that I gained any of the new tools for which I went there. In the end, I only gained a little sympathy for myself, though I still maintain that I am undeserving of it. This is what happened.

After we tried to reveal some biases and a few secrets, we were invited to participate in another exercise. We were told we could opt out in the beginning or at any other point. We could walk away or choose to stand there without participating. It was set up as a safe exercise in a safe space. Being an educator, I was familiar with this activity. I had never led it or participated in it, but I had read about it and learned how eye-opening it could be for privileged people who were somewhat blind to their lot.

No one opted out and we all stood side by side in a long line. I noticed that, in this line, I was flanked by two black women. I noticed because I assumed that race and ethnicity would factor into our participation, and we were among a group of mostly white women.

In this line we were to listen to various descriptions and either take a step forward or a step backward depending on whether or not it applied to us. A few descriptions in, I found myself stifling the tears. The exercise was different than I had expected and I was not where I thought I would be. Taking a step forward meant that we had or had been raised with some sort of privilege. Taking a step back meant, well, the opposite.

I took only a couple of steps forward because the wonderful way I grew up was apparently underprivileged. I kept walking further and further back. As the activity progressed, I regressed and all of my colleagues, every one, left me behind.

I am not lying to people when I say that I grew up without feeling the effects of prejudice even though I am a minority. Maybe I'm lying to myself. No. I think I've just been very lucky. I know that, if I do this exercise with a group of people in my city, in my neighborhood, in my building, I might be embarrassed to be so far in front. For many of us, anywhere we might find ourselves in that line seems inadequate somehow.

‡‡‡‡‡‡‡

Yesterday, a group of friends and I were talking about driving. One of my friends, a fellow New Yorker, is moving to Massachusetts and will need to learn how to drive. As several people offered to teach her, I chimed in with the fact that my driver's license is only for ID and that I had passed my road test because I had flirted.

As believable as this may seem, it is actually not true. I did not flirt at all during my road test. (Well, not any more than my normal state of being just has me give off a flirtatious vibe.) I was not purposefully sending out any flirtatious energy whatever. As a matter of fact, the woman from the driving school who set up my road test appointment had arranged it so that I was tested by this particular man on whom she had a crush. She told me that he was married, but that she just loved going to see him because he was so cute. I know that we all have unique tastes, but I think that hers was partially informed by blindness. I saw no cuteness in this man at all.

He, however, seemed to see some cuteness in me. He was very clear about that. He was bold and unexpectedly flirtatious. I really don't know why he was so confident. I remember sitting there trying to ignore him and just take my road test.

Finally, the road test was almost over. I had parked and turned and luckily there were no pedestrians around to nearly hit. When we were headed back, the tester man was talking and I was driving and suddenly he said, "There's a stop sign." There was indeed a stop sign nailed to a tree. That doesn't seem like a good idea to me because it's a tree and should not have things, especially trafficy things nailed to it. Also, people might be distracted by the treeness of it and not notice the actual sign. Anyway, I craned my neck a bit and saw that the stop sign was there, almost, but not quite behind me. Then I looked at the guy and said, "Does that mean I fail?" Yes, I should've failed, but how could he possibly fail me? He knew and I knew that he could not. That's how I got my official government ID.

‡‡‡‡‡‡‡‡

I'm going to talk about breasts and braziers, so excuse yourself if necessary. I call myself crispy because I'm crunchy for some things, but definitely not all. I remove the hair from my legs and armpits and, despite the trouble I have getting a satisfactory fit-style combination, I have been wearing a bra for about thirty-two years.

I have only recently started sleeping without a bra and I just can't imagine walking around without one during the day. I know I've been brainwashed, but I just think it would be too distracting, to me and those around me. While my breasts aren't huge, they are each more than a handful for my large hands and they tend to move when not being wrapped onto my chest by an undergarment.

Once I did a class with an herbalist who probably stopped wearing a bra decades ago. It was distracting, I tell you. Her breasts are larger than mine and, even more noteworthy, they are longer than mine. It reminds me of an old family joke I used to hear as a child about the woman who wanted to commit suicide (Jokes about suicide and breasts were apparently totally appropriate to share with the children in my family. I'm sure that's not what screwed me up.) Anyway, this woman wanted to kill herself swiftly with one bullet so she went to the doctor and asked him where exactly her heart was located to which he responded, "three fingers below your left breast". The next day, the woman was rushed to the hospital with a bullet wound in her left knee. I always loved that one!

So, here's the tale part of my tale. I stopped breastfeeding about three years ago and decided to get myself some regular bras. After I made this decision, much time passed because buying bras is a chore for me. I am very picky and some of the things I like to pick are hard to find in my size. I waited until I got a message. I thought it was a message from the Universe. It came in the form of a post in an online parent listserv to which I belong. Someone was having an expert from a fancy lingerie company do private fittings in her apartment. There would be all sorts of sizes and styles available. I went.

The expert measured me and announced that in her company's size lingo my cup was a size Q, or some other similarly absurd letter. Fine. I don't care what you call it as long as I like it. Then she convinced me that I liked it. I had to believe that I liked this crazy bra that made me look like a different person because I paid $95 for it and left with it on.

By the time I got home I was crying. My husband felt so bad for me, he didn't even get angry. Buying bras is so difficult for me. Maybe I should just let them loose.

‡‡‡‡‡‡‡

Today is my mother's birthday. While I love celebrating people on their birthdays, true to my birth worker spirit, I would like to honor my grandmother instead.

On November 3,1941, my grandmother, hardly eighteen years old, birthed my mother. Pay close attention to these dates and imagine my young grandmother in Barranquilla, Colombia. On November 14, 1940, she had birthed my aunt. Maybe she liked the routine because on November 5, 1942, she had my uncle. She wasn't yet twenty and she had three little ones.

In November of 1943 my grandmother was lazy. She did not have another birth that month, but she was pregnant and had another baby the following March. She had four more after that.

Writing this makes my eyes watery because that's just how I am and also because this is an amazing feat of which I would be in awe no matter who's it was, and also because I knew this person and so much of her story, and also because my two children are more than a handful for me even though I had them after the age of thirty with a myriad of conveniences at my fingertips.

My eyes are no longer watery because I have released lots of tears now thinking of the privilege I had on many occasions to sit with my grandmother and hear her incredible stories. Then, sometimes I would hear my mother's version of the same stories. No matter the point of view, my grandmother always ended up as the heroine against odds I can hardly imagine.

This month marks one year since we lost the opportunity of hearing stories from my grandmother and today actually marks the year since we lost my grandfather, in whose honor I began to write my Tuesday Tales.

‡‡‡‡‡‡‡

I have been moved by music countless times in my life. Music has sent me back in time and brought me to tears. *Sunshine on My Shoulders* reminds me of my mother talking about my father (it's not an actual memory of my father, but that's as good as it gets). *Close to You* reminds me of my cousins (it also reminds me of a supermarket, but that's a little less sentimental). For months in 2001, I cried whenever I heard or even sang *Both Sides Now. What the World Needs Now* reminds me of that time I did that concert and someone advertised it as 'From Bach to Bacharach'. We were definitely doing Bach, but we had to add that song, which probably never needs to be sung in a concert. Then there was that time on vacation when I was sitting in a supermarket parking lot waiting for my husband. His CD of road trip music was playing and on came a song I hadn't heard in years. The sound of Dolly Parton singing *Here You Come Again* punched a hole through my chest and squeezed my heart until my tear ducts overflowed in poignant sobs of the most inexplicable melancholy. I felt like that song must have been playing in the background of my torture chamber as a child. That, or maybe it was hormones. It's still a mystery.

I've been fortunate to be moved by music as a performer as well. I've sung so many beautiful pieces in majestic theatres. There's nothing like singing Peter J. Wilhousky's arrangement of *The Battle Hymn of the Republic* in Carnegie Hall or Hall Johnson's spirituals in a dimly lit sanctuary. My whole life is different because of the wonderful experiences I've had singing marvelous music!

Today's tale doesn't have to do with me performing. Most of you will say it doesn't include marvelous music. I would agree with that, but it was definitely a song that touched me for a special reason and it almost got me in trouble.

I had recently started dating the man who would be my husband. We were sitting in his living room and through the windows we could hear the neighbor's music. This was so common that my husband donated a bunch of records to him so that he could at least have some say in the music we were forced to listen to. On this day, the neighbor put on *Missing You* by John Waite. I probably sighed and stared off into the distance as the music brought me back to another time. My new beau noticed that I was no longer entirely in the room with him and, for the first time, he seemed to be upset at me. He thought I was reminiscing about another romance. He was not pleased.

In fact, I was nostalgic for my past romance with the Columbia Records and Tape Club. John Waite's album was among the first I received. I can still see it standing atop my record player with his picture on it. Remember getting a bunch of records and tapes for free? Remember records and tapes? I know these thoughts of music past are making you feel some kind of way too.

‡‡‡‡‡‡‡

Weight—a favorite topic for many.

My father is tall and slender. My mother is short and round. I am tall and rounded. I've gained about sixty pounds in a decade and a half and people love to say that it's OK because I'm tall. Tall and wide, people, tall and wide.

Someone once told me I have yang bones and yin flesh. Maybe they said it was the other way around, definitely one of those two, though. A few years ago, when I was met with disbelief after saying I weigh 200 pounds, I clarified that it was actually 197 pounds. My conversation mates made fun of me, saying that I'm the only person to round up to 200 evah. Now I'm quite a bit over 200, so I'm not rounding anywhere. The last fifteen pounds I gained were surely muscle, but I keep the muscle protected under layers of fat because yin, baby (or maybe yang—whichever)!

Anyway, enough of the backdrop. Here's today's tale. I am very flexible and have found that my shoulders pop out of their sockets sometimes. They pop right back in, but this fact doesn't detract from the intense pain I feel, which has at times lasted for a year. Luckily, each dislocation has seemed to make my shoulders stronger and it's been years since this has happened. Quick, everyone, knock on wood or something.

About ten years ago, my mother, weighing over 200 pounds, lost a battle against gravity and landed on her left arm, dislocating her shoulder. Hers did not pop back in. Her pain did not last as long as mine but I dare say it was worse. She wore a sling for a while after the hospital staff readjusted her. During her healing period she was somewhat depressed. She's left-handed and had lost much of the use of that hand. She wasn't eating much and she was losing weight.

One day, she came back from a follow-up visit with her doctor. She was in good spirits and gleefully shared that she was under 200 pounds. She looked like a child when I asked her how much she weighed and her face lit up as she said, "One ninety-nine!" It was adorable. For her, that number meant that she was now in onederland.

‡‡‡‡‡‡‡

Sometimes you date a person and you just know it isn't going to work out. Like the guy who loves your hair in that style you only use when your hair is dirty or the guy who thinks the name you chose for your future daughter is ridiculous (and it's your actual daughter's name now) or the guy who buys you delicious treats all the time because he's actually trying to fatten you up so no one else finds you attractive. Losers, all of them.

Today's tale focuses on one such guy and how I knew that he could never be the one. He had planned an October trip for us to the beautiful autumnal paradise that is Mohonk Mountain House in Ulster County, New York. This place is gorgeous year-round, but during my favorite season, it has the most appeal to me, autumn. Imagine me sitting by the lake in which are reflected the vibrant colors of the changing trees that abound all around us. I have to imagine this too because, unfortunately, it is not part of my memory from this trip.

This boyfriend of mine had usually seen me wearing high-heeled shoes and skirts or dresses. How he thought I might enjoy a rustic hike through perilous terrain, I do not know. Still, he did and off we went. He didn't tell me the plan until we got there and, when faced with steep climbs through jagged-edged rocks, I wasn't completely sure that the plan was not to kill me. I cried. I cried because I was afraid and because I couldn't believe what I was doing. I cried because I thought going back was just as bad as going forward.

I'm talking about a trail called The Labyrinth. I think it's supposed to be fun. It wasn't. It's for normal, courageous, adventurous people. It is not for me. I always remember how weak and wimpy and scared I felt while doing this thing. Even at the end, I wasn't proud of my feat. I just felt traumatized.

Last week, while visiting Mohonk with my friends, I told them this story. We peeked from the scenic path on which we meandered over onto The Labyrinth and my strong, brave friends laughed with me at my memory of almost dying. Then we heard some young, normal looking, possibly even athletic men on the trail remarking on what a stupid idea it was for them to try it. Some of you may have been on The Labyrinth. You may even go regularly. You might think I'm overreacting or even stupid. As for me, I will never go again because I am not stupid.

That boyfriend didn't last very long. He cried when we broke up. I figure he owed me some tears.

‡‡‡‡‡‡‡

My children are homeschooled. Mostly we unschool, as I am confident that they will somehow take in what they need like they take in oxygen. My family does have a history of this type of education, after all.

My savvy, well-read mother attended school for about a year. She may not appreciate knowing that I've made this public to my millions (tens, whatever) of readers, but those of you who know her personally can attest to the fact that by sharing this, I am complimenting her and by saying that she is savvy and well-read I am falling short of a proper description for those who do not know her. She was offered a scholarship and an opportunity for higher education at one point. She declined and let her sister go to school instead, preferring to continue her learning in a way that was more meaningful to her at the time—out in the world.

My grandfather also had an advanced degree in self education. He always had interesting things to say. He could talk about current events as well as events that were current a thousand years ago. He had read about everything. He started reading as a boy in the home of a man for whom he was supposed to be working. I don't know if the man was a family friend or a family member, but I'm pretty sure he showed up in a García Marquez novel at least once.

This man had a room that was full of books. I don't know what my grandfather actually did for this man, but it seems like a large part of his job was to sit and read all day and all night. That's what he did. He read all the books in the room when it was lit and when it was dark.

My grandfather never stopped reading and talking about the things he read and the things he lived. He was interesting without trying to be. I'm so happy that my children are just like him.

‡‡‡‡‡‡‡

Recently, I have seen a couple of articles about musical frisson, chills some people get when listening to music. I was surprised to read that not everyone experiences this. I frequently react to music with shivers and, actually, I react to lots of things that way. Apparently, this sensation is caused by a surge of dopamine, so many of you may not be surprised to learn that I am extra dopey.

I don't have a tale today, really. I want to share the lyrics of a song I sang in concerts for a couple of decades. It is an a cappella arrangement in four-part harmony by Carl M. Steubing. His harmonies never fail to produce musical frisson for me even though I've never heard the song without my own voice adding to the magic.

Part of the chills come from the message of the song, though, taken from a poem by Miles J. Martin. Dr. Martin, an American, met eyes with a stranger while traveling in Asia and was moved to pen the words that flowed from his heart. Because every Tuesday Tale brings me to tears or guffaws, I am sure I don't need to tell you about the state of my eyes right now. I wish the world could sing this song together.

Brothers
Who is that man in garments quaint and rare?
Who is he who speaks in rhythms alien to my ear?
Who is he? Who is he?
To him I am as strange as he to me
and in his questing eyes I read a silent plea.
Who are you? Who are you?
How sad it is we do not know each other,
but when he smiles, At once I recognize my brother.
I hope that he can see in me his brother.

‡‡‡‡‡‡‡

70

Today's weather reminds me of a great road trip I once took because it is so unlike the weather we had that weekend. It was a January in the 1990s. That seems like a different century because it was. It was an entirely different time when people in New York City actually needed to wear coats outside. Imagine.

At this point in my life I had a group of friends with whom I would do various seminars. I planned a trip with one of these friends. Let's call her Gita Punjabi. Everyone called her that because that was her name.

Gita and I had a friend who lived in Virginia and we decided to drive down and visit her. Gita decided to drive and I was just going to sit because (do you know me?), I do not drive. We would head out after a Friday night class that would end sometime around midnight.

My mother was very worried about this trip. I did not understand her concern. I had been driven down to Virginia before and, even though you might think that way back in the 1990s I was a child, I had, in fact, recently escaped that label.

After class, Gita and I rushed around, getting ourselves together, telling our friends about our plans. Everyone had something to say. The thing they all said was about the snowstorm. I had heard that there would be snow. That's probably why I was wearing my three-inch, leather heels instead of my four-inch, suede ones. Suede doesn't do too well in the snow, you know. I didn't know it was supposed to be a storm, but even when I found out, it didn't really mean anything to me. Gita seemed to be equally unperturbed.

The snow had just started falling as our drive began. It was beautiful. It was still beautiful a little while later when we stopped to use the bathroom and the snow was around my ankles, even though my ankles were pretty high off the ground, perched atop skinny, leather heels.

We marveled at the fact that there were hardly any other cars on the road. Soon we noticed that, even if there had been cars, we wouldn't have been able to see them because everything was white. It's not just that everything was covered in snow, but there was snow everywhere. Snow was falling from above and also whizzing sideways and blowing up and all around us.

The sun came out to greet us as we approached our destination. Soon we were also greeted by our host in a warm, cozy home with a basket of fresh pastries. It was like a movie, a good movie, or the positive all-is-well part at the beginning of a horror movie, or it could even be like a bad movie, but this would have been a really good part of that bad movie. It was nice.

We chatted and munched for a little while. Gita and I hadn't slept, but we were enjoying the warmth and comfort and companionship, also the pastries. After a little while, we wrapped ourselves in blankets in the living room and our hostess read to us. I will never ever forget listening to *The Wonderful Story of Henry Sugar* that day. She read the whole thing. I listened to most of it, but had momentary dozes too. It was perfect.

I've read the story since then. I got the book because I remember it being so amazing. It isn't a bad story, but reading it on my own just wasn't the same.

I imagine that I am the only person who remembers this day. It was so special. I hope I make memories like that for people too. That's all I have for today. Maybe this tale was a dud for you, but my eyes got a little watery for a minute there and you know that's always a plus for me.

‡‡‡‡‡‡‡‡

There is a song that can be heard around this time of year about shoes. It tells a story about a little boy buying shoes for his dying mother. To me, it is one of the worst songs ever recorded. You might disagree, but if you did, you would be wrong.

There are much better stories I can think of about shoes. Maybe I'll write some shoe songs myself one day. In the meantime, here are some shoe tales, and they all have to do with my mother.

Her shoe history starts at a very young age. Among her earliest memories, my mother carries one of her father shining his shoes obsessively. For many years into her adulthood, the predominant feelings that accompanied this memory were disdain and disappointment. She remembers seeing her father polishing his shoes during the day, when in her mind, he should have been working. She felt for a long time that the only thing her father was good for was shining his shoes. One day my mother realized that my grandfather polished his shoes every day so that he could wear them every night to work. He was a well-dressed, shiny-shoed singer who performed at night. She felt bad about the contempt she had harbored for all of those years. Shoes.

The next story about my mother and shoes is much more straight forward. It's actually quite common and one others, maybe some of you, can relate to. It is really just the product of poverty and a pair of feet that keep growing. My mother has big feet. Today, in the U.S., it is easy for her to find adequate footwear. When she was growing up, if she had been in the U.S., it would have been much harder. Since she was in South America, it was almost impossible. Even before her feet were too big, they kept growing to attain that goal. The acquisition of better fitting footwear never seemed timely enough. It wasn't uncommon for her to squeeze into shoes that were too small for her. I've done that too, but only because the shoes were fabulous, not out of necessity.

Next is one of my favorite of my mother's childhood stories. It plays in my head like a movie on the big screen. For my mother's year or two of schooling, she was in a Catholic school. There are lots of tales about that, and one might wonder if her dislike of religion has anything to do with her Catholic school experiences. Let's stick to this story about shoes for now. My mother has always been clean and neat. She polished her shoes daily (she had a good precedent for that) and her uniform was clean and pressed. On this particular day, she would be a fine example for the special guest that was to visit the school. It was a bishop or cardinal. It was some Catholic dude who walked around getting lots of respect from the peons. This day was no different. The whole school was in the yard to greet his excellency (I think that title works, right?). Everyone began to genuflect and, as they did, my mother realized that the sandy soil beneath her feet was not a good match for her clean neatness, especially her shoes. She stood there straight-legged as everyone else dropped until, in the multitude, she was the lone stander. Everyone looked up at her from their lowly poses. At that point, it was too late for her to give in. The nuns pleaded with her to kneel, explaining the importance of showing the man respect. He was just a man, though, and her shoes were shiny, so their pleas just made her dig her heels in further, not literally, of course, as her heels had been polished too.

Finally, there's a story of my mother's first experience of snow and her choice of footwear on that day. I had been born in September in a hospital that was not far from the apartment where we were living. My mother walked to the hospital on the day that I was born and for many appointments after that. A few months after I was born, there was a snowstorm and my mother went out by foot to her appointment at the hospital. The snow was new to her and it delayed her walking a bit, but she had to get where she was going. It was really no big deal. That is until she got to the clinic and everyone reacted to her with shock and horror. She had walked in the snow in her pointy, very high-heeled shoes. She hadn't thought to do anything different and, if she had, she likely couldn't have because of her limited selection. The staff at the clinic took up a collection in order to send her home in a taxi that day.

Today, my mother has lots of shoes in her size, even snow boots. Her feet have reacted a bit to her ill-fitting shoes and very high heels, but she manages pretty well. She also, gained respect for her father and, I would guess, that she would even go barefoot to walk alongside him today.

‡‡‡‡‡‡‡

Some of you have urged me to compile my tales into a book. This is not an announcement of such book. I've had a weekly tale for thirteen months and some of them are stinky so there's work yet to be done.

Some of them are stinky because I am a lazy, non-proof-reading writer. I love editing others' work, but rereading my own is tedious. I regret it when I see my deplorable errors, but that regret is very short-lived. Part of the appeal of my tales is the content, particularly when I write about my family. Theirs is a rich history and my best tales are about people who came before me, I think.

Another reason you may like my tales is because of my writing style. It is a somewhat unfiltered thought-to-keyboard approach, albeit my little phone keyboard usually used while

I'm traveling underground from one appointment to the next. It is a little filtered because, otherwise, my tales would be too long. I love to spill my stream of consciousness on a page, but you might like it less when you realize you've wasted so much time reading my nothing of a tale. I remember being praised for this style by several teachers, all named Richard, throughout the years. The first one was in sixth grade. He loved my writing. He was Canadian, though, so I figured he might not know what he was talking about. In high school there was another Richard who appreciated my ramblings. He died the year after he taught me, so maybe he suffered from a lack of lucidity that affected his judgment.

My freshman year of college I took a speech class with yet another Richard. This one really liked my writing and, it seemed, lots of other things about me too. I wrote an essay for him once that was completely off topic by the middle of the first line, never to return. I felt like he was going to love it no matter what. I was right.

One of our big assignments in that class was to give an instructional speech. I will never forget listening to useless information from my classmates. There are only two speeches whose content I remember: the one through which I sat enviously watching as the speaker demonstrated on someone else the proper way to give a neck massage, and mine.

I could have done anything I wanted with my speech. I was the ruler of the writing Richards after all. I decided to teach the class how to properly pronounce my name—verrry useful. I talked about my uncle getting a job when he mispronounced the interviewer, Mr. Major's, name as "Mr. Mayor", a title he actually aspired to gain. Then I warned them that, in a similar situation, calling Mr. Wahl "Mr. Floor" could go terribly wrong.

After convincing them of the importance of respecting people's names, I rolled my tongue, saying Rrrrrrina and cringed at their pathetic attempts in response. I instructed them to use the same movements they used when saying the double t in butter. Being the most pretentious one there, I knew none of their tongues came close to their teeth when saying that word and that, in fact, they made the same sound when saying butter as is needed to roll the r in my name.

Now you know too and I'm sure you are as grateful as they all were to learn how to pronounce my name. Probably as grateful as you are to be at the end of this week's tale. It isn't one of the better ones, but Richard, I'm sure, any one of them, would have probably loved it.

‡‡‡‡‡‡‡

A couple of weeks ago, I almost died, and I almost got arrested, and almost got a ticket, and a cop almost killed me and my sister tried to kill me. All of those things. It was terrible. It may sound like an exaggeration, but you can judge for yourself. Here are the facts.

I took my sister and my mother to see a comedian. He was funny, but I didn't almost die from laughter. Afterwards, we went out for Japanese food and it was good. I did not almost die from food poisoning. So far, so good, but there's more. There's the near-death part, the harrowing part, so you must read on.

I know I told you once that I almost died while flying an airplane and I obviously survived, but this was worse because I was in a car and there were other cars and people and possible incarceration or ticketing or death.

After the show and dinner, my sister had to run an errand. We were in her car. She stopped her car in the middle of 6th Avenue so that she could go into the store. I noticed it was far from the parked cars and commented on this. She said she did not want to block the bike lane. Very considerate. I thought this was a good idea even though it left us in the middle of a lane, in the middle of Manhattan. This must be what people do, I thought. You don't want to block a bicycle lane.

My sister got out of the car and so did I. I walked to the driver's seat and put on my seat belt so it could look like I was the driver. I fondled the gas and brake pedals with my foot, trying to remember which is which. I always forget. Usually this isn't a problem. On the passenger sides of cars there is only a brake pedal. I know this because, although it is imaginary, I press this pedal quite a bit whenever I am in a car.

My mother and I were talking and I was only a little nervous. I would look through the rear-view mirror once in a while and notice annoyance and inaudible foul language coming from drivers who noticed too late that my vehicle was not moving in response to the green light. The hazard lights were on. I was a hazard. Could they not see?

After a few minutes, I saw that the car behind us was a police car. This is when death started pounding on my chest. I heard the voice of Satan, I think, tell me to move the car. I put my foot on the probable brake pedal and put the car into drive with that little stick thingy. I totally knew what I was doing. The car moved a little and somewhere, I can't even remember how I got this message, but there must have been electronically activated words somewhere telling me about the emergency brake being on. I actually knew what that meant and was able to lower another stick thingy to take the brake off. This was taking hours, or maybe a minute, and I was about to cry, when I noticed outside my door, a police officer who was at least eight feet tall. If I had been walking down the street, he would've been cute, but I was in the driver's seat of a car with sweat and tears in my eyes. He was scary.

I tried to lower the window, but I couldn't figure out how. Are you getting that I really don't know about cars? I don't. I had to open the door, hoping the officer would not take this as a threat. I told him that this was my sister's car and that she had just run into the store and that she didn't want to block the bike lane. He said, "You can't stop a car in the middle of 6th Avenue." There wasn't even an opening for flirtation. It was terrible!

I pulled a few meters up to the red light and, when it changed, I bounced the car forward, tapping on the gas pedal. In preparation for my turn at the next corner, I activated the windshield wipers. That was very useful. Eventually, I signaled my turn properly and pulled around to block a crosswalk just off of 6th Avenue. The police officer probably understood how pathetic I was and kept driving.

I called my sister and told her where I was with her death machine and she soon came to rescue me. 2015 was such a tough year!

‡‡‡‡‡‡‡

At fourteen months, my daughter was a frequent milk sipper. In our house, "milk" came from me. There was also "cow milk" and "soy milk", but those weren't called "milk". Months

77

before she was verbal, my daughter made the sign for milk, as we learned sign language together. She made it all the time, as if it was the sign for air. She would have lots of milk in the morning and at night and then pause her activities every few minutes all day long to just sip. This arrangement was fine for me.

For a year after my daughter was born, I did not menstruate. I started again the night of her first birthday, November 6th. I was relieved because I wanted to have another baby as soon as possible.

The beginning of December was normal. The end, not so much. I had had the opportunity to become well acquainted with my reproductive system due to reasons I will describe in a future tale, so part of December was marked by something going on, something I recognized as not quite right.

I visited my gynecologist. We are friends and, although she couldn't detect a problem, she trusted me and my instincts. She had me schedule an ultrasound. I went.

I have had lots of pelvic and transvaginal ultrasounds because I know how to have a good time. Ha! I'm always chatty with the technicians because I'm always chatty with people and sometimes I'm even chatty with things. They are not supposed to give any information about what they are finding, certainly not a diagnosis. Sometimes they have very serious looks on their faces and it turns out that they are concentrating on their job and that there's no concern.

Sometimes, they are lighthearted and friendly and, when they leave the room to consult with their supervising doctor about the emergency situation that is about to explode in your body, they turn the monitor towards you so that you can get a glimpse of the image and perhaps decipher what is going on with the grey blobs found therein. That's what happened this time.

I couldn't really interpret much, but I did see "EDD 9/21/2005"—the estimated date of delivery of a baby I seemed to be making was on my birthday!

After a long absence, the technician came back in and told me to get dressed and that the doctor would speak to me soon. The doctor told me that she had just spoken to my gynecologist and instructed me to go to the hospital across the street, bypass the emergency room and go straight to Labor and Delivery where I would be met by my gynecologist's colleague. As I walked away, she added that I had an ectopic pregnancy and that I was getting preferential treatment and that this was an emergency.

I called my husband from the hospital lobby. He was waiting nearby with my daughter and agreed to meet me there. I was in Labor and Delivery with my family, not looking pregnant, not in labor. My daughter, as usual, was sipping her milk every now and then.

Everyone was very nice to me as they explained that the pregnancy was in my ovary (very rare) and how lucky I was to have caught it so early. Because I had, they were able to offer me a dose of methotrexate rather than surgery. Chemotherapy. A shot in my arm. This drug attacks rapidly multiplying cells. It would stop the pregnancy from progressing. It would also end the breastfeeding relationship with my daughter. Abruptly.

My daughter does not remember nursing. She's actually repulsed by the thought of it. I remember many instances of nursing her. I especially remember the last time and it still makes me teary. Everyone will say that fourteen months is a long time to breastfeed, but we weren't done.

The big needle hurt my arm and the effects of the chemotherapy were hard to handle for a couple of months. My breasts got hot, hard, and heavy. The physical toil doesn't compare to the emotions that flooded my household that winter, though. My daughter wailed. I wailed. My husband had to deal with our wailing.

I was told not to get pregnant for a few months and, once I was cleared, my body made another baby right away. When my son was born, my daughter asked to taste my milk because she couldn't remember what it was like. She liked it, but wasn't interested, to my husband's super relief, in going back to nursing.

When she talks back to me and slams the door in my face, I will always wonder if she's reacting to the trauma of being prematurely ripped from my breast. That must be it because what other reason would a preteen have for such behavior?

‡‡‡‡‡‡‡

Last week, my family went to see the Batmobile, from the 60s TV show, at the New York Historical Society. This was a dream come true for my husband. I was really happy for him and hardly embarrassed at all. While there, we saw a tin toy and model train exhibit, a comic book exhibit and, while my children were writing code in the coding lab, I stood in front of Picasso's immense Le Tricorne tapestry and some other stunning works of art. Yes, toys, comics, computers, and art all together because this is the New York Historical Society in New York City and we can do whatever we want.

I've seen great art in many different places—famous museums, small galleries, private shows, the street, my living room and perhaps yours. Different venues call for different decorum and I like to think that I am usually able to blend in. Unfortunately, I have to say usually instead of always.

When I was fifteen, I went to Italy. There was beauty everywhere. The people, the buildings, the streets, the food, the language—all beautiful. It seemed that even the small corner church in a tiny town was a work of art. Then there's St. Peter's Basilica, worthy of weeks-long investigation and praise just for the building itself, but then they throw in some other art and there's just so much to see.

One of the things to see is the Pietá, the only piece Michelangelo ever signed because he was like, "Yeah, baby, I did this. Look and weep. Uh huh." The faces of Mary and Jesus are serene and beautiful and I felt like I would totally be their friends if it wasn't for the fact that they were made of marble. Also, they lived far away and long ago—definitely a hindrance. Some think they are fictional characters, which would make our friendship all the less likely. There I was, admiring them anyway, because I am totally OK with admiring beautiful strangers. I have even gotten good at controlling my urge to kiss them. Kissing the Pietá would probably be more frowned upon than kissing a stranger on the train. Not that I know from experience how unacceptable that might be because, of course, I have never done that, ever. Not even in my imagination once, everrever. At least the Pietá is protected by plexiglass.

Anyway, let's stay on topic here, people. Back to the Pietá, which is housed in a holy place, a place of pilgrimage, an important shrine to so many. Even leaving all religiosity aside, the Pietá and the basilica merit reverence, in my opinion, and they were getting it on that day, as I stood silently in awe and admiration among a group of tourists, following the unspoken rules, unspeaking being among them because any noise in this place would be magnified a gajillion times, disturbing many a prayer and mindful contemplation.

There we all were looking and admiring, many of us taking photos. I had taken many, many photos on this trip with a camera I borrowed from a friend. Remember, I was fifteen, so this was a different century. Things were primitive. The camera I borrowed used rolls of film, and I couldn't even use it to make phone calls!

I would like to say that this is where my tale ends, but there is one more thing for me to share. As I stood there in solemn veneration with other respectable tourists, I took a photo and suddenly I became the main attraction, as my camera decided to wind up the roll of film, creating a noise that reverberated into the domes and crevices of the whole humongous place. I tried to muffle the sound with my hands and clothes, adding a bit of buffoonery to the spectacle because, hey, there wasn't already enough for these tourists to see in this amazing place.

☩☩☩☩☩☩☩

On Friday, a friend invited me to a Broadway show because she had an extra ticket for the next day, the day we were expecting a blizzard. She said, "You're the only person I know who would enjoy a trip to the city to see a show in a blizzard." She seems to know lots of losers, but that's not the point. The point is that she gained this knowledge of me through experience.

The year was 1996. It was a Sunday. I was working as a singer at a church at the time and the person who would often give me a ride there told me that she didn't want to drive for fear of having a hard time getting back home, when it was supposed to be snowing. Oh, was it going to snow? I hadn't heard.

The night before, I had meticulously prepared an extra-large version of my fine tiramisú (I always pronounce it with the accent over the u, as should you, at least when you are in my presence.) as a birthday cake for my dear friend with whom I would be celebrating. Since it was sure to be a delightful event, I was bringing along my childhood friend and my mother, who also happens to be a childhood friend, my first I would say.

Sure enough, after my church gig, I found that it had already snowed a great deal. As interminable as some of the church services seemed, I had only been indoors for about four hours, and the amount of snow that covered the streets and the, well, everything didn't seem to compute. That is, until one noticed that the snowflakes seemed to occupy every space where there should have been air.

I got home and prepared to head down to lower, lower and way east Manhattan, one of the points in Manhattan that is farthest from my home. My mother, my friend, and I got on the train, me toting my delicious cake. I don't think we even considered not going.

When we got out of the station, my excellent sense of direction froze as I was forced to inhale only snow. The sun had set, yet everything was brightly white. We were the only ones in the street and we couldn't tell street from sidewalk, east from west, north from south.

We got a great fifteen-minute workout trudge-walking the usual five-minute walk to the apartment. When we arrived, we found that the festivities had begun in a warm location with equally warm people. It was great fun and the cake was delicious. I know I already mentioned that, but it really was so good.

On last Saturday, the day of our 2016 blizzard, I went out with my friend to see the Broadway show. Right after we arrived at the theatre, the show, all shows along with everything else, was canceled. We had a good time walking through Times Square with only half the usual number of tourists, maybe two million. Eventually, we hopped back on our train before the service was shut down and, when I was almost home, I called my mother.

My mother was hysterical and relieved. Apparently, the news she was watching had informed her that I, along with anyone else who dared be outdoors, was teetering on the brink of death. Whatever could I have been doing out in the snow!?! I reminded her about the fun we had had in 1996 and how we had somehow survived. I think she's still upset at me despite the fact that I made it home and proved that miracles can happen even amidst precipitation. Apparently, being in a blizzard is better than watching one on TV.

‡‡‡‡‡‡‡

People have asked me if I write Tuesday Tales in advance, if I have a few stored that I can just post on any Tuesday. Nah. I always quickly jot something down, sometimes while on the subway. I'm sure you can often tell.

Then there's today, a Tuesday, and two words which I will dance around to spare you from being victimized by TMI—food poisoning.

You recently read that, if I had to save my life by driving away from danger, I'd probably die, likely from drowning in my tears. Speaking of drowning, maybe sometime you'll read about my swimming (dis)abilities. I'm usually fine in a pool, but if I had to save my life, again, I'd just sink. When it comes to ridding my body of toxins, though, I'm a pro. I guess I'm not good at using my brain when it comes to life preservation. Yeah, so I put something bad in my body and it gets really dramatic about expelling it.

I remember that lovely brunch I had with that cute boy from Buffalo. The hollandaise sauce was extra tart. The next day was not so lovely. There was also that strongly oceanic crab I had at a family dinner once which made me strongly nauseatic the next day. Good times!

I spent the weekend in Clearwater Florida. I had a great time. When I wasn't working, I was eating. They have lots of seafood there. Perfect. Oysters, scallops, mahi mahi, shrimp, mussels, lobster, and grouper. All delicious. All but that one oyster. It practically introduced itself right before I ate it. You know, "say hello to my little friend" style. I never even saw that movie, whichever one it is, but I know that was not a cordial introduction.

Fast forward a few hours and I'm in bed, not asleep. The feeling in my stomach is wisely keeping me awake so I can make it to the bathroom in time. I know how things will go and I'm thinking about 1) not making noise in my hotel room 2) having to board a plane in fewer than twelve hours. Way to party on my last night in Florida.

During the night, I got a little bit of sleep and a lot of exercise as I walked to the bathroom and ended up showering a couple of times. Sometime around 4 I even washed the sink. Let's leave it at that. I was parched, but even though there was a full glass of water on the nightstand next to me, it was too far, and drinking from it necessitated a little bit of uprightedness from my body, which only wanted to be swallowed by the mattress. By 6:30am I was feeling pretty well. I was awake and things seemed like they were going to be just fine. I WAS WRONG! The little oyster had contaminated all sorts of stuff in there and it all wanted to escape simultaneously. I don't know how to say this politely. I was sitting on the edge of the tub at one point and that was just a bad idea. Luckily, the tub and the toilet were right next to each other. Yeah. The deft maneuvering I would have needed to make less of a job for myself afterward was not a part of my survival plan. I cleaned up very well and took a long shower. I left a good housekeeping tip just in case.

After that, I felt practically fine because what was there left for me to feel bad about? Nothing, I'm pretty sure. I drank a bunch of water and got ready for my day. Oh, yes. I was going to fly in an airplane. I had planned to get to the airport early and do some important work and then do some important work on the plane. My brain doesn't function, though, when I'm trying to save my life, remember? No important work got done. I couldn't even spin this tale with some hilarity. I was planning to do that for you. Really. I'm dehydrated, though, and brain no worky. The good news is that nothing came out of me on the plane. Also, I weigh four pounds fewer than I did before my trip. Really. I just weighed myself. Way to diet!

‡‡‡‡‡‡‡‡

Let's talk about egg foo young. Really, you'll be reading, right? Just make believe you can hear my voice telling you this tale because, it may not be such a great tale, but my voice is lovely. Also, I'm not even sure I'm talking about egg foo young here. It could've been something else.

When I was little, we often ate at Chinese restaurants. Sometimes we ate at the Chinese Cuban place where Spanish-speaking people would go and distort their tongues in order to approximate the pronunciation of their Asian meal only to be answered by the waitstaff with, "¿Pa' comé' aqui o pa' llevá'?" in a perfect Cuban accent. Usually we ordered family style, sharing several large plates. Frequently, we ordered familiar things. We knew what we liked. That's what we had.

Today I'm focusing on a particular day. We were celebrating someone's something and we were at a new place. I remember being seated upstairs in a dimly lit dining room. It all seemed a bit formal.

I remember sitting there, looking at the menu, talking to the other children. I've never really liked eating cow, pig, goat, or lamb, but there was so much from which to choose and, other than those exceptions, I ate all sorts of things. There was also the usual, which was good and that's what I'd probably end up having. This fancy menu did something to me, though. The words tickled my eyeballs and danced with my soul. I was seduced right there at the table at the tender age of something less than eight. Eight sounds good. I can't remember exactly.

Not only was I hankering a new dish, but I wanted the other children at the table to join me in my orgy with this exotic meal. I was never the ringleader, but somehow I managed to convince all of the other children there that evening to order the exact same thing. This was uncharacteristic of me and I'm not entirely sure we were not actually at an opium den. It was all very strange.

When our orders arrived, each child got their own small, aluminum, lidded pan. Upon opening them we each found an egg atop a very unappealing mixture of I-don't-know-what. I was not a picky eater. Somehow, I had managed to choose the one thing on the menu with questionable palatability. It wouldn't have been so bad if I hadn't also forced (and I really don't know how I did) the other children, all my seniors, to order the same thing.

None of us ate it and the adults sort of punished us for our foolishness in not diversifying our selections by not letting us have anything else. I blame the other children. Why had they listened to me? Morons.

Happy lunar new year, everyone. Don't be a monkey see, monkey do. Order your own delicious food and eat it so you don't have to resort to fried noodles and duck sauce.

‡‡‡‡‡‡‡‡

Do you remember Valentine's Day 2007? I do. Here's what happened. My husband was upset at me that day. This is often the case. Some might say that I give him lots of reasons to be upset at me. Others might say that he gets upset at me for no reason. Only some of you would be wrong. Let's not get into that too much because now he'll be upset at me for writing this. The reason for his upset on that day, nine years ago, is that I went out in a snowstorm with my newborn son. You might be on his side now, but you'll be on mine soon enough.

My son was born on January 14th. I wrote a lovely Tuesday Tale about that magical day. I probably wrote it in January of last year. Go find it. It was a good one. Anyway, this tale is about the very unmagical days and weeks that followed. "Unmagical" is not a word, but I'm trying to stay away from "torturous". It was only torturous when I was nursing and he was only nursing most of the time, so I don't want to exaggerate.

My nipples bled and my son was not gaining weight. I was getting his weight checked regularly because it is generally frowned upon for a newborn to lose weight and not gain it back. I cried and shrieked and persisted and never really sought help because I'm some sort of martyr moron or something.

My nipples were bleeding or sore for several months, but sometime between weeks three and four, there was a shift. I was still in pain, there was still blood, but I know that my son was doing better and that he was gaining weight. His next weight check was scheduled for February 14th and I just knew he'd pass and that it would be his last.

On that day snow was blizzarding in New York City and I had to take a trip down to the pediatrician with my one-month-old. On a clear day the trip takes an hour and includes a ten-minute walk. I strapped my son onto me, beneath my coat and off I went against my husband's and my mother's wishes.

When I showed up to the office, I was told that the pediatrician hadn't come in that day. I guess she does a better job of listening to her husband than I do. It was OK. I just needed someone to check my baby's weight.

Eventually, I was brought into a room and answered some questions. A nurse took my son and weighed him. The scale was not only a different scale than had been used the previous week, it was not an infant scale. According to that scale, my son had lost a little weight. Seeing my watery eyes, the nurse explained that this happens sometimes and that it was normal.

I have a hard time being confrontational and getting what I need. I sat there crying, waiting for a doctor I did not know. When he showed up, out of my mouth came the words of someone I didn't know either. I demanded that my son be weighed on the same scale as last week and I said I wouldn't leave until that happened. I acted like a strong mother who knew what was right for her child even though I was shriveled up on the inside.

Of course, on the right scale, my baby's weight was just fine and we did not have to go back for anymore checks. I was so proud of myself and my husband was happy that it had all worked out. A little snow was nothing for this determined mother. I ended up breastfeeding my son for five years. Valentine's Day was just the beginning of that loving relationship.

‡‡‡‡‡‡‡

One of my sisters in Colombia sent me some photos of my father and me. I thought it would be nice to write a tale about him, but I've spent a total of about two weeks with him outside of my infant days, and I already posted a couple of memories from those visits. What to write? Remember those times I was embarrassed and laughed at? I do.

When I was eight, I went to Colombia to meet my father. I was fluent in Spanish. It is, in fact, my first language. I don't think this was cool to him, though, because among certain of his friends he did not want me to speak Spanish. He wanted me to be the cool Gringa or something. It was so weird that his friends in the bowling alley would say things that I understood and I would have to act like "No hablando espanol."

One night we were in the bowling alley (because in my one week there we must have gone half a dozen times) with one of his friends of the female variety. The three of us were sitting on one side of a booth with me between them. Maybe we were having dinner. (They did have good food there.) I was literally in the middle of a conversation I was not supposed to understand, but I did. Boy, did I. I was embarrassed and wondering if my father was embarrassed as his friend told him of her pregnancy right there, practically in my ear. I never mentioned it to him because no hablando, you know.

In February of 2000, I was met at the airport in Barranquilla by my father and four siblings. Three of them were his wife's children and the other was, well, not. There were tears of joy and lots of excitement.

We all crammed into a car and my father started asking questions about my relatives, who he hadn't seen since I was a baby. I reported on the aging and the successes and the offspring. He inquired if a particular uncle had managed to have any children and I responded, "Oh yes, he has five, and imagine! After so many years of not being able to have children, his girlfriend had a baby a few months before his wife. They're the same age!"

The silence only lasted for a second, followed by uproarious laughter. They were all laughing at me and my naïveté. Two of my siblings are the same age too and they aren't twins. Baby-making seems to be my father's superpower. Of course, it is relatively easy for men, so maybe not.

‡‡‡‡‡‡‡‡

I complimented a friend the other day by saying how impressed I was with the amount of thought that seems to go into the things he says. That's a normal compliment, right? I am not that way. Words just come out of my face hole with seemingly no connection to my brain sometimes.

There are times when this works out for me. I'm often the first one with a funny comment. It's not because I've carefully composed these comments. They just slip out and often work. Other times, my words don't work as well and we just end up laughing at me because I'm like a jester or funny-looking or there's the pity thing too, I suppose.

There have been times, of course, when my mouth-brain disconnects have been just sad. The first time I remember this happening, I was in first grade. In the days, perhaps weeks, before this word-vomiting incident, my family had been watching a biographical film about Elvis or Caruso. I'm pretty sure it was Elvis, but there's a chance it could've been Caruso and why risk being wrong? It could have also been a completely fictional character. There's also a chance that I made up the memory of the film after my mouth-inflicted trauma, but let's go with a movie about Elvis. That's what we were watching.

In this movie, the Elvis character was on stage and his wife had had a baby. Someone in the audience managed to communicate that he had a baby girl and he couldn't contain his emotion and blurted out, "It's a girl!" I can see the scene vividly in my mind, but even if it never happened, you can all relate to not being able to contain yourself, right? Is it only me?

Well, there I was in first grade and there was some amazing piece of information that just had to be released from my soul and mostly my mouth. I called it out, whatever it was, before consulting with my brain.

I was a goody-goody type of child, so when my teacher told me to stand and face the window as punishment, my eyes did not consult my brain before releasing a stream of tears. I was embarrassed that the teacher now thought less of me. After a while, when the teacher told me from across the room, that I could sit down, I stood perfectly still as if I hadn't heard her because I always strive for perfection, so if I was going to be a victim, I was going to be the best victim possible. I stood there for a long time, a perfect martyr.

The next day, I explained to her and my mother, because this all necessitated a little meeting, what I had seen in the movie and how I could relate to the passion of unbridled speech. My teacher wasn't moved and probably wondered what I was even talking about, as she seemed much less devastated by the events of the previous day than I.

Despite my trauma, my mouth has continued to pay little attention to propriety or decorum or even my brain on a regular basis. It's mostly working out for me, but give me time and you'll catch me red-faced for sure.

‡‡‡‡‡‡‡

I have lived in the same building for thirty-six years. Yes, it is possible that I am more than thirty-six years old. I know you were wondering.   I regularly wish I could live somewhere else, but I know that if this place ever releases me, I will break down and sob. In this building I learned how to show up, literally and figuratively.

When Joel invited me to her birthday party, I went even though I didn't want to. I didn't count her as a friend, but I climbed a whole flight of stairs to get to her apartment and showed up. We had fun and ate a bunch of cake and ice cream by ourselves, butter pecan I remember. So delicious. It was just the two of us and we had a good time. If I hadn't gone, Joel would've had all the ice cream to herself because no one else went to her party. That memory blossoms easily in my head as it is watered by my tears.

When I was a little older, I somehow committed myself to accompany a neighbor on a job interview. I wasn't sure what I'd be doing on this errand, probably because the commitment had been made by my mother. On the morning of the interview, I did not want to go. My mother told me I didn't have to go and then quoted my great grandmother. If you ever want me to do something, just say a catchy phrase and tell me it's what my great grandmother used to say. I went. It was a beautiful day. I remember the dress I was wearing. It turns out that my neighbor didn't speak English and didn't exactly know how to get to where she was going. I was her interpreter and her guide. That day, people complimented me when they found out I was not her granddaughter, that I was helping my neighbor. She got the job and held it until she retired decades later. That was more than thirty years ago and I wonder how much she remembers about that day. I remember it as if it was yesterday.

When my family moved into the building, we were one of three Hispanic families there. Much has changed throughout the years and, today, most of my neighbors do not speak English, and my husband is one of the few people who does not speak Spanish.

When I go to Chinatown, Koreatown, Little India, Little Italy, I embrace each culture and marvel at the smells and sounds and, my favorite, the tastes. What a delight it is to be immersed in a different culture, I think. I don't have the same affinity for the sounds, sights, and smells in my own neighborhood, however, and they are distinctly cultural.

I am frustrated by my neighbors who don't speak English. The woman for whom I served as interpreter has been in this country as long as my mother and can hardly say "hello". If she spoke only Chinese, would I be more tolerant?

I am frustrated to hear music blasting in Spanish. To be fair, I don't like music blasting in English either. Perhaps I'm just self-conscious about being lumped into this group by outsiders because I am Spanish speaking too. I don't know.

If I was living downtown, surrounded by immigrants who shared my parents' homeland, maybe I would feel the same way about them, while embracing the differentness of the Spanish-speakers uptown. I don't know.

Why am I so hard on the people that are most similar to me? This building has more to teach me and that must be why I'm still here. I hope I learn quickly. I wish I had learned last year and had been able to move because I'm on the top floor and the elevator's been broken for five months. There's lots of complaining going on in Spanish.

‡‡‡‡‡‡‡

I was on the train with my children the other day. It was the beginning of the after-school rush hour. Three girls got on the train, calling attention to themselves with their foul language and high volume. Their combined age was not more than forty.

My triad caught their eye. As is often the case, there was clearly a leader of this pack, but she couldn't be a leader without followers. There they were, in front of us, harmless yet menacing because they were like one big blob in their group. I don't believe any of them would have been troublesome on her own. I have a particular disdain for the group dynamic that breeds this behavior, perhaps because I've always striven to be an individual, not swayed by peer pressure.

My son was reading a big, fat book, as usual. They had something to say about how weird that was. Thankfully, he was completely oblivious.

I said "excuse me" to my daughter when I didn't hear something she said. "Why she gotta say that? I slap my mother if she say that to me." I was younger than they when I learned to be polite and not say "what?". How is that a big deal to them? It's sad.

My legs were daintily crossed at the ankles and my feet were tucked underneath my seat, propped up on my toes. I was wearing ballet flats which hung off my feet a bit in this position, exposing my heels.

This to them was scandalous. They started talking in Spanish, sort of telling me to put my shoes on, but not directly, of course. They might have thought I didn't understand what they were saying. They even commented on the size of my feet. They are big, proportionate to the rest of me. One of them said, "If you have big feet that means you have a big..." I couldn't hear the rest. I wish I had because I'm not familiar with this idea. The fact is that my everything is big. I am a big woman.

"Make it a Better Ride for Everyone." This is one of the catch phrases for the Metropolitan Transit Authority's current PSA. Signs with these words were above my head and they caught the attention of my young friends.

"Does it say something about putting your shoes on because she gotta put her shoes on."

I couldn't take it anymore. I got up from my seat and put my face close to that of the loudest girl and with a very intense yet controlled voice, in a volume just above a whisper, said, "Does it say anything about children talking nonsense just because they're with a couple of friends who are not brave enough to tell them they are being stupid and disrespectful." I pointed at the "Courtesy Counts" poster and told the two followers that if they learn to think for themselves and make the right choices, they will end up better off than their friend.

I went on and on. It was great. They cried. Other passengers applauded. I changed three lives that day. I am a hero. The only problem is that everything I said was only in my imagination. Part of me wishes that I had said all of these things and part of me trusts that they will grow out of this need to have disrespectful displays in public and end up just fine.

I walked off the train on my big feet and left the girls to harass someone else. I'm sure they did.

‡‡‡‡‡‡‡

Today's tale is for my mother, who never tires of laughing at her parents and who should understand that I don't tire of laughing at her either.

My grandfather was separated from my grandmother for decades and they ended up living in the same building for a long time. He was also separated from his second wife for decades and she lived there too. Sometimes they all got along and sometimes only two of them got along, being a different two depending on the week or month. No matter what, it was easy to get complaints out of any of them about either of the other two at any given time.

Once, my grandfather was complaining about his second wife. He was calling her names and was angry at her because she had done a stupid thing. She had left the door to his apartment open and it had been burglarized. Luckily, the burglars had only stolen one thing. Still, he was furious. His bathroom was near the front door and they had come in and taken the tube of his bathroom tissue dispenser. Yes, he was convinced that this was what had happened. Yes, he was a grown man.

Not long after his ex-wife had caused him to be the victim of the very targeted larceny, he found himself injured by yet another commode calamity. His toilet overflowed. The plumber investigated and easily deciphered the cause of his toilet tragedy.

Somewhere beyond the bowl was found a plastic tube. You know, the kind that holds the roll of bathroom tissue. The kind that a burglar might be tempted to steal if he found that your stupid ex-wife had left your door ajar.

‡‡‡‡‡‡‡

I am probably going to go to the doctor sometime soon, but soon is relative and it may not happen this week. Some people think I need an x-ray and that I should've gotten it a couple of Tuesday Tales ago. These people are wimps.

A couple of weeks ago, as I was just starting my workout, I lifted a kettlebell for the very first exercise, and it attacked me. I'm left-handed and have had some soreness in my left wrist that comes and goes for years. When I work out, I wear a little wrist band, but it isn't much of an issue.

On this day, the kettlebell, knowing how confident I was in its use, decided to test me. We had a little fight and it won. My wrist really had little to do with it. My hand just crashed into my arm. There was a crunch sound. I'm pretty sure bones that aren't meant to touch each other did and did so in a less than gentle way. It was a great way to start my work out!

It's been two weeks since this happened and I'm probably going to call my doctor tomorrow. I just set myself a reminder to do it because I know that some of you are really going to pester me about it. Supportive friends and family can be a real drag.

‡‡‡‡‡‡‡

Last week's tale was cut short because I was on an express train and arrived at my stop pretty quickly, so I got off the train rather than staying on and writing more. Sorry. I went to the doctor yesterday. I am still alive. I may or may not have broken bones. I'll be getting an x-ray sometime soonish. Stop pestering me.

Last week I was going to tell you about my pain and suffering and my grinning and bearing. Here it is. About twenty years ago, I had foot surgery, both feet, one at a time. I am a planner and, when discussing things with my doctor, I was shocked to find that the surgery could not be scheduled for the time period I had anticipated. Somehow, I talked my way into the date I wanted. (I'm good at this sometimes. I can't really explain how. I just think it doesn't hurt to ask. Smiling too helps. I don't know.)

The first surgery was done in July. I was sent home with two prescriptions for pain killers. Strong stuff because, you know, surgery. In July, my student neighbor friend was around. My mother, with whom I lived, was around too. They were both ready and willing to help me as I recovered on the couch, foot elevated.

I told them I did not need the prescriptions filled. I could take it. How was I expected to give birth if I swallowed white pills every time I had a little pain? (I'm pretty sure I said these very words at the time.) I grew up with no medicine cabinet. I have a scar on each thigh about five inches long from two cuts I got when I was eight. I was probably supposed to go to the hospital and get a billion stitches. Instead, my mother took me home and poured some Listerine on my legs and sent me to bed. I know that sounds bad, but it was either going to be Listerine or Lysol, so I think she made the right call.

That night, the one after the surgery, I didn't sleep very well. I don't think I slept much at all, really, but I wasn't going anywhere the next day, so I just went in and out of sleep that day while my friend and mother took care of me. There was much less pain after that and, about a month later, way before my podiatrist expected me to be able to, I squeezed my foot into a shoe and went to a party.

The podiatrist was amazed at my fast healing and in December I had the second surgery, just as I had planned. Again, I was sent home with prescriptions and I laughed at them. Ha ha ha.

In December, my neighbor friend was in school and my mother was having a life or something, so I was home alone. I was on the couch with my foot elevated and my prescriptions were on the floor—not the drug-filled containers, just the prescription orders from the doctor on paper. Now, they were laughing at me. HA HA HA. I remember them vividly because, that night, they were likely wet. I probably drooled on them as I longed for the relief that they promised. I'm sure I cried on them too.

The pain that night was kind of hard to bear. Someone had cut my skin open, broken a bone, moved it over and shaved a piece off. Don't complain of the gory details. It was worse than it sounds. By morning, when someone could've gone to the pharmacy for me, it was too late for the worst of it. Sometimes I'm a dummy.

Yesterday, when I saw the doctor for my wrist, she asked if I had taken my medication. She meant painkillers. I looked at her confused and she said, "Oh." She explained the different things that might be broken. I told her it could just be a sprain. This is how we communicate. She worries about horrible possibilities and I calm her down. I'll be getting an x-ray today or maybe on another day this month or one of these months. If something turns out to be broken, I'll go to my mother's for some Listerine.

‡‡‡‡‡‡‡

This week I will be traveling to see renowned obstetrician, Michel Odent. I've never met him so I hope I don't embarrass myself by fawning too much. This hope was born of my experience. With a cocktail in hand, I once approached Eugene Declercq and said something along the lines of, "My students think I'm in love with you. It's not entirely true, but…" I don't think I finished my sentence because how could I possibly finish that sentence? I hadn't even started drinking the cocktail! I will refrain from professing love and I will also try very hard not to give him a sample of my fabulous French accent. Michel Odent is French and surely has a better accent than I. I should probably sit quietly and just listen. Wish me luck.

It is no accident that professionalism in my field does not require a cubicle, a suit or saying the right thing to a boss. Saying the right thing is sometimes problematic for me.

In January, I attended a retreat for DONA International-approved Doula Trainers. I am a DONA-approved Birth Doula Trainer. There were about fifty of us there. I say "us", but I often feel like it's "them". How is it that I am included in this group, I wonder? It is comprised of some fabulous people who have done amazing things.

In a group such as this, I tell myself to sit quietly and not draw any attention to myself, lest I be discovered and excommunicated. This is really hard! I walk around in bright clothes with my mouth permanently in a flashy smile. My mouth also does other things. It lets forth a loud laugh and words. So many words come out all of the time.

Well, there I was on the last day of the retreat, and there was going to be a raffle. Goody. We all wrote our names down on slips of paper and put them in a basket. Penny Simkin, grandmother of the doulas, was to draw the name. We all watched excitedly and, as she reached her hand in, I yelled out, "It's pronounced Rrrrrrina!" because way to be inconspicuous!

Of course, Penny pulled out the piece of paper with my name on it. The raffle prize was this trip to Florida. Off I go to try not to embarrass myself in front of a whole new group of people.

Today's tale is sort of a love letter to Dr. Scott G. Hartman, the father of my latest baby. He doesn't even know he's the father. Scandalous!

Years ago, Scott approached the doula community with a crazy idea. He was looking for childbirth educators for his patients. Lots of doulas thought he was crazy, so naturally, ours was a good match.

When I taught, I introduced myself as a doula and, of course, had to explain what a doula is. Once I explained, all of my students wanted doulas. They couldn't afford this special care and I couldn't volunteer for all of them, so I started matching them with people who were willing to volunteer.

I ran a volunteer doula program in some form or another for five years. In that time Scott, along with some other wonderful people like Tamara Wrenn, tried to get us funding. He also encouraged me to become a doula trainer and, in an effort to diversify the doula community, DONA International trained me. The organization's vision statement is "A doula for every person who wants one." I am proof that they are really trying to get there.

Several years ago, I found myself having to curtail my efforts as a volunteer matchmaker. My desire to reboot was always there, but it is hard work and the circumstances were never quite right.

They weren't necessarily right when I recently decided to launch the NYC Doula Corps, but I did anyway, with the help of the fabulous NYC Doula Collective. Many people have helped in different ways along the way, but I may not even have known that I wanted to do this if it hadn't been for Scott Hartman. Thank you.

‡‡‡‡‡‡‡

My grandmother tried to kill me once. You are probably wondering how I've managed to survive so many near-death experiences. Some of it may have to do with the fact that I am a descendant of Alicia Mercedes Palacio, my mother's mother.

My grandmother was an amazing woman. She was savvy in business and in dreams. Her fantastic optimism was contagious and she made words come to life when she wove them into a story. If it was a funny story, you had to be patient because she would make herself laugh so hard that she had trouble getting the words out. When she said "white snow" you could practically feel your eyeballs freeze.

Good with business, dreams, and stories. Not so good with children. It's just a fact. Some people do not like children. My grandmother was definitely one of these people.

Another thing. Maybe because of her generation, she seemed to be unaware that it is generally frowned upon to show favoritism towards some of your children and their offspring over others. She did this and it was obvious, at least to those who were not her favorites. I was among them.

I grew up with this as a matter of fact. It wasn't usually a big deal. I often had fine times with my grandmother and sometimes even had good times with her. There was that one day, though, when she tried to kill me. That was one of the not-so-good times.

I remember as if it just happened. It was morning and my grandmother had made soup for breakfast. It had noodles and veggies and eggs, which had been dropped in just at the end so that they were perfectly cooked. I remember the bowls that we drank the soup out of and I remember where I was sitting when I sipped at the deliciousness that was meant to be the end of me.

As I had my soup that morning, I swallowed something sharp. I knew at once that it must be a strategically placed eggshell, tool of my grandmother to be rid of me at last. I slowly pushed my seat away from the table and walked solemnly to the living room, where I perched myself atop the radiator and gazed out the window for what I thought would be the last time. The drama I am trying to convey was fully present in that moment for me.

I was not yet school-aged, so I stayed behind when my sister and cousins left for the day. I was sad to see them go. You know, for the last time ever. I did not speak for what seemed like hours. I sat there in my favorite spot, feeling like I had a sword in my throat.

Perhaps noticing that I had been silent for so long (maybe you can imagine that silence is not my customary way), one of my aunts eventually got me to eat a banana. This banana was the antidote to my eggshell and a foil to my grandmother's plan.

After that, neither of us ever spoke of it. Sometimes we got along and sometimes we did not, but I'm pretty sure my grandmother never tried to kill me again. Maybe she did, and I just survived each time.

‡‡‡‡‡‡‡‡

Today I bring you a tale of two doctors. I went to an orthopedist on Wednesday and a chiropractor on Thursday.

Orthopedist: What brings you here today?

Me: I wanted to meet you. (He did not react at all. He stood there, continuing to not smile. My smile, however, widened and I told him about my wrist injury.)

O: Where does it hurt?

Me: Actually, it feels pretty good today. You do amazing work! (Again, no reaction. Maybe he had a hearing problem. He took my lovely, delicate hand and placed it gently in his brawny fingers. With the other hand he held my arm. I thought he was warming up to me. I was wrong. He proceeded to tighten both grips and jammed my hand into my arm as he twisted.)

Me: Oh, that hurts. It definitely hurts now. Thank you for reminding me that I'm alive.

O: Do you hear that?

Me: The sound of an enthusiastic drum solo coming from my wrist? Yes, I do.

O: That's not normal. You'll need an x-ray.

Me: I got x-rays. They're in your system. (I refrained here from praising him on his observation of "not normal" even though I was understandably impressed by his brainular prowess at this moment. We looked at my three x-rays and he told me he needed to see more and some of the other hand too. After a dozen more flashes of radiation, we met again for a second date. Twenty minutes had elapsed since our first date. I was thrilled he remembered me.)

O: Do you see this space here? It's not supposed to be that big.

Me: OK

O: On the other wrist, it's not like that.

Me: I see.

O:...

Me: Why is it like that?

O: It's the ligament.

Me: What about the ligament? Is it stretched, torn, twisted?

O: It's torn.

Me: OK

O:...

Me: What can I do about it?

O: What's your concern?

Me: Well, it's painful and my whole arm is weak and the pain is keeping me from strengthening it.

O: The weakness is just pain. That's normal.

Me: ?

O: You can get an MRI.

Me: What will that do?

O: It will confirm my suspicion that the ligament is torn.

Me: So it's not really necessary.

O: No, you can wait. You don't need surgery right now.

Me: I wasn't planning on surgery anyway. How about physical therapy? I'd like to be able to use my hand again.

O: I can prescribe you a splint.

Me: OK. I'll take some therapy too.

O: I'll prescribe you a splint and give you a list of physical therapists. You're definitely going to need surgery one day. You'll also have arthritis. Until then, I have better things to do. See ya. (That's what it sounded like anyway.)

The next day I went to the chiropractor for the first time ever. He greeted me with a smile. We chatted and, when I explained how I had injured myself, he actually understood the words I was using. He was very pleasant and even laughed at my jokes. This last part makes me a little wary of his judgment, but let's see how it goes. He thoroughly examined me with his eyes, his hands, and a computer, explaining everything as he went along. He was very impressed with his findings. I am choosing to use the word "impressed". "Surprised" might also be applicable, or even "horrified".

Chiropractor: Wow! This is so interesting. I've never seen someone who compensated so well for their imbalances. Look at this!

Me: I try.

C: I can't believe what's going on with your neck. Does it

hurt?

Me: I have this perpetual knot in my back and for a few months the pain has been going up my neck.

C: I bet. That knot is actually a rib.

Me: Oh! I have a rib sticking out of my back. That's exciting.

(His evaluation took almost an hour. He explained everything along the way. I loved it. He made me want to become a chiropractor!)

C: Your pelvis is anterior. That means it's tilted this way. (He showed me and shared some of the implications of that.)

Me: Is that why my butt is flat?

C: Sure, (he responded straight-facedly) that can be a contributing factor. Do you have trouble working out your glutes?

Me: Well, it's just that kids used to make fun of my flat butt in junior high school. The trouble working out my glutes probably has to do with laziness.

C: It will also affect your ability to develop your core strength.

Me: Yeah, I don't have a core.

(He proceeded to tell me all of the reasons that made it miraculous for me to be walking around. I don't know how this man got away with pointing out so many of my inadequacies while making me love him.)

Me: It seems like I'm going to be dependent on you for the

rest of my life. (Because a smart consumer will always just step right into an opportunity to spend more money.)

C: Actually, the goal is for you not to be dependent. We're going to create a plan for you and work together.

(He checked my mobility and found that I was not completely broken.)

C: Your neck is amazing. I see teenagers who've lost their range of motion and you're almost 100% in all directions.

(Having a neck like an ostrich is probably the reason. I mean swan. I have a neck like a swan, not an ostrich.)

On Wednesday, I will be going back to the chiropractor. I will probably never go back to the orthopedist. Surprise. I'll be putting comfrey on my wrist and it will be fine before I'm even done with my physical therapy.

‡‡‡‡‡‡‡

I went to the Bahamas once, where they are big on conch. Have you had conch? It is delicious. The locals seem to think their precious conch can only be found there. They tried to tell me I had never had it. I tried to tell them I had.

Growing up I ate lots of water animals, not just seafood, but river, lake, and bay food too. I guess these are all referred to as seafood, right? Sometimes, I ate seafood by the sea.

I remember once being on the beach at the end of my grandmother's street. The street where she had bought a house that would soon be purchased from her for a large sum so that it could be torn down to build casinos, according to her. This never happened. She was the only person who I ever heard talk about this. I don't know where this idea came from.

Well, I was on the beach with my cousins and along came my grandmother with (my mouth is watering as my brain forms the words) conch ceviche. She served us all and then she told me to accompany her as she offered some to the lifeguard. I was supposed to be interpreting for her, but I was useless.

There was no one else on the beach, so the lifeguard came over and ate what my grandmother called "concha" in Spanish and "concha" in English. The lifeguard, not speaking Spanish and not being from the Bahamas, had no idea what it was, but he liked it.

The first time I went to Spain I was with two bus-fulls of teenagers. I, being like my grandmother who feeds the lifeguards, befriended the bus drivers, of course. The day they drove us to the airport, they whisked me away from my charges for a treat. They bought me a bowl of hot chocolate (bowls are the way to go with that stuff) and churros. This was a delicious way to say goodbye. They swore I had never had churros. Although they were right, I refrained from telling them that I could purchase them in the subway station back home if I wanted to. They were much better this way, though.

I tried to be brief today, really, but it seemed very important for me to communicate how people want to think that their food is new to us. It's not. I mean, it's not important.

‡‡‡‡‡‡‡

My husband was very clear when he shared his idea on viewing iconic movies with the children: You can only see a movie for the first time once and you need to be the right age to really appreciate it. I've recently discovered that it's possible to see a movie for the first time twice.

Just before May 4th, 2015, I convinced my husband that it was the right time for my children, aged eight and ten to see *Star Wars*. Everyone was excited. As we watched, I waited for familiar scenes and they never came. There was one part that rang a bell, but it was probably from *Indiana Jones*. Then, suddenly, it was the end of the movie. Where was Yoda? Where was Jabba the Hutt? I wondered if I had actually ever seen this movie. I assumed I had. I still don't know.

We had to wait until this May to see *The Empire Strikes Back*. That's how we do things in my house. Reading one Harry Potter book a year takes a long time, but when they were first out, that's how you had to do it. We have very patient children.

Again, I watched, waiting for recognition to connect the images on the screen to my brain cells in that special way. When Yoda appeared on the screen (I can't imagine that this is a spoiler for anyone!), I thought, "This must be a Yoda-like creature who will be introducing Luke to him," because he was not familiar to me.

Even when Luke and Darth Vader are in that scene together, that big important scene, it looked totally different than the similar scene I have in my memory. Maybe there's one like it in *Return of the Jedi*. I know I've seen that movie. I know I have.

I have lots of scenes from *Return of the Jedi* stored in my brain place. Next May I will find out if they are accurate, but there's no doubt that I've actually seen that movie because my memory of the viewing experience is a special one.

I don't know how many times I've seen *Return of the Jedi*, but two or three is a safe bet. It was my second (maybe first) viewing that stands out. I was at Carmen's house around the corner. I don't know where the girls were, but that day I was hanging out with Ray. He's a few years older than I and I never spent much time with him, but we were definitely friends.

I remember that Carmen was in the kitchen and Ray and I were in the living room. He put on a movie, and it was immediately clear that he was somewhat familiar with the film. *Return of the Jedi* is more than two hours long, and for the full length of the movie, my friend Ray perfectly delivered e v e r y   s i n g l e word that any character said.

I'm sure this sounds terrible to you. As an adult, I would've probably smothered him with a couch pillow. It is one of my favorite memories with Ray though, and it is one I fondly recall when I think about *Star Wars*. I'm pretty sure he doesn't even remember it.

‡‡‡‡‡‡‡

Capitalism almost made me a murderer. For once I will admit to my hyperbolic tendency while I clarify that my feeling was and still is sadness more than rage. I have had some sadness about this every day since last Wednesday. Almost a week of thinking about this one event that, I say, emanated from Capitalism.

On Wednesday, my son and I were headed home at a different time than usual. It was apparently the beginning of rush hour. As we descended the stairs in the train station, I saw a mass of people boarding a train. When the doors closed, a few people were left behind. We remained on the platform, standing where the doors of the next train would open when it pulled in eight minutes later. I moved my son close to me, wrapping my arm around his chest, telling him that before the next train arrived, the platform would be full again so we had to be careful. I also told him that, if the next train was too crowded, we would wait for the following one, which was only four minutes further away.

Less than a minute before the train pulled in, another arrived on the opposite track, spilling people onto the platform, some of whom would want to get on our train. One of these people positioned herself right in front of me. I regularly see people crowd around to get on the bus hurriedly. I am happy to stand back, knowing that the bus won't leave. We'll all get on. On the train, at rush hour, though, we might not get on. This attitude of hurrying to board a vehicle bothers me. People with this mindset don't notice one another. No one helps the old woman with the heavy bags. People shove in front of the man with the cane. I try to be careful. I show my children how to notice others. I don't always get it right, but I try.

When the train arrived, my son got swooped in ahead of me with the interloping passenger between us. My long arm enabled me to grab his shirt so that I wouldn't be left outside. Being my child, he headed for the middle of the train as soon as he got in. I managed to reach him there and we ended up right next to my platform friend. Many people came in behind us and soon a man looked in my direction from the door asking if there was room. I responded in my way, with a cheerful smile, loud enough for most to hear, "There's always room in the middle. Come on in." I said this because there is often room in the middle. Unless the train is actually packed, there is always room in the middle. People like to stand in the doorway. I don't understand why. Perhaps they want to be prepared in case there is an emergency evacuation. In my forty-two years of riding the subway I have known one person who had to evacuate once, so this makes perfect sense. My husband once admitted that, before he met me, he used to stand in the doorway, thinking nothing of it. I do understand, yes. That is the problem. It's not that the door-lovers are maliciously blocking the entrance and the exit so that people are only able to move in a single file, delaying the ride for everyone and then complaining about fare hikes and slow service. Usually that is not the case. The truth is worse, I think. People just aren't thinking of others. If they walk into the train and feel comfortable in the doorway, they will just stay there, not thinking of people behind them or of people who might be getting off or on later. Maybe it's my mother's fault that this upsets me so much. "Consideration" was a big idea for me growing up. Thinking of others should be important to everyone.

Back to the tale now. We were on the train and platform lady had a large backpack which she chose not to remove from her back because, why make room for another human? My son's face was in this backpack so I had him switch places with me. Being of body type not-small, I brushed against the backpack. I hardly touched it, really, even though the train was pretty crowded. I touched it enough that my new friend noticed and reacted. She began speaking in Spanish to no one and anyone who might understand, myself included, though apparently unbeknownst to her. "This woman is missing a screw. First she uses her boy to get on the train and now she's using him to push me. What is wrong with her? She's missing a screw." Maybe she wanted to help me find the screw on the crowded train floor. I don't think so. She added in English, "It's good to talk two languages." I responded in Spanish, "I speak three." I knew this wasn't a linguistic competition, so I went on. "I'm sorry if you're in a bad mood because you're going home from work, but please don't take it out on me." I'm not sure what she actually said in response because all I heard were curses. I don't understand cursing. I think there are better words to use instead, even when expressing anger. It doesn't usually matter to me if other people curse, though, unless they do it in front of my children. People used to be mindful of that once, but more and more lately, I feel they just don't care. I loudly told this pal-o-mine not to curse in front of my son. When I said this, everyone in the car heard me. I imagine this was due to my volume. She started yelling about me acting like I was the ambassador of the train, telling people who obviously fit to board the train. She repeated "ambassador of the train" a few times before I told my son to start walking because we were getting off the train and waiting for the next one.

We stood on the platform and, before the train departed, several people caught site of me starting to cry. I stood there and sobbed with my son. We got on the next train and I sobbed some more. You might think it's silly. I know some people on that train thought I was silly. I don't. I'm not trying to be the ambassador for a train. I'm trying to be an ambassador for niceness. I know our society is devolving. That's the saddest part for me. The inconsiderate people are raising children who will be adults with mine. What will that future look like? Things are getting worse in many ways. Many of us go to work for someone else, making them most of the money and keeping a little for ourselves so that we can buy junk and make believe we're happy with it. When we spend all day doing that, making money by working hard so that we can spend it on unnecessary stuff that's supposed to fulfill us, we might be nasty on the train and cause an idealist to get angry and murderous, or at least sad and disillusioned.

I have been heard many a time telling people to only complain to someone who can do something about the problem. Am I practicing what I preach? Will you think of others and help them do the same? Try to do it without getting hysterical. That tends not to help much. I know from experience.

✚✚✚✚✚✚✚

On Sunday we headed out to the beach. Brighton Beach in Brooklyn is where we go locally. It's about a forty-minute drive and, thirty minutes into it, we found ourselves crossing the Verrazano bridge into Staten Island. We had made this drive many times before and we even had two phones with us, which are each little super computers and could have provided some navigating technology. Still, we found ourselves paying a $16 toll to enter the most remote part of New York City. We rerouted to a beach in Staten Island, looking at Coney Island's parachute drop from the opposite direction than we had set out to.

Some people think I don't like the beach. That's not entirely true. What I don't like is the heat and the sun. I don't like the water if it doesn't have big waves but, if it does, I'll want to be there all day. Give me a wavy beach in the shade and I'm all set. When my husband started taking me to Brighton Beach, that's what he tried to do. He bought a big canopy, the type one might rent for an outdoor wedding. Well, not quite, but maybe a barbecue or something. It was pretty big. Whenever we'd go to the beach, he'd drag it out, set it up and I'd plop myself in its shade.

There I was on August 14, 2003, enjoying my shade while I watched my stepchildren play. It was a hot day. We had been there for hours. At one point I overheard two young women near me talking about how neither of them had cellular reception. I didn't think anything of it. I had had a mobile phone in the 90s, but since they weren't that smart back then, I didn't replace it after I lost it in the bathroom of the Plaza Hotel. (That sounds like it could be a Tuesday Tale, right? It's not. I just used to use their bathroom whenever I was in the area.)

After we had spent most of the day beaching, we packed up and left. It was early evening, but the sun in August is reluctant to leave us too soon. The car was parked half a block from the beach. At the end of that block there was a traffic light that was out of order. We drove through it and reached the next intersection where that traffic light was dark as well. We got onto a major road and found ununiformed people directing traffic at each intersection. Something was going on. We turned on the radio and found out that we were having a blackout. It turned out to be a very widespread power outage, affecting ten million people as far as the Midwest and Canada.

Being New Yorkers who normally steer clear of such tourist areas, we decided it would be a great time to drive through Times Square. It was fascinating to see it in the dark. Equally remarkable was the cooperative spirit that was seen everywhere. We drove around Manhattan, watching strangers offering rides and help. When we got home, it was pretty late and we found that many of our neighbors, who might have otherwise been sitting in air-conditioned rooms watching television, had spilled onto the sidewalk to share the darkness and probably drinks. We joined them for a little while before retreating to put the children to bed. I know that blackout caused great loss for many. We were lucky to have our power restored quickly and to only have gotten good memories from it all. It was a great day to experience things in a very different way.

‡‡‡‡‡‡‡‡

As a perfect parent, I would never want to change anything
about my children, not even those not-so-great traits they got
from their father. Sometimes, though, I know it would be easier
if they rubbed off on each other a bit, making the girl a little
less independent and the boy a little more independent. At
eleven, she is ready for college far away. My nine-year-old boy,
however, tries to crawl back in my womb daily.

This tale is about the womb-crawler. When he was three or
four, I registered him for a dance class. He loved to dance even
before he could walk. He started walking at nine months,
probably so he could get to the dance floor. My daughter, the
big-time dancer, wasn't even like this. Anyway, my son loved
the class, sort of. Every week he would hold on to my leg until I
pried him off of me and explained that I would be just on the
other side of the door, the one with the window through which
he could see me.

Every week he assumed his position, squatting down in the
corner. He watched intently and at the end of the class he
would demonstrate for me everything that his classmates had
done. Sort of adorable and definitely not adorable. I did not
sign him up for the following term.

Every year I would check in to see if he was ready for dance
classes and every year he would say no. That's what happened
last summer and I decided not to listen. My daughter was in a
different school now. The staff knew my family, including my
son, even though he hardly spoke to any of them while he hid
behind me.

Luckily, on the first day of class, I was out of town. I was a
little heartbroken, but I also felt that it was probably better
that way. If I had been there, we might've both just ended up
crying in the hallway. Instead, he was with his father who
tough-loved him into his class. He sent me a video to show me
that everything was OK.

Everything was actually more than OK and my son ended
up enjoying his classes. Recently, when I talked about next
year with him, he said he didn't want to go back, though. I
didn't think he meant it and had every intention of registering
him again.

On Sunday he had his end-of-year recital in a big theatre on a big stage. I was nervous. I was nervous for him and I was nervous for me. Would he freeze in the wings? Would he get sick? Would he cry or forget his steps? As I watched the act that preceded his, I started to cry. I was really afraid for him, my tiny little baby nine-year-old. When his class got on stage, I continued to cry and ended up bawling from relief and joy. He did a great job with his class of little girls, all younger than he.

Later, for his next dance, he really surprised me. The dancers' exit included a wave to the audience. He looked out at the house with a big smile and waved as if he belonged on that stage. When the show was over, as he danced around, he gleefully asked, "Are we coming back next year!?!" I'll think about it.

My baby's growing up!

‡‡‡‡‡‡‡

Years ago, my husband and I took my stepchildren camping on Assateague. Part of the island belongs to Maryland and they allow camping. Virginia's part of the island does not. It is ruled by wild horses who stay away from people and prefer that people stay away from them. The whole island has a great diversity of wildlife and in Maryland, while there are also wild horses, the fact that humans hang out there too means that they are used to being petted and fed, though neither of those is allowed.

When my husband made the reservation for our campsite, he probably didn't give them my name too, so when we arrived, we found that there were lots of mosquitoes and no plumbing. They hadn't prepared for my arrival at all. In the middle of the night, I waited as long as I could to empty my bladder, finally braving the elements just outside of my tent. The mosquitos were right there, waiting. They had surely been plotting, watching every sip I had taken, knowing they would be feeding on me while I made the trek to the port-o-potty. Oh, gross. Just typing that word has left a sour look on my face.

When I got to the facilities, there seemed to be a line. It wasn't really. It was a congregation. They weren't people, though. They were horses, about four or five, just hanging out, in my way. They didn't understand my polite pleas and just stood there, blocking me from my destination. We were on the beach. I could've crouched. I could've walked down the dune to the water. Instead, at maybe 3 a.m., I was trying to convince a wild horse to let me by. We worked it out, a hundred mosquito bites later and all was well.

We had arrived on a Thursday and found ourselves to be among very few campers. After my husband and the children set up the campsite (while I made believe I was supervising), we went for a swim. My husband made some comment about it being my first time in the Atlantic Ocean. So adorable. I had touched this ocean before, along with the Pacific and the Ionic, Balearic, and Caribbean Seas. On this trip he had broadened my horizons by exposing me to midnight conversations with new species, though, so there was that.

There was only one other person in the water and two or three others walking on the sand. The beach wasn't paved at all, so there were living creatures everywhere. I mean, if I had worn my stilettos, someone would've had to carry me around. I'm making a mental note for next time! Anyway, there were crabs pinching my fingers and toes and, of course, I said something about it because there were crabs pinching my fingers and toes. If I close my eyes and imagine really hard, I can still see the mark that one of them left on my hand. It was only momentary, but it was proof of my space violation. We had, after all, reserved a camp site, you know. My husband made fun of me a bit and we sort of laughed. Some of us wholeheartedly laughed. I don't think I was in that group.

As long as he was laughing at me, my husband decided to go even further. He told me, with a very serious look on his face, to watch out for sharks, which were known to inhabit these waters. I knew he was joking, but then noticed how serious he looked. Was he serious? Then, he started laughing at me. HI-larious! At that moment, I saw behind him, what I recognized from that great movie of my childhood to be the dorsal fin of a shark, surely a great white, which had probably been told of my deliciousness by all mosquitos of the land, and was now there to get his own taste.

The look on my husband's face changed drastically as he swiftly moved to get his children and himself to safety. It was really scary. He turned towards the other swimmer and yelled at him to get out because there was a shark. The man calmly turned his face toward the fin and said with a smile, "That's a dolphin." Soon there were dozens (hundreds?) of dolphins leaping in and out of the water right in front of us. We watched them for a long time. I had been in the ocean with dolphins before, but never so many. It was beautiful. Them not wanting to eat me was definitely a plus.

‡‡‡‡‡‡‡

I've always been fascinated with words. Looking at literal translations of idioms and trying to decipher abhorrent misuses of language around me was both entertaining and frustrating for me as a child. I played with my own two languages and as many words as I could gather from other languages too.

I remember when I realized that the words we attach to things could be different words without changing the thing. It's all relative and all that jazz. Hold this thought while I introduce a seemingly unrelated topic now and, as ever, be patient with me.

I recommend that prospective clients choose their doula based on compatibility. I also remind doulas how important the personality match is in this relationship. This is my spiel, but people will hire doulas for different reasons, often ignoring this advice. A friend or care provider's recommendation, the amount of experience the doula has, whether or not they've had children, what type of births they've had, how much they charge—all of these, reasons to hire a particular doula. To this list I add the doula's name. Yes, once I was hired because of my name. This is how that went.

I had been contacted by someone whose midwife had recommended me. I told her that I wasn't completely available around the time she was due because I would be out of town for one day. My fee was a little more than she thought she could afford at the time, so I gave her names of some other fabulous doulas for her to contact. She interviewed a few and was not satisfied. She sort of begged me to go meet her.

When we met, she came across as a very spiritual person. Not so much because that's how I saw her as because that's what she kept telling me she was. We talked for a while and I agreed to make arrangements for my out-of-town day, reduce my fee, and be her doula.

I went to see her for our first prenatal visit, when we had agreed she would pay me. As she wrote the check she said, "How do you spell your name? Oh, that's right! That's one of the reasons I chose you." Then she turned to her husband whose native language was not English and said, "Honey, do you know what a Crane is? That's the bird that delivers the babies in its...oh, wait...," and with a much more serious sounding voice she finished her sentence, "That's a stork!" We looked at each other and laughed nervously. I kind of felt like the reason she had fought so hard to hire me had just slipped through my bird feet.

‡‡‡‡‡‡‡‡

The best arrangement for choir of the *Battle Hymn of the Republic* is by Peter J. Wilhousky. I sang it many times in my more than two decades as a singer. It was exhilarating and left me breathless yet with a wide smile. I sang it almost always under the baton of my mentor and almost-father John L. Motley. Also twice with Skitch Henderson and the New York Pops, but he was not quite as good with voices as he was with the other instruments. Luckily, the glorious view from the stage of Carnegie Hall made up for his underwhelming conducting of the choir. The last time I sang this piece was the only time I sang it under anyone else's baton because my dear friend was gone at this point, as we sang at his memorial. I will sing again one day, but it will never be the same. It brought me so much joy, but it will never be the same for me. If you see a video of this recording, you can spot me, on the far right. You will see that there was no smile this time.

Performing with John Motley led me to meet many famous people and many wonderful non famous people too. I have friendships today that were born in those days. He ruined me for concerts. Much of the time I am too critical of other singers to enjoy them. He taught me so much in the rehearsal rooms, on stage, at his piano (given to him by Peter Wilhousky), and in his kitchen. He taught me about music, dirty jokes, and everything in between. I remember exactly the day that he asked me for my phone number during a rehearsal when I was fifteen and took me under his wing. I was privileged to call him a dear friend and still miss him today, five years after I last said goodbye.

‡‡‡‡‡‡‡

My Pilates teacher plays Pandora during class. Her one station has morphed into a compilation of Frank Sinatra, Pit Bull, Louis Armstrong, Shakira, Michael Bublé, Chubby Checker, Ella Fitzgerald and others who fit equally poorly into this group.

Yesterday, during class, a trashy Spanish-language song came on. It was one of those pieces of music that, to me, is not musical at all. In my opinion, it is best reserved for aerobic exercising or, better yet, turning off. Dancing to it is very athletic and kind of boring at once. I do not understand the existence of this song and its fellows, not the listening to it, the dancing to it or the composing of it.

Imagine my disappointment when my teacher said something about the song, referring to it as salsa. Now, there are lots of different kinds of salsa and some kinds even have different names because they are slower or use different instruments. Very nuanced this genre is. This was not any kind of salsa. It was hardly music.

Of course, I don't expect this woman to know the differences among the various rhythms of my people, but calling this cheap song salsa baffles me. I have listened to many of the songs of the Gringos. I would never confuse ABBA and Metalica. One of those is really good and the other much less good, right?

I am such an expert, in fact, that my children come to me with complex questions, and sometimes, I even answer them. For example, once when she was interested in getting a flute, my daughter asked me if there were any groups that featured flautists. She knows my background. She understands that I have sung in venues large and small throughout this land and others. I am super branial. I know things. I quickly responded something like, "Sure. There's Jethro Tull. He played the flute in that group," and turning to my husband I asked, "What was the name of his group." He laughed at me because I am a dummy sometimes too.

‡‡‡‡‡‡‡

Sometime you may meet someone who's from a different part of the country and she may seem odd. She may be quiet and speak slowly. You may catch her staring at you frequently. You may watch her walk and notice that her legs don't seem to want to take her anywhere and that her arms, slightly bent at the elbows, remain stuck by her sides, not swinging or moving at all. They grow out of her hunched torso just so and don't want to make any kind of effort. You may be surprised when she laughs at your stupid jokes. How is your New York humor not lost on her? You may be surprised to get a glimpse into her life at the kitchen table, and you may be shocked at the actual glimpses. Some won't shock you, though. She has a history of mental illness. Uh huh. Twice a day she takes a meal's worth of medication. She's estranged from her parents because they are religious zealots and abusive. Oh. She has Crohn's. Her first husband was abusive to their daughter. She was hospitalized six times in four years for mental illness. She has gone through shock therapy. They still do that! She had a stillbirth. Her second husband died. Her transgender, polyamorous daughter has Asperger's and she agreed to give her hormone therapy at the age of fourteen. Wow. After a short discovery period, she may still seem odd and that's because she is, and that might just be OK.

‡‡‡‡‡‡‡

My family went camping without me. It's probably best for all of us this way. I do like camping, but not enough to actually go every time we go. I can't complain too much because my rugged outdoorsman husband does mostly everything from getting us there to setting up to cooking and cleaning up. I roll up the sleeping bags (I don't know why he is incapable of doing this correctly) and sweep the tents before we put them away. That's about it.

Since he met me, my husband has started to go to campsites that are a little more civilized. Some have even had plumbing! Once we were at a site with electrical outlets. (His brother had booked it.) I ended up only staying one night at that one because I was called to work. I missed out on a huge rain storm the day I left too. Such a pity. I made up for it the next time I went camping, though. Here's why.

If you know me well, you know that I never complain about cold temperatures. Over 72°, though, has me on the verge of negativity. 40° weather is delightful to me. I can bundle up or just stay active. It's invigorating. I feel alive. Usually, I feel alive. Once, I felt like I was dying.

40° in the middle of the night, in the middle of the woods, when you're sleeping on the ground with a rock in your back is a different story, a story I wish I knew nothing about. Unfortunately, I am very intimate with this story. Is it a coincidence that this was the last time I went camping?

I have nothing really more to say. What can I say? I spent a freezing night next to my sleeping family, listening for bears that were surely lurking, listening to the conversations of a million owls. If owls are so wise, why don't they know enough to be quiet at night when they have guests?

The next day, we went out and got some warmer clothing to sleep in and a comforter. Of course, the temperature magically warmed up. The fact that I hadn't slept at all the night before was going to make for some cozy sleep anyway.

I will probably go camping again at some point before I die. It may be the thing that makes me die, but I will go because someone needs to roll up the sleeping bags properly.

✠✠✠✠✠✠✠

Remember that time I got food poisoning right before an interview? That was a hoot! I had time between my last appointment and my next, when I would meet a very pregnant prospective client, so I was sitting at a Starbucks doing some writing, because the best people always have writing to do, you know. While I wrote, I had a cheese and fruit box. Yum. It included Brie. Pregnant people are advised not to eat Brie because of the risk of getting sick from listeria. I was not a pregnant person on this day. Besides, the dangerous thing is not the listeria but the treatment for the poisoning, and you may recall that I have written about food poisoning before. I am a pro at food poisoning (woot woot!). I don't need treatment. My body just gets rid of it. Smart body. Too bad it doesn't recognize fat cells as poison! Anyway, there I was at the

Starbucks in Chinatown, a few blocks from my interview. I was writing something amazing for sure, when suddenly my stomach was like, "Yo! Yo! What did you do!?! Something needs to come out. I'm gonna go ahead and turn myself inside-out for you. A'right?" It did not give me a chance to respond. I would've said, "Not a'right. NOT ALL RIGHT!" OK. Have you been to that Starbucks in Chinatown? No bathroom. Off I went to McDonald's down the block. Many a time my stomach has turned just from walking into McDonald's, so this was perfect, really. The bathroom at this particular McDonald's was a heavenly beauty, full of clean stalls. I made one my home for a few minutes and emerged a new woman, ready for my interview, right on time. I sat with my prospective client, telling her how I would be a good doula for her, how my intestines probably weren't going to explode in front of her. I don't think I verbally expressed that second thing, but it was surely on my mind. I was hired and that birth was one of my more memorable ones. I ended up catching that baby before the doctor arrived, because sometimes our bodies just can't keep things in.

‡‡‡‡‡‡‡

My husband's grandparents had a house in Margate, NJ when he was growing up. He has fond memories of the house and the beach and of the amusement parks on the boardwalk in Ocean City. About a decade ago I decided that we would make an annual trip there with our children. I have lots of good ideas in my super-planning brain.

My brother-in-law now has a beach house in Brigantine. If you're headed south, you will find Atlantic City across the bridge from Brigantine, then Ventnor, then Margate, and Ocean City is across another bridge. A few years ago, we stayed at the beach house and drove through Ventnor and Margate for our annual night at Ocean City. "Margate Police" is like a catchphrase in my family. It makes us laugh today, though, one fateful night, it almost made us cry. It was the night we were almost all hauled away by the Margate Police. You may have heard people say that husbands don't listen to their wives. You should not believe this. It is a generalization and it's just not nice. I would never say that. What I can say, from experience, be it nice or not, is that my husband, more often than I would like, does not listen to me. I have good ideas, remember? He should listen to some of them. Here's one: make sure your phone is charged in case you need it later. Let's focus on that one.

We were piling into the rental car, on our way to Ocean City. It was my husband and me, my two children, my teenaged stepson, and our teen niece. This sounds like a lot of people for a car. That's because it was. My son sat on my lap because, having grown up in the seventies with about fifty-three cousins, one car and no seatbelts, I could attest to both the convenience and safety of this practice. We got into the car with one out of three phones fully charged, my husband's teetering on the verge of just taking up pocket space.

We had our fun at the amusement park. Sometimes we would split up based on our interests and perhaps age or height restrictions. We could always find one another because we had mobile phones with us to facilitate communication. I could say plenty of bad things about this technology, but it does come in handy. After the rides, we traditionally walk along the boardwalk until everything closes down. This we did on this night too. All was well.

We got to our car and drove through the sleeping town. We crossed the bridge with hearts full of new memories and bellies full of fudge samples. All was still well. When we got to Margate, however, we went from being the only ones on the road to being the only ones on the road, but for the police car behind us. Hmmmm. There was a child, who should've been in a car seat on my lap and we were in sight of New Jersey police officers, known for ticketing even their grandmothers.

My husband decided to pull the car over and go for a walk with my son, instructing his older son to just drive. That was a plan. I will refrain from assigning it an adjective. While my husband and son walked aimlessly in the post-midnight darkness, we drove along, trying to shake off our tail. We turned a corner and parked. I got out, pretending to make a call asking for directions and I noticed that the police car was sort of hiding, sort of peeking, definitely watching us. It was kind of like a scene from a comedy or a horror movie. I was coming up with a story in case they approached and asked questions, but in my mind, I could see myself sobbing with my children during visitation hours at the prison. I am no good in these situations.

I would have called my husband, but one of our phones was dead. I won't go on about that. We got back into the car and kept driving in the direction that would eventually lead us home, while my husband and our little boy surely walked toward the abyss where the black sky meets the black, unforgiving water. Maybe they would knock on a door and get some pity. Maybe they would be picked up by the very police we were trying to escape.

What would the future hold, I wondered, and there was no hope in the response. What hope could there possibly be? Here I was, in the middle of my breakdown, when the police car disappeared and, on the sidewalk, appeared my husband and son. They scurried into the car and, a few blocks later, we crossed over into Ventnor, leaving the Margate Police powerless against our crimes. The relief brought tears, a little anger and eventually, a whole lot of laughter.

‡‡‡‡‡‡‡

Yesterday, I was on the phone with a customer service representative. He was in the same country and from the same country, but our communication was strained, and he might as well have been from another planet, one in which things moved slowly, including speech. I found myself needing to explain things repeatedly, with patience and simple words. In the middle of this fun time, the man giggled and said, "That's the strangest noise I've ever heard." My daughter was bouncing on a birth ball (a.k.a. an exercise ball) and it made squeaky crunching noise against her skin. You know the sound well. It would not surprise you at all if you heard it while you saw her bouncing. "I'm imagining all sorts of things," he said. I asked if he wanted to know what the sound was and he giggled and said he preferred to use his imagination. It was odd. I wonder what he imagined. Often, when we get bits of information, we make up stories that fit into what's familiar. When offered the opportunity for clarity, for facts, for evidence, sometimes it is easier to decline and wallow in bliss.

Years ago, I remember talking to another customer service person. She was in the middle of the country somewhere. She sounded like a complete foreigner to me because she had probably never left her hometown. She was very pleasant and we chatted a bit. Towards the end of the conversation she said something unintelligible, partly because of her accent and partly because of the actual words she used. "Is that a cockatoo?" she asked. Ha ha. I felt so bad to disappoint her when I told her that the sound in the background, coming through my window from the street was that of a car alarm. I wish that the lens of my life was not colored with the easy recognition of a car alarm, that I could assume the noises I heard came from animals rather than anti-theft technology. Nah. I'm happy with my story. We need all sorts of stories woven together. We also need to understand that we're not all coming from the same place even when we don't know what the other places might be.

‡‡‡‡‡‡‡‡

Yesterday I went on a 5+ mile hike with my family. Of course I have hiked that far before, it's just usually in high heels in the streets of Manhattan. I am definitely a different kind of hiker than they are. I like to contemplate the moss, look at the mushrooms and discover forms in the lichen. The words, "If you're not sweating, you're not hiking," actually came out of my husband's face hole. Yuck!

Now don't get me wrong. I totally love nature, but it tends to be very buggy and rocky and hilly and unpaved. "Totally love" is probably an exaggeration, on second thought. We were on "trails" the whole time, but they aren't roads, you know. They're just smoother paths where the ground has been somewhat leveled by the pounding of feet, or possibly the dragging of bodies. And the hills! Going up is hard and I can handle hard, but going down is dangerous. As I mention every few weeks, I weigh 200lbs. That basically means the earth is trying to reclaim me. Walking down a rocky hill sans banister can easily lead to rolling down a hill.

Anyway, I got through that and even enjoyed it. After a little more than four miles, we came across some waterfalls. They were delightful. I did get a major gash on my ankle from a waterfall rock attack. It is several millimeters long. I think I'll be ok, though.

Today's tale isn't actually about yesterday's hike. We walked for more than five miles and only came across one other person. This reminded me of a time, nine years ago, when we went blueberry picking. Two adults and three children picked. (Anyone interested in nine-year-old frozen berries?) My son was a baby and my daughter was a toddler.

I did a little picking with my daughter in between breastfeeding sessions with my son, and some of the berries even ended up in the bucket rather that in our mouths. Eventually, I had to go to the bathroom because of my TB condition—you know, tiny bladder. Having a toddler is a great way to get into bathrooms that aren't for the public. If you're ever in need, just borrow a toddler off the street.

I found my way to the house, a little way from the blueberry bushes and inquired with the man outside about the facilities. He told me we could use the bathroom inside and pointed his chin in the direction of the door. I opened it and there in front of me was the cast of Deliverance, all looking at me and my little girl. I looked behind me and the doorway I had just gone through seemed so very far away. One of the men pointed towards the bathroom and I hurried my way in, eyes to the floor. I have never so securely locked a door in my life. I couldn't believe I was there with my beribboned little child.

As is always the case with my tales (so far), I survived. I'm sure they were all fine and decent people. I just wish they hadn't all been wearing overalls and long beards.

‡‡‡‡‡‡‡‡

I've always loved back-to-school time.
The weather changes from my least favorite kind to my most favorite kind. Yay autumn!
It's my birth month. Yay September 21st!
I loved school, so going back was super. Yay school!
Nowadays, I love that all the other children are going back to school, leaving the city, parks, and attractions to those who do not partake. Yay homeschooling!

A couple of weeks ago, my family was checking out at a store. All four of us. Delightful. I greatly disrelish shopping, so by the time I get to the register, I am usually a little disgruntled. Add to this the fact that my children, although they are already eleven and nine, continue to act like children of, I don't know, maybe eleven and nine years of age. Crazy!

There we were, putting our items on the belt, both children talking to me at the same time because I am so good at the simultaneous bilateral listening that they must think I love it, despite the fact that I have expressed to them on multitudinous occasions, in different ways, that I don't generally prefer this practice. On this day, my expression of annoyance manifested itself in a muffled yell through clenched teeth. The tone was clear, the volume was low.

As I looked towards the customer behind me, I turned the corners of my mouth a little to make it look like I was a normal person, not about to rage. She smiled at me and said, "Thank goodness school is only a few weeks away, right?" This comment tickled me.

My children provide advanced gluteal hardship to me on a regular basis, but you, outsider, are not allowed to say so. How dare you? Furthermore, I know that tomorrow they will be gone from me and that I will long for their madness.

I was happy to tell the woman that we homeschool and that I love spending time with my children. Sometimes my love is displayed through clenched teeth, but it is always there. I am so happy not to be able to relate to the relief that so many people find comes with back-to-school time. These days, I love this time of year for other reasons. Did I mention my birthday?

✠✠✠✠✠✠✠

"Santos...Santos......Santos!" We could hear a man calling as one sometimes does in the playground. So many voices, little ones and big ones. We try our best to ignore most of them, lest we end up writhing in a pile of auditory overload. I'm not the only one, am I? Usually we can pick out a call from one of our own. Often, we turn, looking towards a foreign voice just in case, like the people who look at their phones at the slightest electronic alert even if it does not sound like one they have programmed. You never know and, while you're at it, you can check the time and all of the other urgencies of the moment as we seem to have perpetually and forever more.

We all passively heard the man calling for his son, but it wasn't long before we were at attention. It wasn't so much the slight change in volume as the change of intention that got us. I stood up and turned my eyes to the man so that I could follow his gaze and scan along with him, looking for a child's reaction somewhere in the distance. He kept looking and calling, to no avail. "What color is his shirt?" I asked. "No shirt." "How old is he?" I continued. In a heavy accent the man told me the boy was four years old. I wondered if they were tourists in a playground at Central Park, having more of an adventure than they had anticipated.

As is my style in a crisis, I moved very slowly, casting my eyes into the distance. I have been praised for my calm in the midst of chaos many times. So far, so good with that, but if I ever have to save myself, I fear I just will not. I try to surround myself with fast thinkers as a matter of self-preservation at least. Something happens to my heart rate in these situations. I am incapable of moving much at all as my slow breath resounds in my head.

I walked towards a corner of the playground using my keen eyes in search of a nude four-year-old torso. More people were becoming aware of the goings-on and necks began to crane. We all knew the boy was distracted, safely playing, just out of sight. We also knew that he could have been abducted by a stranger. It was definitely one of these. It didn't matter at the time which was more likely or by how much.

It didn't take long for the calls for Santos to stop and I knew they would stop for only one reason. I turned to see the caller on his knees embracing a small child. Santos was fine, and it was at this point that I broke down. As always, my body changed course and I began to cry.

Tears started to flow and I was trembling. We release endorphins in our tears and I surely needed them. For two or three minutes my body had been doing this bizarre slo-mo thing and now it needed to be washed to recover. It is truly remarkable to me every time.

If you and I are ever on the Savannah, please know that you will be the one acting to fight off the predators, possibly even carrying me out of their way. When it's time for planning or slowly sneaking up on prey, however, that'll be all me. You know, right before I cry.

‡‡‡‡‡‡‡

My family hails from a part of Colombia where the people are known for being fun-loving and always ready to party. They are humorous and happy. Humorous, sometimes even if we're not all laughing, as was the case around the time of my birth.

I have had more than thirty nicknames (I counted once). Some of them persist, and this is the tale of two of them. I am still called, by a few people, each of these names.

My father is Italian and, much to my family's displeasure, looks Italian. The fact that I look so much like him came up repeatedly in my childhood, starting on the day I was born. You know how people always say that babies are beautiful, or at least cute? They usually aren't (except for some like my sister, who drew crowds from around the hospital with her newborn beauty), but people say it anyway, especially to the freshly-parturitioned person. (I'm a birth worker, I can make up birthy words if I want! Birthy- there's another one.)

So there was my mother, without her newborn, who was kept in another room because that made lots of sense back then, visible only through a window by her relatives and visitors. My mother is a wonderful person. Not surprisingly, she had lots of visitors. Everyone said I looked just like my father and all but one said I was ugly. While my father told my mother how beautiful I was, other relatives stood behind him, shaking their heads, miming that I had a big nose and mouth. You know, being humorous. Very funny they were. It was from this humor that was born the nickname Maluca. In this case, Maluca means ugly, really, really ugly. That's me. Thanks family!

Once my mother and her ugly baby were back home, we had a visit from one of my favorite uncles, who isn't actually related to me, but being the fun-loving people we are, that's just who he is to me. This man looked at me and congratulated my mother. He knew I was being called La Maluca and did not comment. He didn't join in on this fun, and just declined to say anything about my looks at all. It wasn't until a couple of weeks later, when he visited again, that I got my next nickname. He looked at me and said to my mother in surprise, "Wow, she's turned into a little butterfly!" He wasn't even trying to be funny. While in his comment he acknowledged my initial horridness, Mariposa is a nickname I'm glad has stuck. I'm really ugly still and also little butterfly.

‡‡‡‡‡‡‡

My grandmother would have been 93 today. She died almost two years ago. Her life is deserving of a tale for every day of the week for the rest of my life. We had only a cordial relationship, which perhaps positions me perfectly to share her story, full of heroism, failure, beauty, sadness and, above all, many grand ideas. That story can't be told here. It is an epic novel that will likely be considered fiction. The best stories about my grandmother are the ones she told herself, mostly because of the way she told them. I have vivid images of many of them in my head. Maybe I'll write a screenplay instead! Today, I can't even write a tale. With tears in my eyes and a little laughter at my tears (both common components of my tales, right?), I just want to honor my awe-inspiring grandmother. Happy birthday, Abuelita!

‡‡‡‡‡‡‡

I fell in the street the other day. It was quite a sight, so dramatic and graceful. Only the best-looking people came to my aid and I greeted them with a smile, tenderly placing my hand in that of the one who looked to be the strongest because, you know, 200lbs here. I was fine, having somehow escaped harm from the impact (and so much of my body made impact!) I made with the asphalt and the great amount of traffic found in the middle of the intersection at Broadway and 86th street in Manhattan. I'm so glad every moment of our lives is being recorded because this was truly a beauteous spectacle, worthy of others' enjoyment. It was really the most elegant fall I have ever been a part of.

Falling is not something in which I am well-practiced. It was the fault of some ridiculous shoes I was wearing, which many of you would surely frown upon, even though they do look fabulous. They had clearly made a pact with gravity against me. While I don't actually fall, it is something I fear in certain situations. Being a tall woman with a short torso, my stratospheric center of gravity makes me wary when negotiating steep inclines with no banisters (remember the hike from a few weeks ago?), or when just thinking about skiing. The season is approaching and I know many people who will start going skiing soon. Today I will tell you the tale of the first time I went skiing. It was also the last time, and I doubt that I will ever give it a chance to change its status as such.

It was my much-older-than-I brother-in-law's fortieth birthday about a dozen years ago and he proposed a ski trip to celebrate. I thought it was a great idea, despite the fact that I had never been skiing and that I am generally afraid of such physical activities. I love the cold and, more importantly, I had a really cute outfit for it, so I was ready!

We drove up on a beautiful day with the sun's brilliance reflecting off of the snow all around us. The crisp air filled me with courage as I carried my awkward skis and horrid boots, ready to sway my hips down the mountain. I got myself strapped into the contraptions, grateful that everyone else was looking equally frumpy from the shins down and that I looked a tad better from the shins up. It's just an opinion based on my memory, but let's just go ahead and trust both of those estimations in this case.

I shimmied over to the ski lift. I was ready. This is probably not true. I am a scaredy cat and I'm pretty sure I was really nervous. I can't remember, though, because of what happened next. The mobile chair thingy came along behind me and scooped me up. The view would likely have been breathtaking had my breath not already disappeared along with my courage. Up, up, up I went. As I approached the summit, I realized that my arrival would not be signaled by a stop. Instead, I was to gauge the right place and moment to hop off and scurry away, lest I be whisked up again by the departing chair.

OK. First, I was to try not to fall out as I ascended. Then, I was to fall out just so, so as to resemble a smooth landing. It was that last bit that got me. Don't go crazy with your imagination now. I totally landed on my feet. The problem was that my feet weren't necessarily pointing in the right direction or maybe even in the same direction. I don't know, but in an effort to compensate, my loosely-ligamented knee twisted. It twisted beyond a place of comfort, and there I stood, on the top of a mountain, in pain.

I stood there and watched as my companions skied down without me. I tried to move past the pain and gain the valor I needed in order to get down myself. They kept coming up and going down and I kept trying not to be in pain or scared. Trying isn't doing, though, so finally, I summoned the young man on the emergency snowmobile and had him zoom me down instead. That was fun. I took off my skis forevermore and spent the rest of the day and evening in the lodge where it was cozy, looking through the large window at the snowy mountains and treacherous ski lifts.

The next morning, I was pleased to see that my knee was smoothly swollen like a bowling ball. I was sure everyone had thought that it was only my fear that kept me from skiing. I was glad to have the proof of my injury. The fact is that it was indeed my fear because, had I been braver, my dismount would've probably not caused me harm. In the end, I think it worked out for the best.

✝✝✝✝✝✝✝

I live near The Cloisters, part of the Metropolitan Museum of Art that is dedicated to European medieval art, architecture, and gardens, at the center of which are, not surprisingly, several cloisters. It is nestled in northern Manhattan's Fort Tryon Park, from which there are beautiful views of the Palisades, the George Washington Bridge and, if you're in the right spot, the Tappan Zee Bridge.

I love The Cloisters. Like so many things that I love, my lack of loving expression is all too evident as I run around busy doing innumerable things all of the time. Had I time to sit and number the things, I might be shocked to find that there are so many. I might also be shocked to find that there are so few and that I am just playing the role that seems to have been assigned to us all by our society. We are all too busy, with no time, doing things. All of us, I know. Even you now, reading my Tuesday Tale while your plate overflows.

About seventeen years ago, I took a trip to The Cloisters with a friend. It takes about as much time to walk from my house as it does to take public transportation in the form of two buses. I can see the top of The Cloisters from my window, actually, but my friend, my former friend, was a wimp and we embarked on our forty-minute journey in a seated position.

We got off the first bus and walked two blocks to wait for the second one. When we got on, I noticed it smelled like cabbage. I looked at the elderly people sitting up front, one of whom was asleep, and we chose our seats towards the center of the bus for the seven-minute ride. At the next stop, one of the other passengers approached the man who was asleep and then went up to the bus driver to say something. Then it was the bus driver's turn to approach the sleeping man and retreat. He went back to his seat to communicate with his supervisor before communicating with us. He told us that the bus was being taken out of service. No reason was given.

We all disembarked in silent understanding. All but the sleeping man. He was silent too, but he would remain on the bus. My friend and I proceeded to our destination on foot a bit solemnly, a bit shaken. Once we got there, we enjoyed the beautiful Cloisters and the grounds. On our return, we decided to walk a bit before getting on the bus and, even though hours had gone by, as we passed our previous bus, which was just where we had left it, we saw the bus driver in his seat with his sleeping passenger in a bag behind him.

It was odd to me to see the driver just sitting there. He was busy doing his job. In this moment his job was to sit and wait. Later he would be busy doing all of the things he has to do, barely having time for them, not having time for anything more, like the rest of us. The sleeping man had no more time and all the time and there was now only one thing for him to do.

‡‡‡‡‡‡‡

They say that the face of a child says so much. Really, though, it's the mouth part of the face. Am I wrong? Children say all sorts of adorable, inappropriate, horrible things. Like the time the neighbor came to the door and I told her that my mother said she did not want to talk to her. My mother had said that. I hadn't realized I was supposed to come up with a lie.

Imagine if your wonderful child tells you that you're good at making double chins. They think they're giving you a compliment on your talent. You might feel differently. I don't have to imagine this scenario. I do not. I can just use my memory to see it.

Words just fly out of children, man. I remember once my aunt was visiting from Panamá. We went to the aquarium. I still have a vivid image of the two of us in one of the dark exhibits. We were standing in front of the glass looking at some amazing creatures. Behind us stood at least a dozen people. All of us looking at the beauties of the sea.

I was a child, but not too young. I was old enough to know my mistake as soon as it started reverberating on the many eardrums around me. "Look at the testicles!" I said in awe. TENTACLES! My aunt was young and cool. She was going to shield me from embarrassment, taking me under her wing to the dark safety elsewhere. Just kidding! She guffawed instead. She laughed for a long, loud time at me, her little niece. Thanks, Mayra. I've never forgotten that, notice? At least I'm laughing now, though.

‡‡‡‡‡‡‡

Once, I was hanging out at a café (because that's what the cool people do), probably making believe I was writing while enjoying some milkshake beverage bearing coffee only by drops and name.

I sat there looking quite busy, thinking thoughtful thoughts perhaps about birth, death, or dessert. Death is an unlikely option, though. I am a birth worker and a dessert-eater, so let's assume it was one of those.

There I was, probably not minding my own business, when an older woman shuffled towards me and stumbled into a chair at the table beside me. She sat there for a few minutes, concentrating verily on her smartphone's screen. I could tell from her expression and the smoke emanating from her ears that she was not at all impressed with the smarts of her device.

As her frustration increased, I offered assistance. She told me that she was having trouble accessing her e-mail. She trusted me to help her, so I tried my best. Phone in hand, I entered the password she gave me: "Psychicjean." She replied in the affirmative when I asked if she was indeed a psychic.

She produced a piece of paper on which was scrawled all sorts of personal information. We had no luck unlocking the powers of her device, despite various attempts from different angles. She was not amused with my comment on her, a psychic, not knowing her passwords. I don't know why. It was a hilarious comment. Trust me. I ended our encounter knowing several of her e-mail addresses and passwords and I don't even claim any psychic powers.

‡‡‡‡‡‡‡

I've just scheduled myself to teach a couple of workshops outside of my own area. I don't drive. You must know this. Even if you haven't read my tales describing how sitting behind the wheel of a car causes my vision to blur with tears, you can probably just look at me and tell. No?

My hesitation in planning these workshops was due to my wondering how I will get to them—not just me, but all of my stuff. My teaching equipment all fits in one large suitcase, three large bags, one other humongous bag, several boxes full of binders and handouts, a flat bag of posters, and my large screen. That's all.

Once, on my way to Brooklyn with all of my gear, I called a taxi. I told the dispatcher that I was going to Brooklyn, as it's a bit of a drive, and that I had lots of stuff. This gave him the opportunity to find a driver that was willing to take me that far and whose vehicle could accommodate my things. He did not take this opportunity.

When the car pulled up, I could hardly see it. It was the smallest taxi I had ever seen. Uh, OK. The driver would have to figure out how to squeeze my stuff in there. Drivers know their cars. I don't know any cars. I couldn't help. I figured I'd end up with some things around me in the back seat. That's OK. I had work to do during the ride and wouldn't notice the stuff anyway. Let's go.

As I thought these things, the driver's door opened and out came a woman, much older than I and seemingly less fit than I. I can't be sure. She might have been in better shape than my grandmother, but there really wasn't evidence of that. I realized that I was going to have to load my own things into the car myself with my own hands myself. Myself. I was not pleased.

I asked if she knew I was going to Brooklyn and her loud reaction assured me that, not only did she not know, but she had probably never been there before. Clearly, I needed a different taxi. After thinking for a couple of seconds, she agreed to take me if I gave her directions. Oh thanks, lady. Thank you. Thanks for doing me the favor.

We agreed and she proceeded to open the trunk of the car, which was less than welcoming to my cargo. By the end of it, we had crammed things in all of the corners of the trunk and passenger areas and I sat in the front. She was thrilled that I would keep her company and told me that I would have to talk to her during the long journey. I was not thrilled. Very much so, not thrilled.

During the ride, sometimes I talked, sometimes she reprimanded me for staying quiet, and sometimes she talked. When she did, she told me that I was her first fare of the day and that I had turned out to be a blessing because she's tight on money and this was a big trip. When we got to the apartment I rented, she rushed in to use the bathroom while I unloaded the car. Of course. It was somewhat comical. I ended up giving her a big tip and she hugged me.

You may wonder why I wouldn't just rent a car. Come on, remember who I am? If I rented a car, it would have to come with the driver. Do they even have those? Oh yeah, they're called taxis.

‡‡‡‡‡‡‡‡

I don't post about politics. I don't really understand politics. It's not just that I don't understand politics because it's so confusing. It's that I don't understand. Today's tale illustrates my lack of understanding. It's a short one because I really don't know what to say.

In 2008 my daughter was in a preschool program a couple of times a week. Sometimes I spoke to one of the other mothers, especially after I found out that her wife was pregnant.

November 4, 2008 was the date of a historic presidential election in the US. My children went into the booth with me and I photographed them pulling the lever to cast my vote.

Late that night, we could hear cheering in the streets. It was like New Year's Eve, but better. My husband opened the window and added to the cacophony with his own chants for the winning candidate, whom we felt was the right one.

Before that night came morning, though, and voting was going on throughout the land. In NYC, Election Day is pretty calm and predictable. That morning I saw the mother of my daughter's classmate and she looked at me with a smirk asking, "Did you vote for Obama?" I told her that we were going to vote as a family that afternoon and then asked her if she had. She shook her head widely from side to side saying, "He's not in my party." She is a black, lesbian immigrant from Central America. I just don't understand.

‡‡‡‡‡‡‡‡

Often people contact me wanting to schedule a meeting to interview me or to talk about mentorship or to discuss if the workshop I teach might be right for them. I love meeting with people who are interested in my work. Such was the case with Celina. I squeezed in time for her at a convenient location between other appointments. We would meet at a second-floor café, attached to a yoga studio.

I arrived early and found that the café wouldn't open until well after our meeting time, so I sent Celina a text message and waited outside. The building was flanked by a French pastry shop and Max Brenner's chocolate restaurant. Uhm, chocolate! I looked at both menus and honestly chose Max Brenner's because they serve omelettes and the other place only had pastries. Really, that's the reason!

I waited for Celina, figuring that she had probably seen a photo of me and would recognize the silver streak in my hair as is usually the case. Sure enough, a young lady approached with her hand extended in a greeting, her face lit up. "Celina," I said. She nodded and walked toward the pastry shop and said, "Shall we go in?" I told her I needed eggs and that they didn't seem to have any there and walked her towards Max Brenner's adding, "Also, chocolate."

We were greeted and seated quickly. I asked Celina where she had come from and she asked me. We talked about New York a little and then the waiter approached. He introduced himself as Joe and I said with my over-the-top cheeriness, "I was just going to ask your name! Welcome to our table! This is Celina." I gestured toward her and she said, "Celine." I went on to say my name with a flamboyantly rolled r, then gave him the option of calling me Rina (the Gringo way) and finally added, "You can also just call me G."

Celina said, "G, not J?" To which I responded that I have so many nicknames it doesn't matter. Then she added, "But your e-mail says Joey, right?" I have lots of e-mail addresses, but I knew none of them said that. 'Doula' might sound like 'Joey', but she was talking about what she thought she saw. I told her that my e-mail says DoulaRina. She said, "I'm here for the mentoring program." Of course she was. I responded, "Ok. You want a doula mentor. I'm a doula and you want to find out about being a doula." Nope, that wasn't it.

Our waiter never left our side. He was much too entertained. The three of us burst out laughing and Celine and I headed outside, guffawing the whole way. She headed into the pastry shop where Joey was surely waiting and I easily found Celina, whom I greeted with boisterous laughter.

Celina and I had a great conversation, which was often interrupted by chuckling as I thought about the crazy morning coincidence. It made up for the bad food and truly mediocre hot chocolate.

‡‡‡‡‡‡‡

One of my favorite things to do is to plan. They don't call me the life of the party for nothing. They don't actually call me the life of the party. They might say I throw a great party, though, and if they did, it would be because I had planned it so well. Some of my calendar events are to schedule this or plan that. I look forward even to planning my planning.

My daughter is blessed with this characteristic as well. It drives another member of our household crazy. I won't mention my husband's name, but let's just say this person has, more that once, been irritated because I asked what we were going to do on a particular day and it was too early for him to think about it because it was only the morning of that particular day. You might think we balance each other out, but I really don't see a problem with the scale being tipped toward my more organized side.

Knowing this, you might not be surprised at the fact that I have started cooking today, a Tuesday, for Thanksgiving, which is on Thursday. I feel like some of the prepping could have been done yesterday, but since I've already planned everything out, I know it will be OK. It'll be OK even if I end up in the emergency room or at a birth. I know this from experience.

Thanksgiving is my favorite holiday and I love a big Thanksgiving. That means lots of people, and lots of food, all made by me. Sometime ago, I was preparing the feast for more than a dozen people. I had planned in advance, of course, and spent Thanksgiving morning just finishing things up. At some point, my body had some suboptimal sensations. I put the turkey in the oven and only needed to cook and mash the potatoes and finish the gravy. I got into the shower and, by the end of it, I realized I should go to the emergency room. I waited for my husband to come home from work so that I could tell him I didn't want to go and he could force me to go.

He did. We went. I gave instructions for the turkey, potatoes, and gravy. At the hospital, I was seen pretty quickly, misdiagnosed, and sent home. Dinner was about half an hour later than planned, but it was still delicious. I got to do it all because of careful planning. Too bad the trip to the hospital wasn't a trip to someplace else instead. Brussels comes to mind.

A few years later, I was called to a birth the night before Thanksgiving. I spent all night there and the next day, arriving home in time to say good night to my half dozen guests, not having had to entertain, yet able to take their praise because I had, in fact, prepared the meal in advance, leaving careful instructions for the things that still needed cooking. That was a great post-birth meal and I wasn't even expected to clean up afterwards!

‡‡‡‡‡‡‡

Last week I made my delicious chocolate-covered stuffed figs. Last time I made these I almost killed someone. While you're probably accustomed to hearing me exaggerate, turning a trip and fall into a near-death experience, this time it's actually true.

It was Thanksgiving of 2006 and we were headed to my husband's aunt's house. I am always eager to please and definitely wanted to make a good impression. I, however, am not the type of person who can reliably depend on her personality for any kind of positive impressing. No, I'm going to show off somehow, maybe shower you with gifts or favors. Rather than seeking therapy, I'm going to cook for you and go out of my way to be nice. I'm gonna work my way into your heart and you're going to like me because I am lovely, gosh darn it.

I arrived at the family house with a beautiful apple cobbler and a tray of my stuffed figs in their crisp chocolate shells. One was for dessert and the other, an appetizer. I was also making a human, my second offering to add to their clan. How could they not like me? I'm sure they did. Well, at least until I almost killed their first-born. I don't know. Maybe that's why we've never been back. Probably not, though. That couldn't be it. Could it? Maybe I should send them some freshly-baked bread or something.

It was a pretty casual affair and I was in the large kitchen. I was mostly listening to the conversations (lest I talk my way out of their favorable regard), and giving my input on the food preparation as requested. There was a table of hors d'oeuvres not far away and my delightful figs were on it. There were more than a dozen of us there and people were raving about the figs. These were clearly people with fine palates.

Suddenly, my husband's cousin approached me, eyebrows up to her hairline, eyes wide, mouth full, saying, "These are SO delicious." Chew, chew, chew, "They don't have any nuts, do they?" Uh, yes, nuts. They are stuffed with orange peels I candied myself, along with almonds and walnuts. You know, nuts. Most of the treat was already gone, but as she quickly disappeared, I saw her spitting out little bits into her hand. Apparently, there was a problem.

I really hesitate to blame a victim, but if I am deathly allergic to something, I'm probably going to inquire about ingredients, especially if we're talking about stuffed something, before I put it in my mouth. This cousin was in med school at the time and her father was a doctor. Surely, memories of this Thanksgiving would not include a death. At least I hoped.

It took much longer than I was comfortable waiting for everything to be OK. She ended up absconding the deathly grip and we all enjoyed dinner. Well, you can't say I didn't make an impression!

‡‡‡‡‡‡‡

Last week's tale reminded me of the time a teenager almost had a fatal allergic reaction right in front of me while in another country, while her mother was back home. True story.

Technically, I suppose it wasn't almost fatal since the reason she didn't die is that a little time went by. In my head, though, it was a really bad situation. Not just in my head, though. Let me tell you what happened. Otherwise, this'll just be a Tuesday Tease.

I was on a little concert tour in Europe with about 85 high schoolers and a handful of adults. One morning in Hungary, we were sightseeing. A bunch of people were eating ice cream. Not a problem. As we were getting on the bus, I learned that one of the students had had two ice cream cones. Not a great choice, but also not a big deal in my eyes.

It was a big deal, though, because this student hadn't had any breakfast, only these two ice cream cones. It gets worse, of course. It turns out that the ice cream cones had peanuts sprinkled on top and that she had a peanut allergy. I'm not sure how allergies work exactly, but I wonder if it has something to do with your brain shutting down before you ingest an allergen. I think I'll look into that. Why did she eat the peanuts? I don't know.

Of course, her mother had sent her on this trip with an EpiPen, which she used and all seemed well. Later that day, during a rehearsal, I took the recovered student out to the street, several blocks away, to a pay phone with a calling card so we could call her mother and let her know what had happened and that everything was fine. This is how we had to do it in the nineties, kiddies. We were both in the phone booth and I spoke to her mother first. Everything was fine. Smooth conversation. No concerns from anyone. Great.

I put the student on the phone with her mother and they spoke briefly. As the conversation was wrapping up, just as they were saying goodbye, the young lady's face started to change in a way I had never seen before. While purple is a color I tend to like, in this case, it was not. Her face turned purple and, as she hung up the phone, she fainted right there in the phone booth with me. Good times!

We walked outside and sat on the ground on a sidewalk in Hungary. She was actually lying down while people walked around us. We stayed there for a while. I did not have a mobile phone in the early nineties. I did not speak Hungarian. Waiting seemed like the only thing to do. We waited and time, and eventually a little orange juice, healed everything.

Her mother laughed when I told her the story. Thanks, lady. Thanks for raising a daughter who's allergic to peanuts and thinks it's ok to eat them while traveling with strangers in another country. Thanks for laughing. I laughed too, later. Later. During, it was a little bit crazy.

‡‡‡‡‡‡‡

I've had a hushed secret, a sort of family secret, since I was about five years old. The secret was to be kept from my uncle, my aunt's husband, and we've just lost him this month. It may be that in the decades that have gone by, someone else told him the secret. It's possible, even likely, but for more than thirty years, I've felt like one of my aunt's protectors. I don't know exactly from what we were protecting her.

I have a vivid memory of the events of that Christmas Eve, and I also recognize that they may be all wrong. Since this is my tale, though, you will nod and grin at my reality that could be no truer to me.

It was the seventies. Sometimes I used to ride in the front seat of my aunt's baby blue station wagon between her and another passenger. If I was lucky, I'd be piled in the back with my sister and cousins. I mean the back back, where there were no seats. I don't think any of us had ever heard of a seatbelt, so there's no way to know, at this point, if this car had any. Many of you know exactly what I'm talking about. Those of you who don't, probably also only think of Times Square as a Disney production. Tsk. Tsk.

On this afternoon, I was in the back seat of the car with my cousin and her little brother and my aunt was driving. I'm not sure why it was just us. My aunt had a habit of taking a million small trips to the market or for errand-running before any event. Maybe we were headed to Little Italy for olives. I fondly remember eating black olives from Little Italy in that station wagon. Maybe it only happened once, but the recollection of it happening all of the time is as real as the tears that are obscuring my vision right now. (You know me!)

I was the middle-aged child in the car at the time, and my little cousin was not yet two. I'm guessing that there was something wrong with the car door. My family's cars often had little quirks. One was even missing half the floor in the back, Flintstone's style, but much more dangerous in real life. Having long legs, I had a particular dislike for sitting behind the driver in that car.

The vision I have of the scene places us at the extremely busy intersection of Fordham Road and Webster Avenue in the Bronx. I hope this was not the case. I hope it was a smaller, calmer, normaler intersection. We drove east and a stranger in the middle of the street got my aunt's attention. My little cousin had gotten out of the car and was in the middle of the street, cars swerving around him. I don't know how my older cousin and I didn't notice. Maybe we had. I do not know. Did he fall out the window? Did the door open and close? I don't know. I remember him behind me. Then I remember the woman telling my aunt to stop the car. That's all.

I'm sure it was terrifying for everyone. Luckily, my cousin was fairly unharmed with only an abrasion on his cheek a few inches wide. I think I was scolded. I'm not even sure. I am sure that, on this Christmas Eve, a handful of us had a secret from my Tío Elias. What did they tell him? What did he think when he looked back at the red patch on his son's cheek in the holiday photos? No clue. I've only ever talked to my mother about this, but today, the secret has come out.

My uncle was like a father to me for years. I don't think it would have been too bad to have let him know what happened, but he certainly wasn't going to hear it from me.

✝✝✝✝✝✝✝

Letting children travel alone—it's dangerous. They might die of embarrassment. When I was ten, I flew down to Panamá with my mother. She decided to vacation without me back at home while I stayed with family down there for a little while longer. A couple of weeks later, I was to fly back home by myself.

I went to the airport with a huge suitcase that is baffling to me today as I am usually a savvy carry-on-only traveler, a Polaroid camera around my neck, and a handmade wood and leather children's rocking chair for my cousin. When I reached the airport in New York, I picked up my humongous suitcase and, when asked if that was all I had, I said yes because I was tired, the rocking chair wasn't mine to remember, and I had had a traumatizing flight. Only minutes of the flight were traumatizing really, and traumatizing surely isn't even an accurate word here, but more than thirty years later, here I am recounting the events, so let's just go with it.

At almost eleven years old I was just shy of 5'10". Still, I looked like a child and supposedly had supervision on this flight. I think I got a little winged broach. Maybe it had a mini camera. That would've been a great idea. Anyway, I sat down in my seat, next to the aisle. A little while later, a MAN made it clear that his assigned seat was the one next to mine.

I'm sure I acknowledged his presence somehow with my gaze fixed through the floor because he was a man and, for years prior and decades to come, I was afraid of men. More than once in my life was this fear justified and once, in my twenties, my self-chastisement as I told myself this fear was baseless was proven dishearteningly wrong. That's a tale for another day.

Here's the trauma part. It's not so bad, but to a shy ten-year-old, it couldn't have been much worse. Apparently, my seat mate wanted to watch the movie and his headphones didn't work. Seeing that I wasn't using mine, he asked if he could use them. My ears were stuffed with airplane noise and fear and embarrassment and I thought I heard something along the lines of, "Are you going to use those," to which I responded, "No," and even smiled.

Many minutes went by and the man did not touch my headphones. I realized that he had asked if he could use them and, though I had been very polite in my response it was still negative. I realized this and allowed more time to pass, gauging my humiliation, noting for a long time that it was too high for me to correct the situation. Just before my mortification exploded all over the Eastern Airlines jet, I managed to communicate to the man that he could indeed use my stupid headphones. I have many vivid memories of this vacation. A few of them, I wish I could forget.

✝✝✝✝✝✝✝

On Saturday I found myself gleefully thinking, "Christmas is almost over!!!" I like the decorations and I like the food, but otherwise, I'm not much of a Christmas person. It's my cousins' fault.

When I was little, my large family got together and my many cousins and I made great memories. I would get a nice gift from my mother and a couple of things from uncles and underwear from my aunt or grandmother. The best part was the family, though (right up there with the panties). As a matter of fact, it didn't have to be Christmas for these good times to be had, but let's stick with the theme this week. Then, my cousins grew up and moved away, and now they're just losers and I'm a bitter, old woman.

I'm not a pagan, I'm not a Christian, and I disrelish consumerism, so if I didn't have children, I wouldn't participate in Christmas at all. My children do love the holiday and it makes me happy to see them enjoy it. The worst part for me is seeing how people feel obligated to go out and buy junk. As if it wasn't bad enough throughout the year, the shopping frenzy during the holidays really drives me mad. Luckily (and sort of unluckily), my husband buys junk all year long and does very little shopping after Thanksgiving. Still, it has taken me sixteen years to get accustomed to the amount of stuff that comes along with Christmas every year. It hardly upsets me nowadays, just a little.

In the absence of my dozens of family members, having dropped the ball myself by breeding only two children, I decided to make some holiday traditions to call our own. Well, there's only one really. You might laugh because it's so pathetic, but it's a hit in my house. On Christmas morning, we always have bagels with cream cheese, lox, capers, and red onion. If Jesus had been a New Yorker, he would have totally had this on more than one birthday, I'm sure. We also have Colombian hot chocolate, the kind that is made with milk and a stick of cinnamon and has a layer of oil floating on top. The wisest of men would have brought this to a new mother for sure.

This year at around 10am, while my husband napped and my children put away their gifts, I was inspired to scrub the kitchen cabinets clean. That made for a very happy Christmas morning. I know you know my style and have likely read that sarcastically, but really, I'm thrilled. Clean cabinets and lox to start the new year—almost as good as happy times with my cousins!

‡‡‡‡‡‡‡

Last month, both of my children became glasses-wearers. This, despite the fact that they possess some of my stealthy genes, and my vision is better than 20/20. Eye exams assess that my vision is at least 20/15 (sometimes 20/10). This means that, at a distance of twenty feet, I can see what is seen at fifteen feet by a mere 20/20 seer. It's pointless to brag about something over which I have no control, but it seems that my own achievements are rarely noteworthy, so go ahead and praise me. Call me a visionary!

Perfect vision, nevertheless, in the middle of October, I almost went blind in one eye. It was a beautiful Saturday morning when I got a very sudden sharp pain. I thought it was a headache, but it was actually in my eye, which is in my head, surprise, surprise, so we could still say it was a headache, technically. It took me a little while to figure out the pain was in my eye anyway, as I explored the sensations, pressing here and there. My right eyelid seemed to be covering a mass of disgruntled nerve endings about to explode.

Sometimes I get a pain in my head. It is on the left side of my face and is cured by sleep. This was different. It was sharper. It was on the other side. I noticed I was also nauseated, so though I am always reluctant to seek medical care, I consulted with Dr. Google.

The interwebs said that, if I had sudden pain, nausea, and blurred vision, I was practically knocking on death's door, but I would have a good tale to tell if I came out of it alive. Nah. I'm exaggerating. It did say that it could be an angle closure episode which could lead to blindness in a short amount of time. Short is relative. In this case, it meant hours, sometimes minutes. Exciting! In addition to the pain and nausea, the vision in my left eye, was not just blurred, but possessed a slight yet uncomfortable umbrage, as if my eye was shutting down.

My mother has glaucoma and, because it's hereditary, I'm considered a glaucoma suspect. I could be suspected for much more thrilling things if people only knew what to look for. For the moment, this is what I've got. This was an emergency. I knew it was even before my online search.

My husband, who usually pushes pain killers, suggested I nap. Our roles had reversed, because there I was, urgently heading out the door, for help. I speed walked to the closest optometrist and then to the emergency room, which did not have the proper equipment to examine me. I went back to the eye doctor and told them I would give them cash if they would give me answers.

The doctor confirmed that the issue was emergent. Of course! I wouldn't be speaking to a doctor if I didn't think so. She said I needed to have a hole lasered into my eye right away. I told her I was on call and would gladly do it in a couple of weeks. No. It needed to be done right away.

A few days later, after much prodding of my eyeballs, I had a hole made in one of them. Good times! Beforehand, I asked how long the procedure would take. Zap, I figured— a mere seconds, for sure. Ten minutes to an hour, they said.

Apparently, some people need a dozen pulses and some people need many, many more. As I settled into the chair/contraption/laser thingy, I said, "Let's aim for seven pulses." They were shocked to find that I only needed seven pulses exactly. Visionary indeed! Good thing because I could actually feel the pain and there's some blood, and also, it's my freaking eyeball!

I will be having my left eye laser-holed on this Thursday because I know how to start the year off right. You know, keeping blindness at bay.

‡‡‡‡‡‡‡‡

Lately, my children have been randomly saying, "Ready?" It usually means they want me to look at something or that they are about to do something to or with my body. I have learned that I need to always respond, "No, I am not ready." I never seem to be ready. This is not a tale. This didn't happen to me once. This is my life. This is my life with children. I am never ready.

My son will have his tenth birthday on Saturday. I am not ready. My daughter is taller than I am. I am not ready. My children correct me rightly all too often. I am not ready. They comfort me without prompting, with understanding and maturity. I am not ready for this either.

Babies come when they are ready. Some come before they're completely ready, but they never come when we are ready. We are never ready. I tell clients all the time so that they know that, practically, they will not get everything done before the baby is born. Still, they are born and we are not ready. There's more to it, though, so much.

I remember holding my first child, recognizing a new love that surprised me. I could never have imagined it. I can't describe it. I wasn't ready.

‡‡‡‡‡‡‡

Last week, while sitting in the crowded waiting room at the optometrist, an older Caribbean woman came in. Her feet seemed to have trouble shuffling under her weight, so she limped a bit. Apparently, she did not have an appointment. I don't know how good her eyesight was, but I suppose she at least felt that she had seen the light. She walked in with booklets in her hand, love in her heart and religious proclamations loudly rolling off of her tongue. She leaned heavily on the receptionist's counter, pivoted a bit at the shoulders and offered everyone her good news. Her uncoordinated effort led to her dropping at least a dozen booklets on the floor. I sprung from my seat to collect them for her and handed them back. Before her words had completely escaped her mouth, my back was to her and my cheery, "No, thank you!" Another patient said, "Man, you were really clear about that." Everyone laughed a little.

This woman did not upset me. I know she feels that it is her duty to enlighten others to the truths she has found for herself. I'm sure she just wants to help everyone out. I disagree with her, but we can both be in the same room together and I will always be happy to pick up her booklets even though I think they are a huge waste of paper and that she should be resting or exercising or being taken care of rather than hobbling around the streets and sitting at bus stops, but never actually embarking on any buses that come.

Yesterday, on an 8 a.m. train, another older woman got on. She had the same ambition as the other woman, but hers was even louder and much more persistent. She seemed to be on an express track to heaven. She stopped in front of each individual person, handing out her pamphlets. She walked away only after her contribution had either been accepted or rejected. I declined her offering. She moved to the man next to me and repeated three times what she had to say, each time a little more loudly and insistently. I turned my head and stated the obvious, "He's sleeping." "He is not. No," she retorted. Everyone was watching now and I proceeded to claim my spot on the throne of obviousness saying, "If he's not asleep, then he doesn't want your pamphlet." Then, because sometimes those who are really resistant to reality need to have different neurons triggered, I repeated it in her native tongue. She took herself down the train as she continued to snap at me, while still waving leaflets in people's faces. I don't think she was so successful at that end of the train car. That was not my intent.

My neighbor thanked me. I felt a little bad, fearing that I might have seemed intolerant. I don't think I am. I totally understand where these people are coming from as obligate professors, but do forced acceptors end up on the same road to paradise? I can't help but think that one should really be at least a little willing to take that journey.

‡‡‡‡‡‡‡

When I was entering fourth grade, my mother sent me to private school, despite my protestations. I made some good arguments about cost and such and some not good arguments. I remember saying that the girls wore their skirts too short. Ha!

She should've reminded me of that one six years later when my long legs were almost fully exposed even on the coldest days.

A few weeks into the school year, I heard people excitedly talking about a "pepper alley". Obviously, I didn't know what this was because I thought it was a pepper alley. There's probably no such thing outside of some small passageway somewhere in a sleepy town.

Soon I saw a big banner outside of the school gymnasium. It said, "Pep Rally," which frankly did not clarify things for me at all. Nonetheless, I let someone talk me into participating in my first non-teacher's pet type school activity.

I showed up and crossed to the far side of the bleachers to sit with people I knew. Right away I could tell that this wasn't my thing. It was in a gym and wreaked of sports. Blech! Still, I made believe I belonged by not being myself or something. I don't really remember.

It wasn't long before a couple of older girls on the other side walked towards me, stopped midway and beckoned to me. I recognized one of them from the building around the corner from me. I didn't know what they wanted, but I got up and went over to them anyway. I still can't say I know what they wanted, but thinking about the next twenty minutes or so still makes me teary. (Surprise! You know me.)

I was being accused of walking down the street with one of these girls and talking to her and calling her sister a f@&*ing b#*~h. I didn't know this girl. I didn't know her sister. I certainly didn't say those words. Did you notice I couldn't even type them into my tale? It's because I don't talk like that. I just don't, and I definitely didn't back then.

These girls wanted me to go outside and fight. With my hands. At least that's what I'm assuming. Having a sister who was eight years older, I was an experienced defender. I knew how to put my long arms around my head to protect myself from the blows, but I certainly didn't know how to fight. I had never been in a fight in my life. Well, not as an actual participant.

I was terrified. I used logic to no avail. I explained that I don't curse and they thought I was just trying to get out of it because I was nine years old. What kind of hogwash was that about me cursing? I told them they must be mistaking me for someone else. One of them was white and the other black. Maybe Latin Americans all look alike to them.

I do not know why they ended up leaving me alone. I don't know what saved me. Were they just having fun? Did the planned festivities take over, blurring their memory of me and my alleged potty mouth? I have no idea. In my mind, I narrowly escaped being beaten up by a stranger that night.

I cannot tell you if that school ever had another pep rally because I surely was never going to go again!

‡‡‡‡‡‡‡

The other day, while walking west on 23rd street with my daughter, she said to me, "You are either the complete opposite of socially awkward or completely socially awkward." Why would my darling child say such a thing? Perhaps I gave her good reason. The fact is that I don't really know which of those it is. I think one causes the other and I don't know which one comes first or which one I end up being.

Sometimes I am just bold with strangers because laughing is good and sometimes people will laugh at me or even with me. Sometimes they won't and that's ok too because they obviously have a problem, a not-being-able-to-laugh problem. Rarely is this boldness at another's expense, but there was that time in a mall in Massachusetts when I loudly asked my friend how her gonorrhea was doing. She was a little mortified while her laughter simultaneously roiled the air. Malls are boring. We would have forgotten that outing had it not been for her made-up affliction.

My daughter has witnessed much less controversial outbursts from me. There was the time a young man was Face-timing at a bus stop and I stood behind him making funny faces. His friend was laughing for a long time before he even noticed. Then he was laughing too. My daughter was down the block, not laughing.

The day on 23rd street, there was a group of about seven people standing near the corner. Each of them was delighting in a donut and one of them held the open, not-yet-empty box. As we approached, I said loudly to my daughter that they were giving out donut samples. Maybe they didn't hear me, but more likely, they didn't speak English. Perfect! I love giving tourists a NYC story. I approached the group, thanking them as I reached for a donut. Of course, I didn't take one. I didn't want one. They were all amused once they got over the momentary shock. It was hilarious.

My daughter, I think, even thought it was funny. Not that it matters much, but I suppose it's good. She's getting older and I don't think I'm getting any less socially awkward or more, whichever may actually be the case.

‡‡‡‡‡‡‡‡

I have a relatively good handle on the English language. Technically, though I was born in New York, it is my second language. I like to say that I talk all the time just to make sure I've got it down. There are basic words and terms with which I am unfamiliar, especially idioms. I grew up with idioms in another language and, you know, they can't be translated. I say things like "fix the bed" and "open the faucet." My kitchen sink is called a dishwasher and your comfort food is not likely to give me a warm, cozy feeling at all.

I like to say that we're all different and some of us are just more different than others, but that's just me being funny. It's hilarious, right? Really, even though we are all basically the same, we are all just different. The biggest differences are ones that are formed really early on. These can be the hardest to change and to comprehend and we'd all get along better if we understood that.

We'd also get along better if we didn't make assumptions. Maybe our sophomore math classes would be easier if assumptions weren't made of us. Maybe we wouldn't still remember that stupid probability test twenty-eight years later if Ms. Applestein had been a little more sensitive to the differences that make each of us who we are!

Two years earlier, in junior high school, I was tutoring others in math. Me, I was a math tutor. High school math was like another language. Even though I'm a polyglot, high school math was like zebra language. I had a good handle on probability, nonetheless. I remember where I was sitting in which classroom. I remember math was my first period. I sat there, looking at the test paper, wondering if I had missed the lesson that discussed how many cards were in a deck, how many cards there were of each suit, etc. Why was I expected to know this? This wasn't casino school!

Ms. Applestein had no sympathy. I was the only person in the class who didn't know. My mother used to spread cards out on her floral ottoman, playing solitaire for hours while I watched television. We were in the same room, but I never played because solitaire, duh!

Today, I know now how many cards are in a deck and I think that there are thirteen of each suit, but that's just a number that popped into my head, so I could be wrong. There are definitely four suits. If I think long enough, I even always eventually remember that the black upside-down heart with the stem is called a spade and that the clover is a club. I would never remember quickly enough for my sophomore math class, however, because some differences are hard to grasp.

‡‡‡‡‡‡‡

Last week, as usual, I found myself in between appointments, in Manhattan. I had a few hours and lots of work to do. I walked over and made myself comfortable on a couch in the front lobby of the Waldorf Astoria Hotel. I am no stranger to fancy hotel lobbies. Even before my singing acquainted me with them, I had frequented them with my family all as a child. Who says NYC has no public restrooms?

Though the Waldorf has been threatened with closure in the past, it has always managed to escape that fate. Not this time. While the long-term future is uncertain, the hotel will definitely close on February 28th. I decided to sit there and get some work done, sharing in its last moments.

Work cannot easily get done with a full bladder. Also, how could it possibly be work without some procrastination? Off I went to the small palace which houses about eight toilets, each with its own sink and stack of paper towels, which could easily be mistaken for a very small, very still white mink. Those disposable hand towels are basically the same quality as my special occasion reusable ones, so a couple of them ended up in my handbag.

I got my work done and, about fifteen minutes before I was due to leave, a stranger invited me into his soul by playing one of the lobby pianos. He played passionately and well. When it was time to go, I descended the stairs and stood at the bottom with a tear in my eye. Not because the Waldorf means so much to me, but because I am a goofball with leaky eyes.

The next morning, I was on the train, trying to be normal, but that's so hard for me! I looked at the people on the bench across from me. One of them was a man in his fifties. He was dressed casually with a dusty black jacket and a baseball cap pulled low over his face. I imagine that he tried to use that visor to shield himself from the world, which had obviously delivered him quite a blow of late.

The man sat there crying inaudibly. I was likely the only person who even noticed. He seemed to me to be crying over the loss of things past. The reason didn't matter. He pulled me in. I wanted to give him a hug. He was sobbing. Every now and then he lifted his scruffy sleeve to wipe his eyes and his nose. I regret letting minutes pass before I took out one of my Waldorf Astoria hand towels, got up, walked over and handed it to him.

He took the towel and nodded in gratitude. I didn't want to attract too much attention to his sorrow, but I'm not sure if that worked. I sat down and looked up at him periodically. I only shed a few tears at his unknown pain, but my heart ached so much. He thoroughly used that hand towel, making it look like a square of one-ply bathroom tissue by the time I arrived at my stop. I saw from outside of the train that he looked up toward my seat and noticed I was gone. I wished I had given him a hug.

‡‡‡‡‡‡‡

I just came back from a week in Seattle. On the way going, the estimated six hours and thirty minutes of travel time ended up being five hours and fifteen minutes. A few people may have been inconvenienced because rides they had arranged weren't yet available, but I don't think anyone was actually complaining.

Yesterday, on the way back, after a very smooth boarding process, it seemed like we were ready to go. We were in fact ready to go, all but the pilots, who were stuck in traffic, on the way. It probably wasn't funny to most of my fellow passengers, but to me it kind of was. I took the opportunity to stand up and visit with others on the plane, talk and joke around with the flight attendants. Eventually, the pilots arrived. I don't know how much time had passed, because you know that flies when you're having fun even if your airplane is on the ground. I was standing right there at the door to greet them and applauded a little bit before I took my seat.

Once they were seated and had pressed the on button, or whatever it is they have to do, the pilots announced that our flight would be four hours and twenty-seven minutes long. Despite the delay, our plane landed only about fifteen minutes later than scheduled. Clearly these guys should stick to the sky and stay away from driving on the ground.

Sometimes things go a little differently, though. For example, there's the time I flew to Las Vegas. When everyone was on the plane and we were all getting settled, a young man came up to the flight attendants. He had just woken up. He seemed confused. After dealing with him, one of the flight attendants, an older man, explained to some of us that they've seen it all. This type of thing happens. They had calmed him down and everything would be fine.

You know when the airplane is going really fast down the runway just before it takes off, when even the flight attendants are required to be seated and belted in? We were at that point when the confused dude ran up the aisle yelling that he needed to get off the plane. It turns out that he had flown from Ireland and had had lots to drink before he fell asleep. I don't know if he might've had something else as well, but in addition to being confused, he was paranoid and definitely not staying on that plane.

Disembarking was definitely the right choice for him. No one disagreed. Luckily, the plane was able to stop before it took off and we made our way over to a gate to let the guy off. On our way there, a couple of passengers inquired about whether or not he had luggage on board. At least three people got off when they found out that he did. One woman did not want to get off and did not want to fly with the guy's luggage still on. She insisted and people were called to dig his possibly explosive suitcase off of the plane.

Three hours later, we were on our way. Three extra hours on a plane that was still on the ground. At least we got snacks and drinks.

The next day, at my hotel, the electricity went out for several hours. There were no snacks or drinks and all of the casino lights and bells were lifeless. I'm pretty sure some of the regulars there would have preferred to have been on a grounded plane.

‡‡‡‡‡‡‡‡

You know how the smartest people know that they know nothing compared to what they could know? That means I'm a genius. I am usually all too aware of my lack of knowledge. I have definitely gotten myself out of situations (I'm not even talking about hitting my ankle with a hammer to get out of field day, though I did do that and wrote about it, you might recall). Other times, I am mysteriously saved from situations.

In fifth grade, I seemed like a great candidate for the school spelling bee. When asked to spell "Wednesday," I didn't only spell it correctly, but started with "capital w" to the annoyance of my non-perfectionist classmates. Not only that, but it was assumed that the one-on-one attention I sought from my teachers would translate to me wanting to be center stage. It's strange that I like to be "center stage", but not actually on a stage.

Ok, at ten years old, my vocabulary was beyond fifth grade level and my spelling matched. I'm not really bragging, because at forty-three, I am not much more advanced than I was then. Each class was to have a spelling bee and the winner from each class would compete in the auditorium in front of the whole school. I think this is a ridiculous scenario for all involved. It's like watching paint dry on a stage, but sometimes mistakenly in the wrong color and it's actually a human, not paint, and that human is a child, your schoolmate. Cringedy, cringe, cringe.

I remember my class's bee. There were two of us left. I know exactly where I was standing in the room. The teacher gave me my word: journey. It sounded familiar to me. Yeah, I knew what it meant. I could not see it in my head, though. It was as if I had never seen the word in my whole decade of a life. I was not trying to sabotage my chance to compete school-wide. I really wasn't, and you should believe me because I have certainly shared worse than that (I'm not even going to remind

you about my couple of food poisoning tales. Oops. Sorry).
Anyway, I don't remember how I actually spelled the word, but
the first letter was definitely "g".

My teacher was disappointed. Part of me was disappointed
because I genuinely did not know how to spell the word in that
moment but, as I sat in the auditorium the next day, I was so
relieved. In fifth grade, there were still many things for me to
learn and I was very lucky that the spelling of "journey" was
among them.

‡‡‡‡‡‡‡‡

My mother lives downstairs. This is usually great for all of
us. She gets to spend time with her grandchildren. I get to not
spend time with her grandchildren. She gets to eat my fabulous
cooking. I get to let her eat my fabulous cooking while
remembering her fabulous cooking of the past. When I'm sick of
her hanging around, I don't feel too bad about hinting that she
leave because she only has to go downstairs.

Yesterday, my mother had cataracts removed. My sister
took care of her right after the surgery. I was in charge of
bringing her to the follow-up appointment this morning. Never
mind that the city was closed down due to doomsday in flake
form: winter storm Stella. It is safer for us to go out this
morning in the slushy snowstorm than tomorrow in the ice-
covered everything, and that is what we shall do.

I hardly slept last night. It was likely a combination of
thoughts, but one of them was definitely related to my mother.
I wondered how she was and if she needed me. Finally, I got
out of bed at about 5:30, showered, dressed, and went
downstairs. Until that time, I was vacillating between wanting
to make sure she was ok and not wanting to wake and disturb
her. By 6 a.m., I figured it was close enough to our departure
time that I wouldn't be a bother.

I was really concerned about her being in pain or needing to
eat or something, anything, and not knowing about it. You
might wonder why I would be so concerned. We are in the same
building and we both have phones. Surely she could make her
needs known. No, not so surely. I know from experience.

About twenty years ago, my shoulders had a habit of
popping out of their sockets and popping back in. Delightful

memories I do not have of these times. Anyway, I guess my mother was jealous of this, and so one day she fell in the street, landing on her shoulder and dislocating it. Hers did not pop back in until it was adjusted by a medical professional. She wore her arm in a sling so that it could set and heal.

One Sunday morning, before the set and heal was complete, there was a knock on my door. I opened it to find my pale-faced, wrinkly-browed mother holding her low-hanging arm which had clearly come out of its place in her skeleton. Oh, no!

I got dressed and took her to the hospital and waited with her for someone to pop it back into place. It turns out, though, that my mother had waited hours in her apartment before she came upstairs for help because she didn't want to bother me. That really bothered me!

‡‡‡‡‡‡‡

This tale is going to make some people crazy. It's going to seem to some of you like I'm proclaiming to possess some type of magic powers. That's not what I'm trying to do. I'm merely relating factual occurrences.

When my daughter was a toddler, we took a swimming class together. We befriended another woman and her son. One day, I went under the water and looked at the woman and thought, "She's pregnant," not because she looked pregnant or because she had told me she wanted to be pregnant. No, the idea just appeared in my head. Later, in the locker room, she said to me something along the lines of, "I don't know why I'm going to tell you this. You just seem like one of those people who can perceive these things. I took a pregnancy test this morning and I'm pregnant."

Another time, an aunt was pregnant. She kept it a secret for a long time, but when she finally revealed it, I had already known for months.

Once at a friend's house, my brain did the same thing with her. Before I left, she announced her pregnancy. It seemed kind of dumb for me to tell her that I knew it and that I didn't know how I knew it. I did anyway and have no idea if she believed me.

Another time, after seeing a friend, I sent her an e-mail. I knew she was pregnant, again for no reason at all, but I didn't want to bring it up. I asked her how she was feeling and she responded, "Bruja!" She knew I knew.

At least one of you will say that I see pregnancy everywhere, so sometimes I'm bound to be right. While this is close to accurate, it isn't quite. I don't get this feeling of someone being pregnant all the time. It's rare, really. It's also irrational. No thought goes into it at all. It's just an idea that erupts in my head.

At a café recently, I saw someone and decided she was pregnant. I studied her, trying to figure out what it was that gave me that impression. There was no physical evidence of her pregnancy. I thought about the handful of times I've seen people out in public and thought the same thing about them, never finding out if I was right because they were strangers I'd never see again. Before I left the café, the woman I had been watching made a call. She talked loudly into the phone, sharing her good news.

‡‡‡‡‡‡‡

I've heard that FaceBook is for old people. Now you know, fogey. If you happen to be a whippersnapper on here, I would like to share with you some information.

There was a time in the olden days, circa 1985, when regular people never used the word "condom." Everyone said "rubber." Maybe this is fact. Maybe it's just that at twelve, neither of those words were coming up much in conversation for my friends and me. Not much, but sometimes they were.

I remember one day, sitting in the dank cafeteria of Our Lady of Angels school with Tara and Margaret. Tara had a book with her. It was, to us, a scandalous novel. I have no idea what it actually was, but I know that it was kept mostly hidden under the table lest the eyes of the Lord on the wall burn it in her very hands.

Tara opened the book to share a passage with her friends. The purpose of her oratory generosity was not to corrupt nor to titillate, but to mock. Apparently, the book was very old. If not, it was at least old-fashioned. Right there on the page, was the word "condom." We found it so funny, I don't remember anything else. Surely the context was more exciting than just that word, but not that day, not to us.

Little did we know that soon, probably less than a year later, Dr. C. Everett Koop would be saying the word "condom" during every prime time commercial break. Thanks to Tara's salacious literary tastes, I knew what he was talking about and probably only laughed once.

‡‡‡‡‡‡‡‡

My main Pilates teacher is Anne. I'm pretty sure she knows my name, but she always calls me Gorgeous. I figure she has good eyesight and can see beyond the reflection in the studio mirrors, which were surely purchased from a fun house supplier.

Anne is in her sixties. We often chat before and after class. We're friends. Yesterday, we talked about having lunch and, as I was leaving, she handed me something. It made me laugh to see that she had written her name and phone number down on a piece of paper. People don't really do that anymore, do they? One person usually calls or texts the other, right? Looking at her name written down reminded me of another Ann I used to know.

I knew Ann for a couple of years around 1990. I'm not sure when, really. Ann and I flirted. She was attracted to me and said I reminded her of someone she once loved. One day she told me their story.

Part of the account involved a court martial. Ann had been in the army and her lover was a woman. I don't remember the details, but it seems that perhaps someone was asked and someone definitely told. At this time, homosexuality was seen as incompatible with military service. Ann was going to be involuntarily discharged.

Somehow, Ann's many love letters were brought in as evidence against her. She had affectionately signed each letter "Anno." This wasn't exactly her nickname. This signature had developed somehow, maybe unknowingly for the purpose of saving her one day. My friend argued that she couldn't have sent these letters because her name was Ann, not Anne, as seemed to be penned at the end of each amorous epistle.

If Ann hadn't handwritten and signed her letters, her story would have been very different. Maybe I shouldn't have laughed at Anne and her piece of paper.

After last week's tale, someone commented that I have an excellent memory. It's true. I often even remember what I was wearing during moments of my life, some of those moments being quite insignificant.

As adults, time seems to move more quickly as we have fewer novel experiences and are impacted less by things that would have been great in our youth. Of course, things are bigger in our memories too. The hill near Decatur Avenue that my cousins used to sled down was a disappointing slope when I visited it ten years ago.

I cling to the past, my own and that of my family's, regularly mourning the loss of traditions, sayings, and recipes, perhaps recalling moments with more fondness than they deserve.

My husband and I planned an educational trip for my family to the southeastern states of the Union. Reluctant to head south in August because, basically, I melt, we decided to take advantage of March's resistance to transform itself into spring and headed down now. Here we are, on the road, and I am only partially melty.

Our first meal out was lunch in North Carolina. My daughter was tickled by our server's accent and, being particularly sensitive to my predictable reactions to the idiosyncrasies of humans who are not me, she watched me as she halfheartedly attempted to stifle a laugh.

My children rarely have soda as I rarely did at their ages, though they have it more often than I did because one of their parents didn't go through the trouble of perfectly making their bodies and is more permissive than the other. They knew that, during their first vacation meal, they could probably have whatever they wanted, so they each ordered a Coke.

When the waitress turned to me, I asked what drinks they had. She said, "We have all of the drink products." "Do you have lemonade?" I asked. She responded, "Nope." When my husband asked for coffee, she said they had just dumped it. Good thing they had all of the other drink products!

We both had water, which was a great choice for me because, a few days later, when asked if I wanted sweet tea or lemonade, I opted for lemonade thinking that the sweet part of the tea was probably going to be too much. Turns out that it was pink lemonade and it was more pink than lemon, for sure. Water is going to be safer for me until I get home, I think.

You may be thinking now that I've just jotted down a bunch of unrelated thoughts. If you are an observant reader, you probably think this at some point whenever you read one of my tales. You'd be right in thinking this, I suppose, but allow me to introduce myself as a guide through the circuitous tangents of my thoughts.

One afternoon in the summer before my ninth birthday, I found myself in the picturesque town of Zipaquirá, Colombia. It was beautiful, but being more than 60°F, a little warm for me. Buying into the company's ad campaign, my mother thought to buy me a Coke. Yum. Dark syrup over ice—how refreshing!

I remember walking up a small hill, towards a shop that was very white and contained very little stock. The woman behind the counter gave me a cold, small bottle of coke. I took a sip and prepared to exit, but was told I had to stay. I needed to drink the contents of the bottle and return it before I left the store. I felt bad that we were now stuck in the store. My mother helped me finish my beverage.

We recommenced our tour of the town, and it probably wasn't long before I was thirsty and hot again. Still, I will never forget that little bottle of coke. It tasted of cold and sweat, of embarrassment and impatience. It was sweet and beautiful, just like Zipaquirá.

‡‡‡‡‡‡‡

My family and I are on our way home from a ten-day road trip. You might call it a vacation, but it was an educational trip, a journey. I had done the grand planning and my husband decided where we would go, basically the day before we left. There were several things we definitely wanted to do. Among them were going to see President Jimmy Carter at his Sunday school and visiting some historic markers of the Freedom Rides and other historic sites of the Civil Rights movement. On my husband's list of must-dos, was also a visit to Okefenokee swamp. Swamp visits are never on my list of things to do. I wasn't looking forward to this part of the trip, and my husband tried to mollify my trepidation by mentioning how fun it would be to see all the alligators in the swamp. Sometimes I wonder if he knows me at all!

On the dreaded swamp day, I smeared myself with sunscreen and doused myself with bug spray. Still, I did not feel prepared. My husband asked the boat rental lady if she thought we might see any alligators and she said derisively, "Oh, I think so." Yay?

I was able to successfully board the boat without tipping it over, though I was never convinced that it would not be upended until four hours later, when my feet were back on the ground. Before we even left the dock, there in the water, right in front of us, was an alligator, swimming ever closer with hungry eyes. Maybe it wasn't hungry, but it looked hungry to me and it looked like it wanted to eat humans. Being the meatiest of the four humans in the boat, and surely very delicious, I was scared. This may sound funny to you, but the possibility of alligator-mauling was very real to me in that moment.

We took the boat through a narrow passage to get to the large swamp area and immediately started saying, "There's an alligator," over and over. Soon, it was pointless because there were so many alligators everywhere. Then, my brain did something I can't explain. Instead of getting more nervous as the threat increased, I got comfortable. It was nice to see them swish their tails back-and-forth, even when they weren't going away from us. There were alligators all around!

This brought to mind Alligators All Around by Maurice Sendak. The book always reminds me of my sister, but the song reminds me of my kindergarten commencement ceremony. This was our graduation song. We rehearsed the song in advance while our teacher, Mrs. Howser conducted. One day, my beautiful long-haired, reminiscent-of-Carole-from-the-Magic-Garden teacher-angel asked me to be the conductor during the ceremony.

I remember how I felt and the white dress I was wearing and how long my legs looked in it. I was five and probably more than five feet tall. My legs were long then. They still are. I am happy to report, however, that they seem to be unappetizing enough to alligators that I was actually able to enjoy my day among them. It is a memory I'll recall happily like that of my kindergarten graduation.

‡‡‡‡‡‡‡

So often people tell me to have fun when I'm on my way to do Pilates. Do they think I'm saying I'm going to do pirates? That might be fun, Pilates not so much. The right word makes a big difference.

Unfortunately, it's hard enough to control what we say. We certainly can't control what others hear. Too often, the words we use are interpreted differently than we've meant them. Once they are filtered through our listener's lens of life and experience, we might be having two different conversations. Sometimes, though, it isn't as much a matter of interpretation as it is of actual hearing.

I was hosting a homeschool gathering with lots of fun and food. I had made all sorts of great treats and one of my friends had made "mushroom balls." She had told me she was bringing them because they are delicious and everyone always loved them.

There they were, on the table, among the many other offerings. I had some, along with most of the other guests and they were received with various degrees of amorous appreciation. I might not have ever thought much of the mushroom balls again if it weren't for the arrival of one last guest.

This last guest came in and greeted everyone and, before she had gotten a chance to get a plate or even settle in, the mushroom ball-maker friend told her to have one, cheerfully proclaiming their deliciousness. The last guest obliged, popping a whole one in her mouth.

Moments later, I found her in another room to which she had quickly retreated. She looked at me and struggled to straddle between the need to whisper and the need to fervidly express her query. Her entire face helped her ask, "What WAS that?"

I answered very calmly that it was a mushroom ball. I know that we all have different tastes and that seemingly innocuous ingredients might be unpalatable to some of us, but the most striking thing about these mushroom balls was their blandness. What was going on here?

"Oh! I thought she said, 'marshmallow balls!'" Yeah, that explained it. Those would've been disgusting marshmallow balls!

╫╫╫╫╫╫╫

Sitting in Washington Square Park the other day, right before we dined on Mamoun's falafel, which has hardly gone up in price since the 1980s and is still quite delicious, and before we saw a tear-jerking production of *Of Mice and Men*, though I can't imagine there being a production that doesn't make for leaky tear ducts, during "family read" time, my children followed in their own books as their father read from *The Old Man and the Sea* about the pot of yellow rice with fish. This reminded me of my mother's recounting of having, in her youth, dusty, dirty fish by the sea.

My mother's uncle, Manuel, lovingly known as Tío Mañe, was a genius electrician and mechanic. This uncle had an amazing talent for repairing anything. People would call him on the phone and run their appliances and he would tell them what was wrong and how they could be fixed. My mother talks about her late aunts and uncles who died young as if they were saints. They're lucky not to have outlived their fine reputations. Tío Mañe had genius going for him and a great sense of humor, but his talents were limited in the sea. He was not a fisherman.

He sometimes took the family on predawn trips to a beach near Cartagena to watch the sunrise and spend the day. One day, he got the idea to go fishing. He made a deal with a man to take him in his canoe. The deal involved a bottle of rum, which the man looked at with eyes that crossed with longing as it was set before him. Do you know the saying about paying the band before they play? You're not supposed to because they'll go out and get drunk. Imagine if you pay the band with a bottle of rum. Yeah, that's what happened.

The rest of the family stayed and played on the beach, tossing in the Caribbean waves, under the equatorial sun. That alone makes for great hunger, beach hunger. Add in the fact that the trip had started before the sun was up, and you have a sad scene, as it was now afternoon. They waited, cooking tubers and roots, for the fish to arrive. My mother says that her little brothers looked like the ones on t.v. ads in need of sponsors. My Tia Magaly was crying from hunger, though this wasn't the first or last time she'd shed tears for want of food.

When the sun was no longer high in the sky, Mañe was seen dragging the drunk fisherman off of the boat. He could do this with both hands because he didn't need them to carry fish. There were no fish. "He can't drink. He gets sick," said the fisherman's wife, perhaps a little too late.

My mother was resigned to eat yuca with yuca even though she could tell that the yuca wasn't good. It was a certain kind of not good that I don't know how to say in English. Then, the fisherman's wife said, "Well, I have some little fish here I can sell you." She lifted her arms and reached for some fish that were hanging on a wire, clapped them together and put them in the pot. My mother watched the clouds of dust that rose from the clapping and then settled into the pot along with the fish from which they had been stirred. She was disgusted only moments before she had the most delicious yuca and fish she had ever tasted. Her Aunt Nora gobbled up a couple of bowls after declaring that she "was not going to drink that soup." My mother remembers the chipped enamelware plates that were surely laden with harmful bacteria and she also recalls that, "The banquet was done in a minute."

On the way back home, everyone was stuffed, no thanks to the fishing trip. Sitting in the back of the pickup truck, my mother wondered how had it not occurred to anyone that it was a bad idea for someone who had never fished to go out with a drunk fisherman. Like most of us, I suppose, Tío Mañe was only a genius for some things.

‡‡‡‡‡‡‡

Rules. We all have different types of relationships with rules. I'm going to share today about my two very different children. I won't say which is which, not that either should be embarrassed anyway. They are who they are.

A few weeks ago, we had a little time on our hands. I wanted the children to do some running around, but I definitely did not want to do any running around myself. I proposed a game of Mother May I. They had never played it. I explained that the person who was it, me, would tell them what kind of steps to take and how many. Before moving, they needed to ask, "mother, may I?" Easy. We started to play.

Each round shouldn't last that long. One of the players should reach 'it' fairly quickly. As the mother of the only two participants, I figured I would have to make sure it seemed fair, balancing my instructions, making sure neither of them was always the obvious winner. This proved a little challenging.

It turns out that one of my children never, ever, ever, ever, ever remembered to ask for permission to move. That's a little bit of an exaggeration, but only a little bit. In thirty minutes of play, this child only remembered twice. It was really funny, really interesting, and we all had a good time laughing, even though, in the back of my head, I was pretty concerned about this child's future. That child managed to win one round by creatively taking humongous steps.

Then there's the other child. The child who follows all of the rules, and makes up rules if there aren't any to follow. A couple of weeks ago, this child was taking a standardized test. We are homeschoolers and, if we choose to, we are allowed to administer the test ourselves in our home. That's what we did.

My husband explained the instructions. He mentioned something about the sample questions in the beginning of each section, and not being allowed to flip the page to go ahead. The rule-follower understood this rule, along with all of the others. Ready. Go.

The results of the test were well above average. In reviewing the few questions that were wrong, my husband discovered that, for the math section, there had been a graph with about half a dozen questions that went along with the graph. At this point in the test, my child, rather than using the graph while answering the questions, studied the graph, turned the page and answered the questions from memory because the rules said you weren't supposed to flip the page. They hadn't realized that was only for the instruction-reading before the timer started. Amazingly, this rule-follower did really well even on these questions.

I think they'll both be ok. Probably they will rub off on each other a bit. At least, I hope.

We just had another Mother's Day. My mother is amazing. As a parent myself, I marvel at what she did on her own, wondering how she possibly managed to raise two children as a new immigrant by herself. She even did a really good job on one of us!

I still can't figure out, though, how it is that I am qualified to be a parent (To do any adult thing, really. All of that childhood wishing I was older really snowballed into crazy fulfillment!) I have definitely done a handful of really cool things as a mother: I chose a great father for my children; I taught them baby sign language; I breastfed for a really long time; I homeschool; I feed them well; I dress them well; I take them on cool outings. That's it. The rest of the time, I don't know what the hell I'm doing.

Then there are those little moments that clearly make me a bad parent. They comprise the majority of this mothering journey for me. The one that stands out right now happened on my daughter's fifth birthday.

My daughter went to kindergarten and attended fairly regularly when she wasn't skipping class to go on homeschool trips. On the day of her birthday, I had arranged to bring in cupcakes and treats for the children. My daughter was donned a gorgeous vintage dress which I had purchased before she was even born. I made delicious cupcakes, each one with an M made of honey tuille, so delicious!

In addition to my gourmet treats, I brought in goody bags, one for each child in the class, except my daughter. I left hers home because we'd soon be going back and it made sense to me. It did not make sense to her, however. This was evident from the tears that streamed onto her reddened face. I don't think her teacher understood why I had left it home either. I felt so bad, I shed a few tears myself, and I didn't even cry the time she broke her leg and it took me almost a week to take her to the doctor. Of course, that's a story for another day.

My children took part in the 11th annual Dance Parade last weekend. I really dislike parades, but I'm so happy they did it. My daughter danced on the main stage at the parade's culminating event and my son danced down the street for about two hours.

I sent my husband a video clip of the parade dancing and he noted that my son looked "sharp though others looked confused." This was true, and the confusion was on the part of one of the other, older dancers. I explained that she has a developmental delay. She was part of the parade, not really dancing, and everyone was happy to have her there.

A few years ago, while helping in the dressing room for the end-of-year recital, I was making a bun for a gregarious little girl. Her teacher was next to us, fixing another dancer's hair. I complained to the teacher that the girl couldn't keep still. She responded, "No, she can't. She has spina bifida. If she stops moving, she'll fall over." She went on to tell me how, in the show, even the bow had to be choreographed around this challenge.

Both of these girls are being greatly helped by their dance instruction, by their patient teachers and peers. They too are helping the children around them as well as the adults, I believe. My children's dance school has excellent dance instruction and it also has a big heart. We are privileged to be a part of the Ballet Hispanico family.

‡‡‡‡‡‡‡‡

I remember when I first had my ears pierced. I yearned to have a grand collection of beautiful, long earrings. I dreamt of this. I actually remember quite vividly several dreams in which my ears were extravagantly adorned. Such simple longings.

It makes sense that innovations will be tested before they are implemented. This happens with many things and most of us aren't aware of this when it happens as we are not usually among the testers. My friend Noel was one of the testers in Staten Island before the MetroCard was available to the general public in the nineties. That was cool.

In fourth grade, Jessica Velasquez was a tester too. Her home phone had call-waiting before anyone in the universe had ever heard of it. This was cool a little, but mostly it was enviable.

It wasn't really that I wanted call-waiting for myself. I was, at that age, busy just wanting a bunch of beautiful earrings. That was obviously more practical. The issue was that Jessica and her mother, for no reason at all, had been deemed worthy of accessing this Jetsons-like technology. What the hell? I think I just didn't want her to feel special.

I remember talking to Jessica on the phone and being put on hold. I never told her how I felt and I certainly didn't lie and tell her I was also testing call waiting myself. Well, "certainly" is a strong word there. As is "lie," to be frank.

Once, I was on the phone with Jessica. It was a shiny, yellow phone on the wall of the kitchen, next to the doorway. I remember like it just happened saying to her, "Oh, hold on." Then I waited about a minute and put the phone to my mouth again and said, "My grandmother is coming over this weekend." I didn't tell her I had just gotten a call from my grandmother on the other line, but that's what I really, really wanted her to believe.

That was so dumb. She probably either didn't know what I was talking about or thought I was being stupid. Little did I know that, before my age would quadruple, I'd be making video calls like Judy and Elroy and have a fabulous stock of earrings. Metrocards are bound to be replaced by some chip thing in the near future. Are any of you testing those yet?

‡‡‡‡‡‡‡

Pareidolia—you may not know what it means, but I'm pretty sure you've experienced it. Our minds try to make sense of things we see or hear by transforming random or unrecognizable sights or sounds into ordered, familiar ones. We might see a face in a jumble of dots or lions emerge from geometric patterns. At these times and whenever we see figures in the clouds, we are experiencing pareidolia.

When the movie Awakenings came out, I could never read the sign properly. Every single time I saw it, I would read "awakeningas," like it was some indigenous herb of the Amazon. This was maybe reverse pareidolia (or just stubborn stupidity).

It took my mother decades to realize that the Batman logo did not contain fangs. It doesn't, does it? It must've been a relief for her brain to stop trying to figure that one out and just see the bat.

I remember when my grandmother saw an animated version of the NBC peacock. That was such an eye opener for her. She said she always wondered why the rainbow design had a white notch cut out. Yeah, Abuelita, that's a peacock and the notch is its beak.

I suspect that pareidolia is unique to each individual, incorporating each person's personality and experiences, perhaps. When I first trained to become a doula, while we were discussing the interview process, the trainer suggested that we bring a short list of references to offer to prospective clients.

Ok, cool. I totally got that, except that I didn't at all. Maybe it's because English is my second languish or maybe it's because I'm just a nice person. I'm not sure how it happened, but for my first two dozen interviews I always brought a list of referrals with me. Before leaving, I'd tell people about a few other great doulas they might want to interview.

It's funny, but it didn't work out poorly for me. Prospective clients got the sense that I was in the doula business to help people, which I am. I don't think that was really pareidolia as much as my generous spirit working things out for me.

‡‡‡‡‡‡‡

A Couple of months ago, I was at Thomas Jefferson's historic home at Monticello. On display there was a bed with a blanket on it. It was labeled as such. The blanket looked like a sheet. None of my blankets are that thin, and I dare say that none of yours are either. This reminded me of the towels I used when I was in Hungary.

Today I said goodbye to a friend who will be traveling to Hungary for a few months. In her bathroom, she had a plush, luxurious towel, you know, a normal towel. I didn't warn her that she might have a different experience of post bath dabbing while away.

When I was in Eastern Europe, I went to a Kmart for the first time. There, I purchased beautiful, fine crystal. Great quality crystal was plentiful and inexpensive. In Hungary, there was intricate embroidery to be had for very little money in small shops everywhere.

Crystal and embroidery seemed to be very important to Hungarians. Towels, not so much. I still have a couple of the hotel towels. I took them and left a big tip. I needed them to protect the crystal in my suitcase. If you come to my house, you can ask to see them. You will look at white dish clothes with orange and blue stripes and those will be my Hungarian towels. Really, they are the size of dishcloths and they are not made out of terry. They're like a Monticello blanket.

Sarah, you should take your plush towel with you. When you come back, use it to protect the fine crystal in your suitcase!

‡‡‡‡‡‡‡

Last week I went to a concert by the New York Philharmonic. I enjoyed it. I like that type of thing. People who know me know that about me. I know a couple of two or three things about classical music.

Twenty plus years ago, I was even singing classical music myself. I did this for more than two decades. I sang lots of different kinds of music. I enjoy lots of different kinds of music. I don't enjoy all kinds of music.

Let's go back to age nineteen or twenty. This year there were three different times when I thought I was just hanging out with friends and it turned out that my friends were attracted to me and wanted something more. Sometimes I am stupid in this way. Perhaps I'm not unique.

One of my I-thought-we-were-only-friends people told me he had a surprise. His name was definitely Victor or definitely Carlos. I know it doesn't matter, but I am as sure of it having been one of those two names as I am unsure of which one. He asked me to get dressed up. We went to lunch somewhere and then he took me to Lincoln Center.

He had gotten us tickets for a chamber ensemble concert or something. I don't know exactly what it was, but I know it was a group I didn't know playing music I didn't like. It was so boring.

I suffered through the concert, feeling really bad. I realized that he was trying to impress me because he liked me. I did not like him in that way and I definitely was not impressed. Not only had he spent money on these tickets, but I know he definitely didn't enjoy the concert as he wasn't at all familiar with classical music, and it didn't even work as a tool to win my heart.

I have no idea what happened to Varlos, but he never got another chance at a date with me. He was probably relieved, anyway, that he wouldn't ever have to sit through such a concert again.

‡‡‡‡‡‡‡

Last week, I went to a baseball game. Someone actually laughed out loud when I told them. I posted about it jokingly on FaceBook because it isn't my usual thing.

In 1986, I watched half a season of baseball all by myself just for the heck of it and the Mets, for whom I was cheering, just happened to win. Same thing in 1987 with football, when my hometown Giants won. It would be unfair to teams outside of New York if I regularly watched sports, I think.

I can't remember what got into me that year, but it was definitely out of the ordinary. Outside of that year, my life has been spent avoiding sports—no watching, no participating, no talking about.

I know that I'm not alone, but sometimes non-fans seem like quite the minority. Once, in fourth grade, Ms. Sheridan, who would later become Sister Patricia to the astonishment of her young students, assigned us an essay to be written on the spot about our favorite sport.

I liked writing essays. I always remember my masterful paper in first grade on something I wish I could change in the world, the "Clucluxclan". I'm pretty sure I had just seen an episode of All in the Family or something. Anyway, I liked writing when I had something to write about, but this time I did not. It wasn't even that I disliked sports. I just needed to find a way to fill my page with the sentiment "what is sports?"

Instead, I chose to write about a sport my cousin liked, gymnastics. I thought I knew something about this sport, but apparently, I did not know enough.

As I wrote, I decided to focus on my favorite event in my favorite sport—the "floor dance," known to everyone else in the

169

universe as the floor exercise or floor routine. I have never had a paper get so marked up in my life. My teacher not only corrected my invento-wording, she also had lots to say about the descriptions I used, which seemed to be made up. You know, the descriptions I made up.

Finally, she asked why I had chosen to write about a sport about which I seemed to know very little. Uh, because your assignment was stupid and presumptuous, lady (Sister), just like the time in high school when I was expected to know how many cards there are in a deck and how many of each thingy and such. Hogwash!

Compared to my knowledge of other sports at the time, I was an expert on gymnastics and the floor dance! Thank you very much.

‡‡‡‡‡‡‡‡

On July 4, 1991, I spent the day and night at the South Street Seaport in New York. It was a hot, sunny day. The air was thick with the invisible, moist weight that has been part of every July 4th I've spent in New York City as long as I can remember.

The area was being developed at that time and the event authorities directed me and about fifty other singers to our holding area—storefronts that were empty and some still under construction. They would, in the coming weeks, welcome tourists with unnecessary treasures and exorbitant price tags. Even in their underdeveloped state, they exuded their mystique among the pristine cordoned-off streets of what seemed like a ghost town that day, but for the giddy teenagers, shuffling around to claim a spot for our belongings. We each had a garment bag with a tuxedo or a white gown, and a lunch from home.

The sun shone brightly as we walked over to rehearse. The stage, covered with a canopy, practically met the water, a little too closely for my comfort, but my place was up front and the orchestra was behind us, so the percussion and brass sections would have been the first to go anyway.

We warmed up under our own familiar baton and were then handed over to Skitch Henderson so that he could coordinate us with his New York Pops. We had sung with them before under the gilded brilliance of their Carnegie Hall home. We knew what to expect, remembering that we had scoffed at him the first time because he had never performed with Peter J. Wilhousky, the arranger of the big piece we were to sing. We knew it better, but we also knew to follow the conductor.

As the sun set, we were escorted through the crowds back to the stage. We sang beautifully, I'm sure, ending with our awe-inspiring rendition of the *Battle Hymn of the Republic*, the last chords of which elided with the boom of fireworks in the waters behind us. Afterwards, we made our way back through the sea of people, acknowledging the praise with satisfied smiles. The girls held up our white gowns as we walked gingerly on the cobblestones, making our way back to our secluded area, which hadn't yet been enhanced with electricity.

We changed into our civilian clothes in the balmy darkness. Knowing we had done a great service to our audience and growing from the service they and the music had done for us.

✠✠✠✠✠✠✠

Son: What's your Tuesday Tale gonna be about?
Me: It's going to be about the time I almost got squeezed to death by a boa constrictor.
Son: No you diiiidn't.
Me: Well, in my imagination...

Of course, that totally counts!

My children met Fitz last week, their cousin's bearded dragon. She told them some interesting facts about the reptile and they were surprised, upon touching it, at how soft it was. That's always the way with reptiles, it seems.

I have a friend who's a herpetologist. In my teens, he had many reptiles and amphibians living in his home. Once, for no reason that I can come up with now, I found myself in that home with him and his pets. He was much more enthusiastic about me touching them than I was.

A dragon that fits in the palm of my hand is not at all menacing. A boa constrictor, longer than I am tall, is very different. Sometimes I have trouble expressing myself oppositionally, so there I sat, on the bed, as he lowered the very heavy snake onto my shoulders and around my neck. Good times!

As he did this, I felt it scrape against my earring. I remember the earrings I was wearing that day. It was the late 80's. They were fairly big earrings that were made up of lots of flat pieces of wood and some wire. Totally cool, they were. Anyway, once the snake was wrapped around me, my friend looked at my long, polished nails and told me to be careful with "those" so that I didn't scratch the snake. That would be very dangerous, he said.

I sat there and waited for the snake to live up to its name. I was scared and I figured freaking out would be counterproductive. I also didn't want to tell my friend because I figured he'd get upset at me. I just sat there and waited. For minutes, the snake crushed me under its weight, but here I am telling this tale because it, in fact never strangled me to death. Surprise ending, right?

‡‡‡‡‡‡‡

I love good food of all sorts. I can be particular, however, even in some ways that are different than what most others like. I don't like crunchy cereal, for example. Growing up I couldn't understand why some companies were advertising cereals that didn't get soggy in milk. Yuck. Who needs all that noise while they're eating?

I learned to expertly make French toast when I was very young. This is the only thing I ever remember my mother actually teaching me to cook. I didn't learn how to make pancakes until I was a little older, and on this day, the day of the ruined pancakes debacle, I was about six.

There I was, sitting at the table, with my plate full of beautiful pancakes. I always ate them the proper way, making a little puddle of syrup on one side, into which I'd dip each delicious forkful before enjoying the syrupy yet not soggy delight. I even always evaluated my meal (I'm using the past tense here, but this technique is too good to ever abandon. Trust me.), figuring out which side of the pancake was the most deserving of being the last bite and positioning it furthest away from me on my plate.

On this sad, sad fateful morning, my uncle came out to break his fast with his adorable niece. He was living with us for a little while and I was learning some new things. Maybe some of them proved useful in my life. I suppose the one that has inspired today's tale really just taught me to be careful with my food because other people might just not know what's good.

My uncle sat down with me and told me that the best way to eat pancakes was to poke them repeatedly with a fork before pouring syrup on them. He assured me I would love this horrible technique. I did not. The syrup disappeared! The pancake pieces were heavy. I can't believe I wasn't completely turned off of breakfast foods for life on that day. It was worse than the time I had French toast at the diner and I mistook the blob of butter for egg.

Later in life, I would hear my family making fun of my uncle, Tío Toto, for his overuse of ketchup. I wish I had known at age six about his unpalatable idiosyncrasies and culinary inadequacies. Sometimes we learn too late and end up with a ruined pancake meal never to be forgotten.

✝✝✝✝✝✝✝

I used to wear pantyhose all the time. It's been quite a while since I regularly wore them, but I have some vivid memories of those days. I'm tempted to change course now and tell you of the horrorful heat-of-DC-pantyhose tale. You're going to have to come back for that one, though. Today's tale is much more tame.

Last time I wore pantyhose was more than a year ago and I took them off halfway through the event. Maybe they were uncomfortable. Maybe I got a run. I can't remember. It was a sweet sixteen party in the spring and it was evident that I didn't need to be wearing them, so off they went.

I'm not sure if it's in my imagination or if there actually was a time, not long ago, when any leg that was seen beyond a hem was covered by hose. (Of course that was the case! It wasn't long ago at all that our hems dragged along the floor, not leaving a hint of leg in sight.)

It was during this time that I was at an engagement party with my dear friend. I was an obligate hosiery donner. The engagement party was on a spring or summer afternoon, but it was in a fancy hall, so there I was with all the other decent women, in a dress and pantyhose.

It was a huge affair. There were several courses of food and dancing and fanciful fanciness galore. I can only imagine what the wedding was like. Really, I can only imagine it, because I wasn't there. I wasn't invited. Maybe it has something to do with what happened during the engagement party.

There we all were, partying it up. There were a couple of hundred people there and I knew about a handful of them, but I'm friendly. I had fun. I had fun until things changed for me. They changed because my friendliness sometimes is manifested in odd ways, in ways that leave me friendless even.

I walked up a grand spiral staircase, to the ladies' room and, as I walked through the gilded doorway, I saw two women crouched over what could've been a soldier's wounded leg in the trenches. It wasn't a wounded leg, though. It was a wounded pantyhose leg. It had a big hole in it from which emanated a long run and a few runettes. I don't know if those women were religious, but those hose were sure holy!

Upon seeing this catastrophe, I said in my chipper, optimistic way, "What run?" That's what I said. I said that to these strangers and then noticed that the victim of the torn legwear had probably been crying. They gave me the nastiest look, I can still see it.

After I used the bathroom, maybe I tried to patch up the awkwardness, maybe I just ran out of there. I can't remember. After that, I spent lots of time sitting at my table with my intact hose hidden under the tablecloth. Those women probably don't even wear pantyhose anymore.

‡‡‡‡‡‡‡

One of my children is a little obsessive about cleaning up. That one needs help. The other one, never notices that anything needs to be cleaned up at all, even if the contents of every drawer and shelf are strewn all about (which is sometimes the case!). That one needs help too.

As an adult, I am more obsessed about everyone else cleaning up than myself. I mean, I want everything to be neat and tidy all the time. I just don't want to have to do it myself. It should just happen automagically!

When I was a child, I was definitely the neater of the two siblings, but I don't really remember cleaning up. Maybe I just didn't leave messes to begin with. I used to love doing dishes, though. Someone once told me that they like to feel the steam on their face like they're at the spa. Ha! That's my least favorite part. I'll take a real spa day after I've done the dishes. Thank you very much.

I used to like to do the dishes and I used to like to clean the windows. I definitely did not like to fix my bed, though. I think it was mostly a matter of logic. I was always going to be messing the bed up again that evening, so why bother?

My mother had a different idea. Not only did she want the beds to be fixed daily, she wanted them to be fixed to her standards, which she seemed to have made up in some fantasy world where there's nothing better to do.

This actually worked to my advantage. I never aspired to gain her approval, but I did feign interest in learning her peculiar ways. "Mami, I don't know how to do it that way. Can you show me again?" My bed always got fixed with no effort on my part, as I watched and "learned." Thanks, Ma.

‡‡‡‡‡‡‡

My major in college was Early Childhood and Elementary Education. I went to NYU and the program was very liberal. I took twenty-four credits most semesters and many of them were music classes—performance, history, and appreciation classes. It was great.

For a few semesters, I only took classes on Tuesdays and Thursdays, except for one "class" on Fridays, jazz ensemble. It was just a jam session with about half a dozen people for which we got college credit. Pretty sweet.

One day we were talking about *How High the Moon* and I brought up Ella's version. I love me some Ella Fitzgerald! Her musicality was amazing, even eclipsing her lyrical amnesia. Good thing she could scat, because words often just seemed to escape her. In the recording I was referencing that day, she goes on for about eight minutes as follows: thirty seconds of correct lyrics, two minutes of inventolyrics and the balance, Ella genius. At the end of the discussion, I was assigned *How High the Moon* for the following Friday. This particular version. Have you heard that mess? At one point she actually says, "I guess these people wonder what I'm singing." Somehow, I got away with a different song. Not that I couldn't do it. I totally could, ok?

On another memorable day, I was singing an Ella song yet again. I didn't sing only her songs, but today I'm writing about her (also, I sang a lot of her songs at the time, so many). The studio where we jammed was on a floor where there were lots of sound-proof rooms for piano lessons and voice lessons. There was also an office. I imagine that our room was sound-proof because we made some serious music—singers, pianist, bassist, and drummer.

Most of you have never heard me sing. I get tremendous stage fright, so you probably never will. When I do sing, though, I'm pretty ok. On this day, I was comfortable and singing something fabulous. Towards the end of my song, the secretary from the office walked through the open door. She had probably worked for the school for a dozen decades and wore the same coiffed do on that day as she wore the day she started. I remember seeing her standing there with her mouth open and her hands on her cheeks. She came in because she thought she was listening to a recording of Ella Fitzgerald and, halfway through my piece, began to wonder.

I couldn't believe that I was not just compared to but mistaken for Ella. After all, I knew all of the lyrics.

‡‡‡‡‡‡‡

I have a plethora of embarrassing or shameful memories from my childhood that would make great tales, but perhaps you will have to wait to read them in an anonymous collection revolving around regrettable bodily functions, circumstances, and actions. Sometimes bad decisions and uncontrolablenesses make for good stories.

Today's tale is about a bad, bad thing I did when I was about eight and how it didn't take me long to regret it for the wrong reasons. It is shameful, but not enough to keep me from sharing it here.

I wasn't a doll type of girl when I was a child and still don't understand the appeal of doll play. I remember the four dolls I had and each of them probably merits its own tale. They never existed at the same time in the same place. You might imagine them sitting on a shelf, playing among themselves, but there was never more than one at a time. It's so odd that the acquisition of each doll does have a memorable story for me.

Today's tale is about the Barbie head. Many of you would argue that it wasn't even a doll. It was an almost life-sized bust with long, blonde hair. She came with make-up and a mechanical tool that twisted two portions of hair and then twisted the two portions together. I wasn't interested in the make-up, but I learned how to braid on that doll. My hairstylist mother taught me. I think she figured it out that very day because she has since always claimed she does not know how to braid hair.

Joel, from the fourth floor, had the same doll. It made perfect sense. She was Jamaican and I am Latin American, so we practiced braiding blond hair and applying blue eye shadow to pale skin.

One day, I noticed that Joel's doll had longer or maybe denser lashes than mine. The envy that these plastic eye hairs erupted in me is inexplicable. Naturally, I asked if I could borrow her doll head. I can't imagine what reason I gave her, but it seems to have been satisfactory. Later, I gave her my doll in return. (The shame! Don't judge me too harshly please.)

After a while of having my more glamorous-eyed stupid Barbie head, I noticed that the feature that was important to me had been mutilated. Joel had cut her doll's hair! I don't know if she noticed that seemingly magical follicles had sprouted longer locks on the one she now possessed.

I've blocked out the memory of what happened next. I probably just didn't say anything and I surely shed some tears. Dolls are stupid anyway.

‡‡‡‡‡‡‡

Well, I guess I'll write about the eclipse—a big deal and not a big deal. The universe is amazing. Sometimes it merits walking through the streets of Manhattan, looking for a bald patch of sky where the buildings are not climbing, but it's always amazing. That's just its nature.

I had an appointment yesterday that I couldn't change. It had the potential to go from 1 p.m. to 3 p.m., perfect timing. I was hoping to be done by 2:30 and was lucky enough to be out by about 2. As soon as I was outdoors, I got very emotional. You know why? Yeah, neither do I. I have no problem with unclaimed tears. I shed them frequently and they are very satisfying.

I made my way towards Madison Square Park and was not disappointed. Hundreds of people were there to greet me. Not really, but they were there and so was I. As a matter of fact, no greetings were exchanged, but we all talked anyway. I did not have solar eclipse glasses. Neither did maybe two thirds of us there. Nonetheless, every one of us got to look through these special glasses repeatedly. We also looked through homemade pinhole cameras and I even sent a bunch of people to marvel at the moon images on the ground, among the shadows of the tree leaves.

I moved among these people periodically so as to hide my tears a bit. These, my people, were making me cry again.

I was in touch with my family, making sure they were experiencing the wonder too. My children told me that my mother said she saw a solar eclipse forty years ago. I think that maybe she was thinking about the black out (because she was not in the right place at the right time for even a partial solar eclipse). Same thing. Except not at all. In a blackout, the lights go out. With an eclipse, the heavenly bodies are just going about their business, not changing at all. The sun doesn't actually do anything special. The moon doesn't really either, but she asserts herself and reminds us of her power.

Though she may seem dark and cold, she is formidable. She affects us constantly and we don't often take notice. Once in a while she gives us a nudge by maybe casually passing in front of the sun. I have friends who cried like me, others had headaches or strong cramps. "I am powerful. Remember me," she cried.

My children and I started the day by celebrating the way we do a New Year. Eclipses are times of new beginnings so it felt right. I have some good beginnings brewing. I hope you do too.

‡‡‡‡‡‡‡‡

I can write lots of tales about my mother, but she's my FaceBook friend, so I need to be careful. You know. Also, I don't want comparisons to be so readily available in the future. Being told I'm just like my mother is often a compliment, but of course, not always.

My mother loves to explain things. I'm not even sure that's an actual truly factual statement. It's more like a habit, I think. It is not one of my favorite habits of her, by far. I mean, why do I need to hear her reason for going to the bathroom or for needing a glass of water? Why? My mother and her freaking explanations!

Lately, she has taken her habit a little further. She'll end a sentence with, "because imagine." What? Why do I need to imagine the explanation, lady? It's yours to give and mine to ignore!

I really do not like explaining things. Usually, when someone tells me they don't understand something I've said, I will look at them and wait to see if a moment will help things land in the right brainular patterns. Then, I'll usually sigh to give myself an endorphin boost before I do the dreaded deed of figuring out how to fit my idea into their head. Ugh, abhorrent.

I don't know why I'm like this exactly, but let's blame my mother. Let me explain! When I was a child, I remember my mother telling me that it was always better not to give explanations. She accompanied this advice with a little story about a woman who was visiting Europe somewhere. When the woman went to check into the hotel, she was told that the only room available for that night had half a bathroom and that she could upgrade to another room on the next day. The woman began to respond, "That will be fine because I never bathe," she noted the look of horror on the man's face before she was able to add, "at night."

I don't know where my mother got this story, but I will never forget it. I wish she would remember it too! Good thing she reads all of my Tuesday Tales.

‡‡‡‡‡‡‡‡

When I started dating him, my husband used to say I was hoity toity. At the time, I had never heard the term, but I could tell by the way he used it that it was a bad thing. He said it jokingly because I'm a bit fancy compared to him.

On our first day trip, we were with my husband's sister-in-law. I didn't realize I needed to try to make a good impression, so I just spoke honestly. Imagine! The subject of IKEA came up and I went ahead and shared that I don't particularly like what I consider to be disposable furniture. I went on to praise solid, heavy pieces.

There was a moment of silence before I learned that I was the only person in the car who felt this way. Furthermore, the other adults not only liked IKEA, but really liked IKEA. My husband told me later how that probably lost me major in-law points that day. Oops.

I'm not sure if I made up for it by agreeing, later, to fill my house with IKEA furniture. It's so hard to be hoity toity nowadays!

‡‡‡‡‡‡‡

Since I started writing my tales, I've had several gems in my head. They live there in tangible memories from my childhood, narrated by my mother's mother, the matriarch of my clan. When I count my elders, they are all strong women, led by this one, my grandmother.

The stories of her life play vividly in my head. They include sweat and sorrow, joy, and flirtation, hope and disappointment. For more than nine decades, she was a wild woman.

I'm definitely going to share stories about her, her gains, her losses her grand ideas and dreams, but I've come to realize that I can't share the stories she told. They don't work in writing. To me, they don't work unless they are heard in her voice.

I can't possibly convey the tac, tac, tac sound made by the exposed nail in the heel of her shoe in the dark, silent streets of her little town on the way back from the movies and how it made her laugh and laugh. It's making me laugh now just thinking about how she couldn't get through that story without cracking up herself.

I remember the way she'd look towards the distance while she described her escapades in foreign lands and how she'd bow her head as her laughter began to bubble up until her shoulders and chest were bouncing, while her eyes were only slits formed from her mile-wide smile.

This month she would have been 94. She lived quite a life. I wish she could have told you about it. I'll tell you a little here and there. Come back next week.

‡‡‡‡‡‡‡

About two decades ago one late September day, I called a man in Puerto Rico. I asked for his son and told him I had been in the army with him. He caught me up on his goings-on and I gave him a name and a voicemail number to pass along to his son. Of course I lied. I mean, can you picture me in the army? First of all, those clothes—not cute, also all the same. Hello? Individual star power, anyone? Then there's the whole physicality problem. Such hard work. Also, the fighting. I cry during just arguments. Maybe I could stand on the front lines and drown the enemy with my tears. Anyway, I had spoken to this man several years prior and I knew that the truth would not get me to my end.

It wasn't long before I received a message from the man's son in which he left me his own phone number in Florida. Tears flooded my, well, everything. Part of my mission had been accomplished.

I regained my composure and called the stranger back. I immediately confessed that I had lied and told him my real name. Then I told him that he should come to New York and spend Thanksgiving with my family and me. When he asked why, my response got stuck in my throat and then came flooding out, "Because you're my uncle." I didn't know what he knew and how much I would have to explain. By the end of our conversation, he had agreed to come meet us before Thanksgiving. Now I will share with you what I know. Luckily for me, he was already familiar with some of his own story. Let's go back.

At the age of eighteen, my uncle tried to leave Puerto Rico for the first time. He was smart and driven and was planning to study abroad. Due to some requirements for his passport, his parents were then forced to tell him the truth. His mother, the only one he had known his whole childhood and now as a young adult, hadn't birthed him. I'm glad he knew that much, because can you imagine a stranger calling you up to tell you that!?! What had I even planned to say? No clue. I'm glad that's behind me!

My grandmother had met his father, a dashing, young Puerto Rican soldier in Panama. In her twenties still, she already had a handful of children. They were, of course, more than a handful. She had five living children at the time and had lost one.

Soon, she had a baby with the soldier. My mother recalls that the baby was always meticulously dressed. She'd like to share more memories of him, but she can't. Before he was a year old, his father took the baby to meet his grandmother. He would never return.

When we were all united that November evening, it was as if we had known one another all along. My family is very familiar that way. We cried and we laughed and we marveled as we took photos of my new uncle with one of his brothers who could've been a twin.

I imagine my grandmother's life, working hard for her young children. I imagine her life when one of them died. I imagine her life when one of them was taken away and her knowing that he was probably better off. My imagination is a little misty, of course, but in the center, there is a strong, beautiful woman who did her best. Her best got so many people so far, even the ones who were taken afar!

‡‡‡‡‡‡‡‡

In September, because it's the best month, a dozen years ago, my husband and I celebrated our union with a wedding. An autumn day in New York City seemed like a great idea. The weather was going to be perfect, crisp, and inviting of hugs from the couple of hundred guests. I designed and made a long-sleeved dress of ivory peau de soie. Each of the tables had about twenty candles and a beautiful arrangement of flowers in autumnal colors nestled in a few inches of freshly harvested cranberries because it was going to be a beautiful autumn day. If I could have, I would have planned to have a few fireplaces with wood crackling in them, casting a glow upon the faces of our loving guests, a warmth upon their hands and hearts and filling our nostrils with the redolence I so love in the chill of the cooler months.

Good thing I couldn't do that, though. Good thing because the temperature on that day was freaking 83°! Oh, here's a great idea. Let's pack hundreds of people and hundreds of candles together on a warm day in a space where the air conditioners won't get going for several hours. I don't think anyone complained about the heat. I was probably the only one wearing long sleeves anyway.

For this affair, my husband and I did almost everything ourselves. I not only hand-addressed the invitations, but made each one, cutting paper to just the right size, nestling it in the other paper I had cut and finishing it all off with a ribbon tied in a bow. I made the party favors and I even did some of the cooking. The night before the party, my husband and I, along with my step children and a couple of friends stayed up way too late to decorate the space, including hundreds of chairs which we covered and decorated to our liking. To my liking, really—a gold bow to match the ones on the invitations and party favors.

I'm getting a little tired thinking about all of the things we did. Fortunately, we also hired a few friends to help us out. A couple of people crammed into the tiny kitchen and helped us arrange all of the food beautifully. Another couple were assigned other tasks like, "Put this there after the cocktail hour and make sure you set the favors out after dinner where the family photos are and don't forget that thing under the table." They were much more detailed and all written out clearly on a piece of paper, of which there were at least two copies. Turns out that it didn't matter how detailed they were because the people in charge of reading those instructions couldn't actually read. I figured this out at the end of the night as I tried to make sense of some confusion. I felt bad, but didn't say anything because I imagined my friend felt some sort of way about it himself.

As my husband and I checked into our hotel for the night, he in the $5 tuxedo I convinced him to buy at the thrift store in Bronxville soon after we met because it was the perfect style and cut for him, assuring him that he would at some point likely need a tuxedo if he stuck with me, not that I was thinking of marriage, just other fancy events to which we would surely be invited (still waiting on those, by the way) and me in my peau de soie gown, the young lady behind the desk looked at me and probably thought, "Girl, it is a million degrees out there and you are all wrapped up as if it was actually a nice autumn day." Then she offered to upgrade us to a suite. There was no fireplace, but the air conditioning worked splendidly!

‡‡‡‡‡‡‡

You may have noticed that I don't dye my hair. If you didn't, you probably thought I was trendy. I am not. The only time I colored my hair was when I was eighteen. I put deep purple streaks in it. It was rather subtle, but still noticeable in my dark hair. I thought it looked nice, especially in the sun.

This was in September. I was in college and had just started working part-time as a nanny. The family I worked for consisted of three children and their parents. The mother was mostly around. It's nice to have extra help, though, I'm not sure that she actually needed it. Maybe the apartment's size made it impossible for her to be heard from one end to the other, so an extra voice and set of ears and hands, I suppose, were a necessity. The apartment was on Park Avenue and it was, in essence, a house within a building. Instead of a backyard and lawn, they had doormen and a concierge. Being a couple of blocks away from Central Park made it a good trade, I think.

I added the purple highlights to my hair on Saturday, and the following Monday, I headed to my nanny job. It was a bright, sunny day, but the air was brisk and I wore my matchy matchy purple Gap turtleneck. My mother had bought me that top in 1987, along with a black and purple striped skirt that I would never wear today (horizontal stripes! Eek!) and some plaid lumberjacky button-down shirts. Let's not dwell on those, please. They were soft, but they were plaid. How gauche.

The turtleneck matched the new highlights in my hair, which I had slicked back and tied in a chignon at the nape of my neck. The concentration of hair made it difficult to see the purple streaks unless one scrutinized my head with a judgmental eye. There was such an eye at work that day. It was coupled with another eye and what they saw was mashed up into a harsh brain that controlled a mouth that, on Tuesday, fired me.

My employer told me that, while she had no problem with my fanciful tresses, her husband had been "born in a three-piece suit." She also assured me that they weren't firing me because of my hair. Oh, no. They had decided to hire a full-time nanny, one who wore all white, like a nurse.

Those children were very sweet. They had very light blonde hair, really good for dying. I hope at least one of them got rainbow locks at some point in their life.

✝✝✝✝✝✝✝

I've been thinking about intelligence. I remember, when I was younger, hearing about certain people who were very smart. I'd hear it said that they were book smart and lacked common sense. As I understood it, this was frowned upon by the sayers. I was satisfied with the possibility that I might have this common sense of which they spoke, at least, since I knew I wasn't book smart.

I know lots of trivial facts and I think I also have an uncommon sense. I have a people intelligence. Furthermore, people sense that I do. They come to me with their stories, with their woes. Perhaps you can relate. I suspect many of my colleagues and friends are the same way. We are the ones who sit with people.

Today, I left clients with their newborn, after helping them navigate that journey for about twenty-five hours. They told me that my job was the most stressful job imaginable. I don't see it that way. That's why it's my job and not theirs.

Outside of work, people share with me as well. Oh, the secrets I've heard and the loads I've lightened with just a listening ear and an open heart! I don't advertise this trait, but people know that I know people. Sometimes they are surprised or ashamed by what they share. Other times, they don't even notice they've done it.

I remember Jason and Shirley, the twins in elementary school. I can't remember what they shared, but I recall it was something that weighed heavily on their hearts. Shirley used to get migraines. Maybe she needed to talk to more people or people a little older than her seven-year-old classmate.

Gilbert in third grade, tough kid and a bully, was always in trouble. One day he told me, by the bookcase in the front of

Mrs. Jacobson's classroom, that he didn't want to be bad. When I asked him why he was bad, he cried. Why was he ok crying in front of me? I wish I knew what happened to him. I could do a much better job of listening to him today.

Sometimes I think I want to eliminate negative people from my life. It is an impossibility because they need the listeners. I need to be a listener, you know, because not being book-smart means that when I say things, I probably don't know what I'm talking about anyway.

‡‡‡‡‡‡‡

Last week I tried to convince you of my unintelligence. This week, I'm surely going to win you over to that idea. I have a smattering of multisyllabic words in my vocabulary, but that's like sleight of perception, pure trickery. Really, I'm a dummy and not even smart enough to stay quiet about it.

I'll be traveling to Washington DC this week. Let me share about an embarrassing time I had there once. I don't even know how long it took me to realize that I should be embarrassed about it because, again, I am a dummy.

I was dating a man who lived in downtown DC. I went down to see him a few times. Based on the stupid stuff I said the first time I visited, I can't believe he gave me the opportunity to go back. Here it is. Here's the story. Minor things, but mortifying once I realized that the words I said probably made it through my friend's ears and into his head.

I arrived in DC by train on a Friday afternoon. It was my first solo trip there and my friend picked me up at the station and we walked to his apartment. I'd like to say that I can't remember what he did for a living, but the truth is that I just didn't understand it at the time. It was something to do with finance. It was a very adult thing. I don't know. My first faux pas was related to this mature-like profession of his. We were in his apartment and he said that he was waiting for the markets to close before we went out. I don't remember what words I said, but the fact is that I somehow expressed my delight in this idea because I really don't like shopping. You know—markets, shopping. Yeah, I said that.

Then, he said something about walking on the mall. Now, you may think he was talking about the National Mall, but that's only because he was talking about the National Mall. What else would he be talking about? Are you an idiot? No. No, that would be me. Again with the shopping, I thought. I really don't like shopping.

The kind soul said nothing. Perhaps, knowing how corny I am, he thought I was joking. Wouldn't that have been great? Sure. I wasn't stupid. They were just stupid jokes.

‡‡‡‡‡‡‡

Last night I dined with three colleagues. Two of us are fully bilingual at least. One of us is learning English. She's an obstetrician and doula trainer in the Dominican Republic. She's doing an admirable job. English is a booger to learn and, in the year and a half since I met her, she has come a long way. The fourth diner was a Gringa. Her mastery of her native tongue is sufficiently ample. I can judge here because I spend more than my share of time practicing the English language just to make sure I've got it down.

At times, three of us spoke in Spanish while the fourth jutted her chin out in her intense listening pose, catching much of it and sometimes asking for interpretation. Other times, three of us spoke in English. My Dominican friend made several valiant efforts at manipulating the sounds of the English language into words and even sentences, most of which were met with success.

Once, she said to me, when I paused after what was surely a minutes-long run-on sentence, that I speak too quickly. I don't know that I've heard this before and I generally don't consider myself to be a fast-talker. We chatted about this and I acknowledged that my speech would have slowed down had I been speaking only to her.

We often speak more slowly and enunciate when we want to be understood. You know, like with people who have trouble hearing, because distorting the words makes everything better in that case. We're such geniuses.

My children call my mother Abuelita, the diminutive of Abuela, which means grandmother. Apparently, in Spanish diminutizing words makes them endearing. This is in direct opposition to our apparent ideas about the best size for people, as evidenced by our delicious foods which we eat in abundant quantities.

When my daughter was beginning to speak, she was juggling two languages. When she said "Abuelita," all ears but her own heard "Lala." We all understood what she meant, of course, but my mother sat her down one day so that she could get it right. It was her name, after all, being misspoken by her favorite person in the world.

Face to face they sat, almost nose to nose. My mother looked intently into my daughter's eyes, channeling to her the great concentration she felt was necessary for the task at hand. A b u e l i t a she said, almost as if it was another language, taking care that each letter was carefully woven through the dendrites of my daughter's brain. My daughter, she's a smart one. She caught on right away. Fully aware that her repetition would be a great feat, she leaned on in and just as carefully enunciated Laaaala. In her effort, she solidly positioned those sounds as the most adorable way possible of saying grandmother in our family.

‡‡‡‡‡‡‡‡

When I was growing up, we would get dressed up for stuff. If we were traveling, going to the movies, going to the doctor, and certainly for a party. As a result, I always had several floor-length dresses. It was the style in the seventies.

These dresses made it easy for my mother to transform me into a "gypsy" on more than one Halloween. I'd put on the dress and she'd wrap a kerchief around my head tying a knot at the nape of my neck. She'd pierce the kerchief at my ears with large hoop earrings and paint my lips bright red. There were necklaces and bangles involved too. She did such a good job. Years later, I think I recognized my younger self on the streets of Budapest.

In first grade, I was going to dress up as Snow White. Just like all the other parents all over the place, my mother bought me a plastic costume. Why did we partake in that madness!?!

The body consisted of a white plastic bag with armholes and a neck hole, onto which had been printed an image of Snow White's dress. Then there was a mask. This rigid piece of suffering was made out of plastic that was surely reserved for only this purpose. It had a subtle graininess that I could still recognize today with my eyes closed. The mask smelled of slow death, but the copious amounts of sweat and condensation that accumulated face-side assured us that we were yet surviving. The elastic string that was stapled onto the mask to keep it on our heads was surely designed to be flimsy so that we could easily escape the talons of the afterlife.

Ok, where was I? Yes, first grade. The week of Halloween, we were all told that, we should go ahead and dress up for school, but that plastic masks were prohibited. This didn't make sense because all of the children had plastic masks that year. On the other hand, it totally made sense because they were torture masks of the deathly variety!

My mother was not deterred. Naturally, I had a dress similar enough to Snow White's. My hair, though not quite black, was bobbed and the red bow made it indistinguishable from hers. A little rouge and, of course, red lipstick.

I remember asking my mother if I really looked like Snow White. She assured me that I did and I trusted her because she was a magician, not for Halloween, but always. I don't know how the other mothers pulled it off that year.

✚✚✚✚✚✚✚✚

The other day, I had a baby and yesterday she turned thirteen! So far, so good with the teenage years. You know, it's been a day.

As long as I can remember, my top career choice was to be a homemaker. In seventh grade, we had to do a research assignment on three careers that we would want in the future. I chose teacher, designer, and actor. I knew I couldn't put down what I really wanted because there would be no way to fill in the salary and schooling expenses and such. Also, girls aren't supposed to want to be homemakers. Have you heard?

Still, that is what I wanted. To that end, I started planning and, since I wanted to make a home for a husband and children, when I was about sixteen, I started researching my options for birth. I was going to have a daughter first and then another and then maybe ten more children, or not, whatever.

By the time I was in college, I had planned out my births. By the time I got pregnant, I had spent about fifteen years reading books and researching my options. Pieces of my plan started falling away a few months before I got married, however, and they kept dropping off my map until my baby was born.

She was born healthy and even came out my vagina. Many people think that this is all that matters. Selfishly, I was traumatized by my experience when I should have just been grateful. This is what led me to become a doula. I didn't want a career, of course, I just wanted to help someone every now and then understand things a little better than I had.

I thought this tale was going to be about the love I discovered for my daughter the moment she was born and in the days and weeks and years after. I didn't realize it was going to be about my birth as a doula. It's just as well, though, because there are no words, really, to describe that love and the surprise that it was for me.

‡‡‡‡‡‡‡

On my way home from Washington DC last month, I decided to take a one-hour walk from my hotel to the train station. The weather was lovely and I relish a solitary stroll. I've never asked my phone for walking directions, but on this day, I put my earphones in and listened to Flamenco Chill while Siri interrupted every now and then to keep me on my path.

I selected the longer route, made a left and off I went. Why did it take us so long to put wheels on suitcases? I could walk for miles. Good thing because I had almost four to go.

For the beginning of my journey I just had to walk straight for a while. Siri did her thing, reminding me to head southeast on Connecticut Avenue. I found it curious that she would do this at every corner. I found it curiouser that she was always a little behind. Silly Siri, I just passed that corner. I figured that her lag was due to the internet connection being below my NYC standards.

I went along, admiring the beautiful embassies, humming and singing along to my music. Twenty minutes into my walk, I climbed a small hill. While the spring in my step never waned, the summit greeted me with a little extra heat and a slight elusion of breath.

I stopped there, under the sunny sun, wishing I had worn more than a tank top under my flyaway cardigan so that I could remove it without exposing too much of my stuff. I pulled out my phone to consult my map, lest a passerby think I had stopped to catch my breath.

That's when I noticed that Siri hadn't just been micromanaging my trip and slightly lagging behind. She had been trying to correct my course. I had been walking in the wrong direction all along.

Was this the first time I had asked for directions and heard them but didn't listen? Have I ever thought I was following directions and wasn't? Do I ever go in a different direction than I am supposed to? Do I ever go along with no direction at all?

No. Yes. Yes. Yes. I suspect that's true of you too.

‡‡‡‡‡‡‡

I am aware of the fact that the internet feeds us incessantly what we are most likely to want, often before we want it, so I was only momentarily surprised when Google informed me of the passing of actor Ann Wedgeworth this week. You probably don't know her name. I had forgotten it until I searched for her a couple of months ago.

You may recognize her from other shows, but I remember her only as Lana from Three's Company. I used to love that show. One season, they brought on this new character and she was amazing. She was a new neighbor, an older woman. She was in love with Jack and she showed it.

I don't think that the show could ever be seen as making any sort of feminist statements, likely to the chagrin of co-star Joyce DeWitt, and I can't imagine that Wedgeworth signed on to be such an icon, but her nine-month stint on the show was revelatory to me.

Here was this sex symbol who was older and bigger than most at the time, but most importantly, she went around expressing her sexual desires. Did you know that a woman can go up to a man and give him a kiss if she feels like it? Yes. I saw Lana do it in my youth and I think it changed my life.

‡‡‡‡‡‡‡

If you know a native Spanish speaker, you may have heard this complaint. If you are one yourself, you know what I'm talking about. There are some words that just have no equivalent in English. You can usually describe the idea, but there's no one word that'll do it. Today's tale features the word "empalago." It's pronounced just the way it looks because it's in Spanish, you know, a language that makes sense. Empalago is usually about food—being stuffed, but really referring to excess, often of richness or sweetness, not necessarily fullness. People can be empalagosos too.

Now that I think of it, my tale isn't really about this word, but I already wrote a whole section about it so I'll hold your hand as you cross the bridge with me to make the connection. Sometimes you can have too much of a good thing, right? I'm speaking generally here because I don't frequently have this problem personally.

I started listening to music through earphones about two years ago and listen to one of only four playlists usually: Ella Fitzgerald, Vivaldi, Chambao or Chopin. I will never get sick of any of these. That's just not how it goes with me.

My husband, however, gets sick of things very easily. All sorts of things he'll love and then, one day, he can't bear them. He knows all of the lyrics to every Beatles song. He grew up listening to them and loves the Beatles. Yet, when we met, he owned no Beatles music because he had had enough. I don't understand that.

Sometime in the early nineties, my friend was visiting from New Orleans. I accompanied him and his aunt to see one of their friends. When we arrived, it was clear that he delighted in company. His speech was very high-energy and he had music playing. Soon, the music became the topic of conversation, on and off, for the rest of the evening.

He had a little turntable on which revolved a small, black disc that would, all on its own provide us with hours of amusement. He told us that he had been playing the same song over and over all day. It wasn't a bad song, but I certainly can't vouch for it being a particularly good one. The best part about it was that it played repeatedly all night. Each time the arm of the record player lifted itself up, moved itself over, and landed in the first audible groove, one of us, usually me or this amazing host dude, exclaimed something along the lines of,

"Wow! What song is this?" or "I've never heard this song before!" It was so much fun and we never tired of the song or the game because neither of them was empalagoso. (Welcome to the other side of the bridge!)

‡‡‡‡‡‡‡

I want to write about rainbows and flowers today, but the only tales that come to mind are about rape and race. Really, I really mean rape and race. I have tales about each.

You may have heard me jest that I love people as a group, but individuals, not so much. Sometimes, it's not really a joke. People can be so nasty to one another, mostly I think, this happens from thoughtless actions or words, a lack of consideration for others' feelings or from wrong assumptions.

This isn't a tale today. Sorry. It's just a rant. I recently had an interaction with someone that left me crying. I cried about it for several days. I think it involved thoughtless actions and assumptions.

Where will we all end up? I've always thought about how the future will see us as so backwards based on innovations in manufacturing and technology. Cutting edge standards of today will be primitive tomorrow. More importantly, though, I've thought about our evolution as animals. I know we will get better. I know we can be better to one another and to everything around us. It seems far off to me lately, but sometimes there's a paradigm shift and great change follows quickly. Maybe that shift happens with the individuals first. Maybe we just need to be good to others, not assume the worst, be considerate and positive and all that good stuff.

I want to like people as a group and all of the individuals, including myself. It's so hard to do any of those things. Help me and join me. Let's not wait to see what happens. Let's happen it today!

‡‡‡‡‡‡‡

I remember many years ago using the bathroom at the Plaza Hotel (smart New Yorker that I am) and seeing the PalmPilots displayed in one of the store windows. Remember those? They were very fancy. Eventually, I got one. I loved it. I love being organized and taking notes and writing things down. Reminders are a dream!

For a long time I had my PalmPilot, and then I had a PalmPilot and a phone. One day, I couldn't believe it, I got to have a Palm phone. Two things combined in one. How organized was that!?! It wasn't as smart a phone as most of us have today, but it was a very smart phone, considering a decade earlier mobile phones were the size of a large man's sneaker!

I still miss my Palm phone. One day, I was almost forced to miss it prematurely. It was December of 2007. I left my baby with my mother while I descended the grand Marble Hill with my toddler. (While the hill does consist of marble, the surface is made up of conglomerate rock, cement, and asphalt, and is known locally as Suicide Hill.) My daughter and I were on our way to the store. It was surely a necessity that brought us there because I disrelish shopping most times and truly find it abhorrent in December.

My daughter and I made our way gingerly downward, our small gait keeping us from realizing the nickname of the hill first-hand. When we got to the store, we went over to the customer service department to make a return. I can't remember what I was returning, but it's safe to assume it was something mediocre which I purchased hastily to get myself out of the store and away from the shopping experience.

At the conclusion of the transaction, we turned around and went down the stairs next to the escalator. When I got to the bottom, I noticed that I had left my precious little Palm phone on the counter. Poor thing was surely missing me. Catecholamines made my stomach do a little swirly thing, and I quickly turned around and went upstairs. The two women who had been behind me in line, had just walked away from the counter and responded in the negative when asked if they had seen my phone.

The young lady at the register hadn't seen it either. She offered me her personal phone so that I could call mine with its distinctive Euro ringtone. I dialed and it rang right away, just a few meters from me, in the bag of one of the previously questioned women.

This was unbelievable to me because they had just told me they hadn't seen it. It was also undeniable. I am not good with confrontation, but adrenaline moved me over to them. I told them that my phone must have fallen in their bag because I'm not very good with accusations either and, frankly, would have been fine if they had said, "Oh my, darn that gravity! Here's your phone back. Have a nice day!"

Instead, they insisted it wasn't my phone as I kept redialing my number to keep it ringing. One of them said something about being pregnant and they got themselves ready to exit. I was not going to go after them, outside the store, so I dropped myself on the floor because, though my brain wasn't fully functioning at this point, the dramatics department seems to always be up and running in there.

Sure enough, security became part of the scene. The women were stopped and I was ushered into a small room with my daughter, who was having quite the adventurous day. Soon enough, I had my phone in my hands and the police were asking me about pressing charges.

I kept telling them I did not want to press charges. It was the holiday season and one of them was possibly pregnant. Also, I didn't want to be involved in any of that for a phone (amazing as it was. I really did love it). No, no charges. I just wanted to make sure they wouldn't be outside the door when I left the security room. That was all.

The police showed me the video in which the phoneknapper slyly looks around as she covers the phone with her hand before slipping it in her bag. I have found many nice phones. I always look around before taking them. I look around for their owner and I always get them back to their owners! I've gone out of my way to do this and have even paid priority shipping fees to deliver them because that's what you're supposed to do! This woman was not looking around in that way and it made me angry.

I ended up pressing charges and had nothing else to do with it because there was a video of the thievery. I thought about her often in the following days. I felt bad for her and her Christmas and her family. Maybe I felt worse about it than she did. Thanks a lot, lady. You shouldn't have messed with my beautiful little Palm.

‡‡‡‡‡‡‡

When I was growing up, I hung out with the Yugoslavian family downstairs sometimes. I learned to eat pancakes with prune butter at their house and how to play a better version of checkers. I watched the father grind the coffee beans for each batch with his small mill and watched the mother cut a bunch of potato off as she sliced away their skins. In the beginning of each year, I'd have some of their special cake into which Angelika had blindly tossed a coin. The recipient of the coin would have good luck that year. I also learned to make eyelash wishes, pressing a fallen eyelash between two fingers and making a wish. Whoever gets the eyelash, gets their wish granted by the universe.

Yesterday, my son found one of my eyelashes on my face. He carefully removed it and held it on his index finger. We had a moment of silence as we pressed our pointers together. I can't imagine that either of us did very much thinking at this point. Don't we all have a core set of wishes that stays with us? I go back and forth between only two.

Once we confirmed that we were both ready for the big reveal, my son held my finger horizontally and slowly and carefully peeled back his. He was very pleased to find that my long, beautiful eyelash still rested on my finger, seemingly undisturbed. He said that he had done it in such a way so that I would get my wish.

I said, "My wishes are always for you anyway." He, gave me a hug and then said, "Would it be the ultimate paradox if you wished that the other person would get the eyelash?" Sometimes I don't think my children need my wishes at all.

‡‡‡‡‡‡‡

I was making confections the other day when I remembered an epiphany I once had when I was really too old not to have already figured out this sort of thing. I grew up with the slogan "M&Ms melt in your mouth, not in your hands." I remember sitting in my living room and realizing that they weren't just referring to the chemical change that happens with the heat of your hands. They were talking about the deliciousness of their chocolates causing their quick disappearance. I love clever advertising, but in that case, it was much less about ad man canniness than limited audience astuteness.

196

I'm happy to think that I'm the only one with late revelations, but I suspect that you've had such moments in your life on more than one occasion as well. The key is to be open to paradigm shifts. Acknowledging the new information or way of seeing things and then embracing it, trying it on and seeing things anew. So exciting!

You know very well that there are at least a dozen songs whose meaning completely changed for you when you heard the real lyrics for the first time. Sometimes your faux lyrics are better, but that aha moment is precious and tickles your neurons and opens up a world of possibilities.

Or maybe I'm taking this too far. Let's just say this is a metaphor for, you know, something meaningful and important. That thing you're going to work on in 2018 and how you're going to be open to new ways of thinking and loving and being. Yes! I'm going there too. So exciting!

Let's do that and let's be good to ourselves and to one another along the way, remembering that we're not all ready for epiphanies at the same time and that "mamasay mamasa mamakusa" are the actual lyrics to that song.

#######

Our first meal of the year was a Colombian treat we call bollos. I made two kinds: one with yellow corn flour and cheese and one with white corn flour, coconut, anise seeds and cheese. The dough is formed into a log and tied in corn husks and then boiled. We eat them with butter and I just realized I forgot to make Colombian hot chocolate to go with them. Please don't show my children this tale because they weren't aware that chocolate was part of the original plan.

I like to preserve memories and culture, so today I asked my mother to tell me about a memorable new year celebration from her youth. I was delighted as we watched the Rose Parade (known to my family as the "flower parade," and roses are flowers, so my family is right no matter how much my husband insists they are not) to hear my mother share something positive about my father. I'm sure, in my life, that she has told me a few other good things about him, but I can't remember them. Now I have this new memory. She remembers watching the parade while she breastfed me and having him interpret for her the explanations of how everything was made from flowers and nuts and seeds and such. I figured she would share some other touching memories.

I didn't want her to lie, so I took what I got. She remembers sitting in front of the house, watching people rush by, everyone hugging and kissing, sharing greetings for the new year. She remembers that so many men took advantage of this time to inappropriately touch women and girls and that my aunt used to hide from them.

She remembers that her grandmother used to buy very fine fabric at this time of year to have dresses made for the girls. That's a good memory. She remembers that these were the special occasion dresses for the rest of the year or two and that, the last time she wore one, she had grown so much that the waistline was right under her breasts.

She remembers that this was the time of year when the children were made to go to their father's house to ask for money for shoes and he never had it. That was the worst part of the holidays, she said.

She knew my grandmother would always send money. That's why she was away, working. She also knew that the money did not get distributed as her mother intended. Then she went on to tell me that my grandmother used to send trunks full of beautiful gifts—chocolate, linens, dinnerware and porcelain dolls. The children never got to touch any of it. My mother says they were given to the rich children, who knew better how to care for such nice things.

I remember crying at the stroke of midnight when I was a child. I cried because my big, happy family was celebrating and it was very loud. I didn't understand. I don't have unhappy memories, though. Hearing my mother talk, she doesn't really either. They are just memories, the way it was. I hope my children will have only good New Year's Eve memories, filled with the scent of sage and sweetgrass burning and not missing hot chocolate their mother forgot to make.

‡‡‡‡‡‡‡‡

At the end of this month the Lincoln Plaza Arthouse Theatre is going to close. For three decades I've enjoyed great films there along with fellow cultured New Yorkers. I practically had a date there with Harry Belafonte once and another with Gloria Steinem. You know, if they had noticed that I existed at all.

Lincoln Plaza specializes in foreign movies and other indie films. Instead of popcorn, you can have lox on a bagel and relatively freshly baked goods instead of the usual movie theatre candy.

This is the place I chose when my then future husband proposed that we go out to celebrate his promotion and my birthday seventeen years ago: our first date. He was to decide on dinner and I on the movie. I chose *Aimée & Jaguar*. I thought we had both loved it and found out years later, when I gifted him the book, that he wasn't so thrilled with it. Lesbians fleeing the Nazis—a tearjerker to be loved by all, I say!

Really, though, I had chosen the venue before the movie. We'd meet behind the theatre and sit on the iron patio furniture to talk by the pond and fountain. I remember as if it were yesterday the very New York City moment we had there as I talked about Ella Fitzgerald. He was surely hanging on my every word and, when I mentioned the boy that had fallen into the water, he looked over his shoulder and quickly turned back to tell me to get up and walk. As we rushed away from the scene, he shared that the boy was his son who was accompanied by his daughter and estranged wife. They did not live in the area, but that's small town living for you.

I have lots of memories of that theatre. I remember watching the *Crying Game* and noticing they had cast a trans actor before I knew it was something to notice. I remember crying during a movie and another and another and another. I remember the same peculiar ushers for years. I remember that every time I walked in there, after descending on the escalator to the waiting area with the big pillars and out-of-place lion fountain, there was always that familiar smell and feeling and the same artwork on the walls for all these years.

Last week I went. I took myself. I paid the million-dollar fee for admission, requisite of all New York City movie theatres, and I sat there for the last time. I watched the aptly named *Happy End* by Austrian director Michael Haneke. I sat there with half a dozen people in a seat that did not recline, looking at a screen just a wee larger than many home televisions.

The last scene I viewed at this theatre was perfect: a woman incredulously looking over her shoulder at someone recording with their phone the emergency towards which she was running. There was a little applause and we left silently. I lingered for a while in the dim, old lobby, reminiscing.

‡‡‡‡‡‡‡‡

I was not an active child. Yeah, nothing has changed. I didn't get skinned knees on a regular basis, so the injuries I attained are only ingrained in my memory.

I got my fabulous Wusthof chef's knife professionally sharpened a few weeks ago for the new year (we all have our own way of celebrating) and, as usual, I bled on it pretty soon after. It was a small, shallow cut on my index finger for which I, of course, did not use a bandage. I grew up without bandages in the house and basically think they're for wimps. Remember, faithful reader, the gashes on my eight-year-old legs that were dabbed with Listerine before I was sent to bed, rather than being stitched up in the emergency room (Tuesday Tale of the past).

There I was with this little cut, surely exposing twenty billion nerve endings, and I had to keep my finger curled in order to preserve my very life. I knew that I should straighten it out once in a while in order to decrease its time as a futile appendage, but I had to balance that with the whole it-bled-every-time-I-stretched-it issue. This reminded me of those few weeks in the early nineties when I practically couldn't use my right hand at all. Luckily, I am of the superior lefty persuasion and my right hand doesn't come in, well, handy very often.

It was a lovely summer night and I was on a date. After dinner, we meandered towards Washington Square Park in the darkedy dark darkness and sat on a bench. It was late o'clock and it was pretty desolate theres abouts. Surely we were enthralled by each other. I'm imagining him responding with glee to my every bon mots and gazing into my sweet yet seductive eyes. I don't know, but somehow my handbag was stolen as we sat there, by some unseen figure who melded into the darkness of the park.

My date walked me to the train station and I went on my way, feeling fairly safe, with no possessions to be stolen. I got home after 2 a.m. I was really tired because, although I am a morning person, it's only after I've slept. I can start the day at 2, but I usually don't want to stay awake until 2. I can't remember where my mother was, but it certainly wasn't at home or anywhere near home. Someone else was living with us at the time (Tuesday Tale of the future) and, as if I hadn't reason enough to dislike him, there he wasn't. I sat on the marble steps with my head in my hand, without my keys, waiting. Hours later, arrived the person I was only ever happy to greet on that occasion, finally.

At this point in my life, despite the fact that my mother always said we would never have pets, there was a cat living with us (Tuesday Tale of the future). This special cat had to be fed at 5:30 in the morning in order to get to work doing nothing. Here I was, hardly awake, not wanting to get up in another hour for someone who couldn't even open the door for me when I was in need.

I decided to open her can of food early and the can, in turn, decided to open me. Across four fingers it gashed my soul. My bed was so close yet so far. Had I gotten into it at that point, I would've drowned in my blood. It was everywhere, which was great because, I was in such lovely spirits by this time, of course I wanted to clean up a mess while simultaneously continuing to make it and being in terrible pain. My hand. My poor, poor hand. It pains me still to think about it. Was the sun up before I got to bed? Maybe. I'm sure I slept well though, my hand wrapped in some towel or maybe bathroom tissue or something because, you know, bandages—pah.

‡‡‡‡‡‡‡

I'm very sensitive to smells and I eschew drug use. Even as an herbalist, I've never smoked marijuana or tobacco, not even a puff. I'm writing this on the train as a young man just sat next to me reeking of a marijuana fest. It brings back memories of an admirer I once had.

He was an accomplished and well-known musician, a conductor and composer. He was the close friend of my music mentor. I met him when I was about twenty-one and I saw him weekly when we sang together on Sunday mornings. He was in his sixties.

It didn't take long for me to realize that he had a special liking for me. While I find sixty-something to be a great age for a man now, in my early twenties, I did not so much. At the time, I remember, the thing I found most objectionable was how our weekly kiss and hug at 9 a.m. marinated my nostrils with freshly smoked marijuana vestiges. No, they weren't vestiges because it seemed to me that he spent every Sunday morning locked in a closet smoking pounds of the herb. This impression was probably formed by my irrationally selective prudish tendencies.

One day I received a call from my mentor who was about a dozen years older than potty dude. The sole purpose of his call was to play matchmaker. I was shocked. I told him I wasn't interested and didn't give a reason. The reason I gave myself was that he was decades older than I, but I'm thinking it had more to do with the fact that he had this crazy addiction. I mean, he was a famous musician. Unheard of!

‡‡‡‡‡‡‡

You know I don't drive. Goodness! How many characters have I used going on about that? I just don't have the temperament for it. My son takes after me in this way. When he's within earshot, I say he's a cautious boy. Really, we're both just nervous wrecks. I could drive if it was an emergency, but the tears would impair my vision and the adrenaline might arrest my heart, so that would just cause another emergency.

I was just in Chicago and my hotel was flanked by buildings with floors and floors of parking. There was one pair of curious towers that had multiple stories dedicated to exposed cars that had been parked backwards. There's a word for that. Too bad I'm not a real writer. Maybe "back-end parking." Let's go with that.

Well, from across the street, one can see these car butts, seemingly inches away from the edge. I figured there had been engineers involved in the construction of these buildings and that these cars and drivers were surely safe, but that didn't make it any less crazy to me. I would never park one of these cars (Oh my goodness! Understatement of the universe for all eternity!), but even being a passenger in a car while it was being parked like this would give me a cortisol overdose with which I happen to be familiar, yes.

In the late 1980s I was in Europe for the first time. For a few terrifying moments, I thought it would be the last time, there or anywhere else. I was on a bus on a pier. Need I say more? Well, I'm going to anyway. I was sitting in the back of the bus with a great view out the windows. That was the problem. While maneuvering the bus into a parking spot, or maybe to just invigorate me to death, the driver started to back the bus up.

I am not afraid of being dead at all, but I do fear the process of dying. As the back of the bus kept going back further over the water, with the driver, far away in the front, obviously not knowing what was going on, I imagined us landing in the water, going under and not being able to escape. This I imagined as a certainty in seconds and it was terrifying.

My shrieks did nothing to help the situation yet, somehow, we survived. When I got out of the bus, I noticed that there were no tires near the back and that the driver probably knew that we weren't going to roll over the edge and land in the water. I wish I had known that. I wish there had been some announcement when I boarded the bus about the driver's competence in reverse, back-end parking/driving. That almost killed me!

‡‡‡‡‡‡‡

If you are walking in the street dragging your heels behind me, I will turn my head to look at your feet, look at your face and hope you see me give you a nasty look.

I'm not an easy person to love and that's ok. It will be easier if you cater to my sensitivities. Have a neutral or mild yet pleasant smell about you. Don't whistle at a disturbing pitch (and trust my judgment as to which pitches are disturbing). Close your mouth when you chew!

I remember my sister talking to me about this last point when I was a child. She told me about how rude it was for one to chew with their mouth open. It turns out that there's more to it, though. Some of us are extra special and can hear your freaking chewing at a distance and it stimulates the homicidal part of our brain. I'm going to go ahead and say that we're superior beings—survival-of-the-fittest ears or something like that.

In my freshman year of college, I registered for a required sociology class. The young adjunct who led the class was Chinese and, while that isn't a problem itself, the fact that I don't think she spoke English was. To be fair, she probably spoke English well, but she had such a heavy accent, I couldn't understand much of what she was saying. I'm good with languages and accents too, but this just wasn't going to work. Before too much time passed, I transferred to another sociology class.

This new class was taught by a man with intelligible English. What a relief. I was set, right? Not so right it turned out. The subject matter was a little dull. Maybe it was the delivery. I can't remember because there was something much more memorable in this class.

There was a light in the ceiling that made the noise of 1000 angry bees. I asked classmates if they could hear it. They cocked their heads and squinted an eye. Some of them said no. Some of them gave me a dismissive yes. Something had to be done. How could people sit in a room with a buzzing light? I don't know because I didn't stick around to find out. I had to withdraw from this class too. I couldn't take it.

Those people, the ones who stayed in the class, those are the type of people who drag their feet on the ground and chew with their mouths open for all to hear!

⧗⧗⧗⧗⧗⧗⧗

It's strange to me that we need sleep. Imagine if we didn't sleep at all. We'd have many more hours to complain about not having enough time.

I like to sleep at night, but not in the morning. My whole life, I've been happy to go to bed early, but I'll often be awake to greet the sun as it appears in my sky. My issue is that I'll wake up early no matter what time I go to bed.

When my daughter was a baby, she was smart enough to take after me. At thirteen, she's a foreigner now though I visit her land with her often. Why does midnight greet us so frequently these days? I do not know.

My darling little daughter didn't only go to sleep early, she was a great napper. She would tell me it was nap time and cheerily go to bed. When I was pregnant with my son, I was thrilled by the thought that my children would nap at the same time together every day.

When my son was about two months old my much-less-darling little daughter decided that she would never again in her life take another nap. She didn't actually say it, but actions do speak louder than words.

By the way, it's almost 10 p.m. as I write this tale and that's why it's a bad one. Also, I'm having that late night delirium because writing that line just cracked me up. Good night.

‡‡‡‡‡‡‡

I went to Saks Fifth Avenue today. Maybe I went to use their bathroom. Maybe I got a $750 pair of shoes. Never you mind those details.

It reminded me of when I was little. We didn't use the bathrooms at Saks when I was a child. We used the ones at the Plaza and Hyatt hotels. What I was reminded of was the time I went to buy knickers (the outerwear, not the undergarments) at Saks. I was eight.

We didn't go shopping frequently. My mother was a single parent who always had just enough money for the things she wanted to buy. When she didn't have enough, she would work a little more and it would come.

Some families who are on a budget buy cheap things, often lots of cheap things. I know someone who will buy the sale items in bulk even if they aren't what he wants. The perceived bargain lures him in and it ends up being a waste of money. In Spanish there's a saying, "The cheap thing ends up being expensive."

Because she worked for herself, needed money seemed to magically appear. The magic, I'm sure, had no mercy for her arthritis. She wouldn't spend money often. She would wait to have enough for the one good thing.

That's how we ended up at Saks when I needed knickers. You may be questioning my use of the word "needed," but it was 1981. Let's all agree that I did need them. After all, I think I only had that one other lavender pair.

Even back then, I didn't like shopping. I saw the pair I wanted and went into the fitting room. I was trying on black, velvet knickers. Black goes with everything and velvet goes with fancy. They were perfect for me. They were the ones I wanted.

I remember the salesperson thinking I was a teenager though I was only eight. She helpfully suggested that I try on a pair of zebra print knickers. I'm not sure if it was around Halloween or what, but I knew I was never going to be walking around in zebra stripes even back then.

I don't know why this trip to Saks has stayed in my memory or why it comes up for me so much. I guess that shopping with my mother was always like a special event. I'm glad they have bathrooms there so I can go in and reminisce. They have nice shoes too.

‡‡‡‡‡‡‡

Someone complimented me on my confidence the other day. They do not know me well and clearly don't read my Tuesday Tales. They don't know that it's all an act like you do, dear reader. Sometimes I marvel at the confidence of others. Maybe some of these people are acting too. Maybe some of them feel that they have nothing to lose.

I'm reminded of Larry Jonas, who I knew in my freshman year of high school. He was a junior. He was long and gangly, with prominent facial features and acne. His voice was very deep but also kind of nasal and he was awkward when he spoke and when he moved and when he just stood there.

Larry wrote stories and was a great fan of Ian Fleming. He was smart and he was very confident. He liked me and seemed to never give a second thought to making it plainly known to me.

We were both involved in the school's big anniversary production of *On the Town*. I was an artist in this math and science school, so I was involved with every aspect of this show, including building sets. One day, during spring break, in a room that smelled of sawdust, I mentioned for some reason in this small group of high schoolers, that I didn't have a

206

boyfriend. Larry asked to speak to me in the hallway. He had asked me months before if I would be his girlfriend and I had told him that I could not be as I was already someone else's girlfriend.

He asked now, in the hallway, why I hadn't told him that I had broken up with my boyfriend because now I could go out with him. The truth is that I wasn't interested in Larry at all. I told him I wasn't ready to get into another relationship and he was very upset. I didn't feel comfortable just telling him that I wasn't interested. My interest, though, didn't even seem like part of the equation to him. He felt that, if I didn't have a boyfriend, that was reason enough to accept him.

He wasn't very nice to me after that. We had a scene together in the show in which he had to push me off the stage, and his forcefulness was not an act, I'm sure.

Larry was gifted in many ways, but he seemed to lack social skills and the ability to integrate himself with his peers. Nonetheless, he was exceedingly self-assured as if he had nothing to lose.

The year after we met, he died of an asthma attack. Some people don't seem like they are meant for this world or maybe this time. Larry, I think was one of them. I wish I could go back and tell him that, though I didn't want to be his girlfriend, he had an impact on me and that I would never ever forget him. If he was alive today, he probably wouldn't even remember me. Isn't that something?

‡‡‡‡‡‡‡

In September, my daughter will start high school in an actual school, after eight years of homeschooling. My thoughts on that are varied. Well, not really. They're just various degrees of fear.

It's March now and we are supposed to hear which schools were smart enough to accept her. She tested for academically advanced schools, auditioned for dance schools, and auditioned for music schools. I have no idea how any of this will go.

When it was my turn to apply for high schools, one hundred years ago, I did what I do with so many things. I decided on a school and tunnel-visioned my way in. I went to a specialized high school, mostly because it was walking-distance from my house.

Maybe I should have gone to a music school. I had planned to audition for LaGuardia for both theatre and music. I did the research, and then was too scared to go through with it the morning of. I would've totally gotten in too. I know it's easy to say that now, but really, I would have. Instead, I went to a science and math school and did all of the few artsy things they offered.

Years later, the courage I lacked as a teen came boiling over into audacity. I went to see an off-Broadway show called *De La Guarda*. It was all energy and movement and presence. I had these things. The performers were all petite and firm. I was, uhm, not petite and not firm. Something called to me, though, so I called to them. I wrote a letter with my hand on paper and put it in the mail. Basically, I told them I should be in their show.

This made total sense to me. I knew they'd just bring me on board. I was close. I received a response with some audition dates and the requirements and some encouragement. I signed up.

I put on some leggings and a t-shirt and dusted off my sneakers and off I went, to an audition. It was such a beautiful day and I was dressed like someone who exercises—very memorable.

I got to the audition site and there were people all over— small, fit people, stretching or showing off or something. I figured they were stretching muscles, so I just stood around because, you know, my body didn't have any of that, so no need.

Eventually, we all went into a large room to warm up. Obviously, I survived, but it wasn't because they didn't try to kill me. There was something about jumping jacks and push-ups, all very confusing because it was, you know, hard. After the torture session, we were to go up on a platform in the center of the room, three at a time, to perform a routine they had taught us.

To me, it was mostly about attitude. I recalled all of my years of stage fright in that moment, summoned my imaginary bravado and climbed (stumbled, can't really remember) onto the tiny stage made for three delicate dancers. I was, at least, commanding attention.

I did a great job. I remember the part where we had to yell and jump to a squat and point. I did that. I was energetic and loud and good. I don't know if I threw the other dancers off with all of the stage trembling my jumping caused, but too bad for them if I did. I was fabulous.   I didn't get cast because I was quite unsuited and unqualified, but I totally showed up, albeit a decade late. My daughter has been showing up for years. She's bold and qualified and suited for so many things. My various degrees of fear for her are ok because I'm the only one who has them.

‡‡‡‡‡‡‡

When I was eight, I went to Colombia with my mother. We were headed to Bogotá and had a layover in my mother's hometown. In the airport of Barranquilla I experienced déja vù. I felt it sort of in my head and sort of in my stomach and I saw it with my eyes and with my heart. This tale isn't about that, though. I'm not exactly sure what it's about yet. Let's find out.

My mother and I stood by the tall airport windows and looked out onto the warmth of Barranquilla. In the distance we could see a woman in a brightly colored dress. She walked normally. Actually, a little bit better than normal because she needed good posture in order to keep the large bowl properly balanced atop her head. My mother told me she hadn't seen that in years. For me, it was the first time. The image has never left me.

From the Caribbean coast of Colombia, that woman is known as a "negra Palenquera." She can be found in and around Cartagena, my grandparent's hometown. Maybe you've heard of this city. It is a former slave port and a well-known tourist destination today.

If you drive southwest from Barranquilla to Cartagena, on a road on which you will likely see a wooden bus, before you reach the old fortresses and fancy hotels, you might make a left. You probably wouldn't, but one might. That's where my grandparents grew up, having nothing to do with the new downtown or even the historic downtown. It was just a poor, simple life of mostly slave descendants there.

Tourists don't go there, but they might dance along, like people do in many places, to a song that tells the story of a slave couple in Cartagena and a rebellion. It's such a good song! Every time I hear it, I think of my grandparents' neighborhood. I've only spent hours in Cartagena, and not even a portion of that was spent in the heart of it.

The Palenquera may look like a colorful oddity, but I know she really looks like my people. The Spanish Colombian looks like my people and the Indian Colombian looks like my people too. They are all my people, colorful like the Palenquera's dress, rhythmic and rebellious like the song.

‡‡‡‡‡‡‡

There are some people who go around bad-mouthing themselves and wallowing in self-doubt. I'm not going to mention anyone's name, but you may or may not be reading one of their stupid little tales right now.

Anyway, these people, you may think, are just fishing for compliments. Well, maybe they are because maybe they need all the compliments they can get to combat all the poo-pooing that's going on in their own self-talk.

So, let's suppose that one of these people jokes around with friends all the time, teasing them and you know that they can't actually insult someone they don't like, so maybe there's just so much self-love, really—the biggest insults going to the most loved kind of thing. Aww, that's a nice idea. It makes me feel good. It almost makes up for this next thing.

Maybe, like totally hypothetically here, one of these people sees a little story that's written about them and it's not a bad story, but it includes photographs in which the person sees them self the way they really look and, it turns out that they are not looking good. As a matter of fact, they thought they looked much better than that and now they're going to have to step up the self-loathing game a bit.

Of course, these people have friends who say things like, "You look great," and "Blabbity blah blah," (one of those is paraphrased). And they know they're lying because they have eyes! Well, they are, of course, just being nice. Good thing they know nice people! These people should keep nice people around always. If I was one of these sorry people, I'd be super grateful for all of my dumb friends who say nice things about me!

‡‡‡‡‡‡‡

The other day a colleague told me about a stranger who opened up to her about their birth story out of the blue. They didn't even know they were talking to a childbirth educator. Maybe they sensed a birthy vibe.

This wasn't the first time my colleague was made privy to the particulars of a fairly personal experience of someone they had never met before. Usually it happens when we divulge the details of our work. Or even not the details. I imagine that even people who say they clean the floors of labor and delivery units (really hard job, by the way) get birth stories spilled all over them.

Many of us consider this a perk. Usually, we love the work we do and relish the stories about it. Sometimes we can laugh with people or marvel at them. Sometimes we just have to listen, knowing that this retelling has brought them a little closer to healing.

I've heard stories from taxi drivers, people on the train, at social gatherings, on the phone with customer service representatives, everywhere.

There are many things I love about birth. One of them is witnessing someone view their partner with fresh eyes. It's like they see the birth of this new person, fierce and strong, along with the birth of their baby. Pretty cool.

A couple of months ago I went to Barcelona. It was amazing, though not as much as it could have been because, in this case, it was a restaurant in New Haven, Connecticut. I was dining alone, though, and the server was cute and he brought me delicious food and drink, so it was definitely a winning experience, albeit more local than I might've liked.

At some point during my meal, I started talking to the couple next to me because, (well how do I put this?) I love strangers! I tolerate people that I know and even like some of them, but strangers are the best! During the conversation, I told them I was in New Haven to train doulas.

As is often the case, I got a birth story out of them. It was a little different than the usual and, while it isn't fair to compare, really, I think it's one of my favorites. This time, I didn't hear about the woman's birth experience. Instead, her husband told me about the day their first child, now my age, was born.

He said he didn't know much about what was going on, but that he remembered how awe-inspiring his wife was. He said he never saw her the same way again. This was pretty great, right? It got better, though. Apparently, in the four decades since this birth, he had never shared this view with his wife. It was beautiful.

I needed to give them a little privacy after that, so I ordered more sangria and a plate of chocolate deliciousness, just for their sake. Doula life has great potential. Sometimes we touch people in unpredictable ways. Sometimes we have to sacrifice for them by ordering dessert even.

‡‡‡‡‡‡‡

A fellow memoirist recently posted a famous writer's Ten Rules of Writing. I'm going to refute each one here, possibly putting on display the reasons for my under-published status, definitely proving that my writing is my own. I am a detail-oriented perfectionist in many ways and notice things like grammar and spelling errors with ease, but I'm also an artist. I think that my writing has a healthy dose of some rules of writing, even if not these, and that it is presented with creative flair. I'm not really trying, though. Maybe I should try.

For copyright reasons, each rule has been paraphrased.

1. Don't start a book with weather. If you're setting the tone rather than describing how a character reacts to or deals with the weather, you should be brief because readers are apt to skim ahead to a part with people in it.

Me: I have memorized a book which opens with weather. It is a seventy-two-page children's book with lots of illustrations, but a good one nonetheless, with an excellent opening. So there. (Have you heard of *The Cat in the Hat*? It's a pretty good one, I'd say.)

2. Do not use prologues: They are irritating, especially if they follow an introduction that has been preceded by a foreword.

Me: I think that each of my Tales is basically a prologue followed by a paragraph or two and a closing thought. Oh, maybe they're just a prologue, introduction, foreword, and conclusion. Yup, I think that's it. Those conclusions are hard to come by too!

3. Don't substitute other verbs for "said": The dialogue is the character's; the verb is the writer's intrusion. "Said" is far less intrusive than more colorful verbs you might use.

Me: "Far less intrusive?" Mine is nonfiction. I know all of my characters. I'm going to go ahead and intrude. Sometimes they respond begrudgingly or inquire tentatively. Why would I just write that they said something?

4. Don't use adverbs to modify "said": It is a mortal sin. It's distracting and messes with the flow of dialogue.

Me: Mortal sinner here. I want you to hear how people are saying things. Mkay?

5. Don't use too many exclamation points: Use no more than two or three for every 100,000 words.

Me: What!?! I don't even understand this sentence. My life! My LIFE, it is punctuated with mostly exclamation points! (And that's when I'm not being dramatic.)

6. Don't use "suddenly" or "all hell broke loose": This rule needs no explanation. Writers who express themselves in this manner, tend to use way too many exclamation points as well.

Me: Yes, please don't explain. Some things are sudden and you know how they happen? Suddenly!

7. Do not overuse regional dialect: Spelling words phonetically and filling the page with accent marks and apostrophes is likely to get out of hand.

Me: How are you going to hear the voice of my people, Gringo?

8. Don't describe characters in detail: Ernest Hemingway did not use any descriptors for the "American and the girl with him" in *Hills Like White Elephants*? The only visual he gives us is, "She had taken off her hat and put it on the table." We know them by their voice and can see them without being told what they look like.

Me: Again, my people. Very colorful they are. There's much diversity within the group and each individual is colorful on their own as well.

9. Don't describe places and things in detail: When you have too many details in your descriptions, it brings the action and flow of the story to a halt.

Me: Luckily for me, my stories are already lacking in action and flow. They're basically just descriptions.

10. Don't include in your writing the part that readers will likely skip.

Me: Uhm, I think that most people just skip my Tales entirely. I'll just keep writing them. Thank you very much.

The most important rule for me sums up all of the preceding 10: If it sounds like it's writing, you should rewrite it.

Me: My redeeming quality—my writing sounds like I'm speaking. Maybe this writer would approve after all. Does it matter, though? I did publish my Tuesday Tales because I got approval, but that's not why I wrote them.

‡‡‡‡‡‡

The other day I was waiting for a bus and an older woman approached a man near me with her little shopping cart partially keeping her upright. She said something to him and then turned to someone else. I could tell she was asking for

214

directions and in response she got a couple of people looking around and pointing this way and that.

I walked over and asked where she wanted to go. She told me she was looking for the number 10 bus. I told her it was only one block away, albeit a long one whose end we could not see from where we stood. I asked which way she wanted to go so that I could specify the corner on which she should wait.

Her voice shook as she told me she just wanted to go home. I said I'd take her to the bus myself and we started to walk. She told me her address and I asked how she had ended up where we were. She said she had walked down the hill, but then she didn't recognize anything. It had probably been more than a thirty-minute walk for her from her posh neighborhood on the hilltop.

As we managed our way along the long block, before we got to the highway overpass, she told me that her daughter was coming over for dinner and she had gone out to buy the food. Her daughter, it turned out, lived just blocks away from her. A little part of me thought, "Well, she should be helping you, fragile lady."

For some reason, I thought to ask the woman if she had a MetroCard with which to pay for her trip. She said she had dropped it the day before and some kid had run by and swiped it up, taking it with him. That was a crazy story, but still, I felt around for change in my pocket and then told her I'd just wait for the bus with her and let her use my card.

Eventually, we got to the bus stop and, as we approached, I could see the bus rolling towards us. Because I've been in the neighborhood for thirty-eight years, and maybe also because I always say hello and thank you to the drivers and sometimes have long conversations with them and some of them know my name and honk hello when they pass me as I'm walking on the street, I happened to know the bus driver. I told him I wasn't staying on the bus and I got my new friend into a seat and paid her fare and disembarked after I told him to make sure she got off at her stop, which was luckily on the corner where she lives, which she assured me she would recognize. Off she went and I walked back to my own bus stop.

Then, last week, I was walking to my children's dance school when I was approached by a man who asked if I spoke Spanish. When I told him I did, he asked me if I knew where something was, but I did not know what he was talking about because it was in neither English nor Spanish. Then he explained it. It was a place where someone could sleep if they were homeless. A shelter! He was trying to get himself and his luggage to a homeless shelter or "chelteng."

I instructed him to go to a place, not far from where we were, which was probably what he was looking for. He was very grateful and explained apologetically that he only needed shelter for a little while. I wished him luck and then stopped for a coughing spell because bronchitis and I are hanging tight these days. He stopped and turned towards me. Pointing to the little grocery store, he asked if he could buy me something to drink. The homeless guy did that. We all just want to help one another.

✠✠✠✠✠✠✠

In November of 1996, on my way home from my job as a nanny, I stopped by the now defunct Barnes and Noble store, near Lincoln Plaza. I was looking for a magazine, about what, I can't remember. I remember what I was wearing, though. A long, grey, pencil skirt and A ribbed, short-sleeved, black top. This outfit clung to my twenty-three-year-old figure just right.

Before I left the store, I stood on line for the pay phone to call my mother. I wouldn't get my first mobile phone until ten months later. There was a tall man with salt and pepper hair on the phone. His conversation was animated and his accent was heavy and thick, like a ton of molasses.

It wasn't long before he was patting his pockets, obviously looking for change so that he could continue conversing. I checked my own backpack and offered him a couple of the coins I had found. He took them and raised his thick, wiry eyebrows in gratitude. I was glad that the entertaining display would now be prolonged a bit due to my monetary contribution.

He took out of his pocket a pen and an envelope which he soon transformed into a proposal. "Would you like to see a movie?" It said in plain English. I took the pen from his hand and neatly wrote, "Quando?" I thought maybe he was Italianish. I was wrong, but that's not the point of the story. (Spoiler alert: there is no point to the story.)

216

His invitation was for a movie that was starting within an hour. I declined, but that was ok because he went to the movies almost every Tuesday. He asked me to meet him the following week and we said goodnight without exchanging numbers. It was a little odd and a little romantic. I showed up that next week just in case, and there he was.

We watched *The English Patient*. I didn't pay 100% attention because he was acting weird. He drove me home in his rickety old gigantoid white van and he seemed to be somewhat ill. We later found out that he had the mumps.

We planned to meet again in a week. Still no phone numbers. Again, romantical it was. Turns out he just didn't have a phone.

On our second date, we went to a restaurant on West 67th street and had delicious food and a whole lot of wine. I don't drink much, so I know that lots of the lot was allotted to him. At the end of the meal, he told me he hadn't had a drink in more than twenty years.

The next time we met, we were riding around in his huge metal box when we started talking about religion. I told him I was anti religion. He asked a few specific questions and I answered in my anti religion way. I later found out that he was a pastor for an ecumenical church of his own design.

I could write so much more about these eight months of my life with him, but all the richness of that era is too much for a tale. It was even too much for the eight months and it overflowed into several years. I may write about it in parts. To close today I will say that the object of this tale is now a very sick septuagenarian. Can you tell from this glimpse that he was quite a character?

‡‡‡‡‡‡‡

You know those sappy love stories that are just unbelievable? Sometimes they're true.

On a beautiful New York day in the late nineteen-nineties, I was walking, as I often do, in the streets of Manhattan. On this day, I was headed to the Science Industry and Business Library from Grand Central Station. I had recently acquired my first e-mail address. I'm not sure who might've sent me a message, but there was a chance that I had gotten an e-mail since the last time I checked it a couple of weeks prior.

Ahead of me, also southbound on Park Avenue, was a young man. I trailed him, caught up to him and passed him and then he arrived at the corner as I waited for the light to change. Once it changed, we started on our way again and I left him behind.

While I can understand people not being able to keep up with my flirtation, this was different. He actually couldn't keep up. I had to hope, as I approached each corner, that the light would favor me and turn red. Having to walk with a stick and a little partial paralysis meant that he always lagged behind a bit, even when I slowed my super speedy New Yorker pace down to something more manageable for an out-of-towner.

We met at the next couple of corners, and I kept leaving him behind. Finally, I turned to him and said, "Are you following me?" I can't remember what he responded, but it was enough for us to develop a conversation. Now I really had to slow down.

I learned on our meander towards 34th Street that he was visiting from Buffalo and was on his way to the Empire State Building. I was going to the library just two blocks away from there so we kept each other company and got acquainted during the long-in-time-if-not-distance walk.

On the corner of 34th street and Madison Avenue, we reluctantly said goodbye. I got to the library and checked my e-mail. Back in the olden days, one could do this without getting entangled in the web. I was soon done and could've headed home, but the flutter in my stomach propelled me to the Empire State Building instead.

I got there and I still remember where I stood as I shared with the security guard that there was a boy up there whom I had just met and I liked him and I was going to wait for him because maybe he liked me too. The guard was touched and hopeful for me.

Before long, out of the elevator came the boy with the walking stick. We looked at each other and it was clear that we were both just where we needed to be. I don't even know how to express how cinematic this scene was.

My exceptional memory can't recall how the rest of the day went, but I know that it was the beginning of a brief and lovely time. It was interrupted by a yucky period whose tale I may never bring myself to write. Before that, though, my friend visited me in New York and we made plans for me to visit him in Buffalo.

It was a whirlwind romance, but it surely would've never worked out. We would've likely killed each other. Once I got food poisoning (How many times has that come up in a Tuesday Tale!?!) and another time, he ended up making a midnight ER visit. I could've also ended up in Buffalo! While I don't mind the weather, I would've totally needed a chauffeur (another recurring theme.)

We never got a chance to say goodbye and that's just one of my many regrets from that time in my life. I will never forget him, and the movie from the lobby of the Empire State Building still plays beautifully in my mind.

‡‡‡‡‡‡‡‡

In his autobiography, García Márquez wrote that, in my mother's hometown of Barranquilla, there is a peculiar custom of addressing people one has just met with the formal "usted," then switching to the friendly "tu," as expected, and back to "usted" when talking to really good friends, this last part being the peculiar one.

I was the first in my family to be born in the U.S. I say that English is my second language because I was born just weeks after my mother got here and my people were definitely not speaking English then. For some reason, though, I did not grow up with some of the linguistic customs of Latin America, like addressing my elders as "usted." I don't know why. My sister, who lived in Panamá until she was eight still uses that address for my mother (as she should) and I'm like, "Pah! She's my mother. I used to be inside her body. We're pretty close."

I remember the day my grandmother sat me down with my cousins and told us that we had to use "usted" and that we had to call out "señora" when they called us from another room. I was four or five years old and this was a completely new idea to me. I accepted, though I don't remember if there was a reason attached. It was just a new rule.

For a little while, all of the children followed the rule with all of the aunts and uncles. I used the formal "usted" for most, though a couple of the youngest ones got "tu" from me. Soon, I felt like I was the only one doing it broadly.

My grandmother would always be "usted" to me. Personally, it wasn't a matter of respect. It wasn't really about fear either. It was a way for me to get on my grandmother's good side, the location of which remained elusive to me even until the end of her life. It wasn't, as García Márquez said, because we had gotten so close. Ever. Never ever.

‡‡‡‡‡‡‡

I started donating blood in high school. With my mother's permission, I could do it at the age of 16. It was great. I got to give my wonderful universally donatable blood to people in need, and I got to pick which class I was going to skip, and I got cookies and juice. I also liked the idea of ridding myself of old blood and replenishing it with newly generated cells. I would have owned hundreds of leeches in the old days because that just seems like a brilliant idea.

Once I was sixteen, I donated blood every time my school had a blood drive. Then I made a habit of doing it every year around my birthday at least. Sometimes, though, they turn me away. They want my blood and I want them to have it, but they fear that I am not a good candidate because I am a permanent resident of Relaxovania. I had someone at a blood bank tell me to drink coffee before I went in once. That didn't work.

My blood pressure is very low. Sometimes my husband gets his blood pressure all up in a bunch when he hears about mine because it upsets him to know that I am chillaxing so hard.

Sometimes my blood pressure goes up. Last week, for example, it was 105/68. It was very hot that day. I must have been stressed about that. Poor, poor me.

The first time I was told I had low blood pressure, there was a big scene and flurry of activity all around me as I sat there calmly (of course), wondering what the commoting was all about. Here's how it went.

The nurse and I had lovely chit chat as I sat in the chair answering basic health questions and likely making tangential comments to brighten his day or some other such charming thing. You know. Then I gave him my beautiful arm and he proceeded to strangulate it with the sphygmomanometer.

Once the cuff was done with the torture, he read the numbers and wrinkled his brow and said he had to do it again. Oh, goody. Yay. He did just that. After our second attempt, the nurse went outside and returned with another nurse. This was the head honcho nurse. She was tough. No machine was gonna mess with her. She strapped me in and pumped me up. She was very concerned with the results. She told me it was a problem.

I think she went outside to find a blank death certificate to start filling out. She only returned when the doctor was ready to see me. When he came in, three nurses stood in the small exam room along with him. They wanted to break the news to him together, I suppose. He shooed them away and then turned to me.

I was a little nervous now. The doctor asked if I regularly got dizzy or fainted. I told him I did not. Then he told me that, as long as I wasn't fainting, my blood pressure was indicative of my status as someone who's going to live forever. That's what he said, that I'm going to live forever. I think that might be stressful and that my blood pressure might end up going up.

I still try to give blood frequently because I can probably get lots of donations in in forever.

‡‡‡‡‡‡‡

Next weekend my children will perform at their dance school's year-end recital. It is a weekend-long event for our family, about twelve hours each day. There will be tech rehearsing and volunteering, dancing, bun-making, backstage shushing, and lots of excitement. Hundreds of costumes will go on the stage. In preparation, I have spent several afternoons, hours at a time, steaming the wrinkles out of them.

I remember the first time I used a steamer. It was my first job and I was working as an assistant to a fashion stylist. My mother was her hairstylist and I had known her for years. I always admired her look and her serpent bracelet and her clothes and her hair, short, spikey, and orange. She was dreamy. When she suggested I work with her, I was thrilled.

The first time we worked together, she had me meet her in an apartment in a foreign-to-me neighborhood in upstate Manhattan. Now I know that it was Castle Village. I had no idea where I was then. She gave me careful directions on paper and I remember walking there in the early morning cool and light. I was nervous to be walking in this strange land and nervous to be going to work with this hero figure. Soon we left to prepare for a fashion show by Norma Kamali. On a shiny rolling rack hung garments in rich red, not tomatoey, but regal. All of the clothes smelled of a luscious perfume, the scent of which I would recognize for years to come. Ahhh. Norma was glorious in my eyes and in my nose.

That day I learned how to use a fabric steamer. I naively asked if there was one way that tops were supposed to hang in a closet because my mother had taught me that they should all hang one way, facing the same direction. My mentor confirmed that there was no proper direction, but that hanging them all uniformly was more organized. Of course. She was a genius.

Being 5'10" and generally mature, I did jobs with my fashion diva friend for people who had no idea I was only 14, 15 and 16. We did fashion shows and photo shoots for magazines and record covers and we had a steady job for a while on a television show for which I got paid $16 an hour, in the eighties, as a young teen!

The television show first aired in October of 1988. We prepared for weeks, picking up clothes and accessories from different designers and fitting the co-hosts and dancers. We filmed at Studio 54 on Tuesdays. The thick upholstery that was hidden in the dark during club hours seemed to want to share a story or two under the lights which were on now as we transformed the ordinary people into television stars.

Being only 15, I also went to school. I would rush downtown every week and work for hours. Sometimes we'd go so late that I was sent home in a limousine in time to shower and dress for first period in the morning. It was all thrilling and it was a gift.

Sometimes my mother would fill in for me as assistant while I was in school. She would brag to the pop stars about her daughter's singing or maybe she bragged about some other daughter thing. I remember a singer by the name of India being happy to meet me one day because she had already heard so much of me.

Every week there were celebrity guests, but the core group of dancers and hairstylists, makeup artists and other production staff were the same. We were all very friendly, though I only remember the co-hosts, Tonya and Joey and Cynthia, the producer, by name. Radio personality, Al Bandiero, was regularly on the show. They used to spray paint his bald spot for TV.

We were like a once-a-week family and many of them knew I was only a child. One afternoon, a group of us was sitting around and someone asked me, as people like to do, what I wanted to do when I grew up. I responded something along the lines of, "Maybe I'll have Madeleine's job." This was meant as praise, assuming that Madeleine would be doing something else, bigger and better if I ever happened to reach her position.

Insecurity created a whole new meaning for my innocent statement. The following week, someone told my mother about the change in Madeleine's demeanor as my words of apparent betrayal slapped her in the face. Not long after, as the show was facing cancellation, I was told that my job was no longer in the budget, that they were restructuring a bit and that they wanted me to be on camera instead. I did that for a few weeks and then that was that.

I continued to work in fashion a bit, but it is only as I write this, decades later, that I wonder if my boss was trying to distance her fifteen-year-old apprentice from her producers for fear of something that is hardly rational. I was hurt to learn that my friend had misinterpreted my words. I was hurt and she was steaming.

‡‡‡‡‡‡‡

I'm prefacing this tale with an unnamed trigger warning because I know that so many of us are delicate in various ways. I am not explicit about anything in this tale that might be a trigger and I'm sure some readers might not rightly interpret my allusion without this here warning. For all I know, it may all be an illusion anyway.

My children had their annual dance recital on Sunday. It was a humongous undertaking from which many of us are still recovering, I'm sure. As their mother, it makes sense for me to tell you that they were amazing as talented dancers, but I will go further now and say that my children, on the stage, performing for hundreds of people, looked normal. This isn't something that ever escapes me and it leaves with me a wistful satisfaction.

While I was a performer for decades, it was a rare person who might have witnessed a solo offering from me. My stage fright has kept me back, in a dark corner for most of my life, but not all of it.

If you've read even a handful of my tales, you've likely gotten the sense that I have an excellent memory. I remember performing with my cousins, both song and dance, for family and friends when we were very young. I remember being featured in a kindergarten performance and being comfortable and I remember being at ease performing in first grade.

Between first grade and third grade, I was in second grade. I think it's safe to say that I was in that grade for ten months. I remember the teacher's name and that's about it. I have lots of memories from every other school year, but second grade seems to have happened to me without my full participation. I do not remember second grade, people.

Now, it's probably not accurate to say that I don't remember any of it because what I'm thinking was the turning point for me as a performer happened in a classroom that my memory doesn't recognize, so I'm going to assume that it was in second grade. It's funny, I can see the hallway in my mind and I can take myself to the door of the classroom, but that's it.

There was, as usual, some show being put on. I was slated to have a major role. I have no idea what it was. I'm sure it involved a display of seven-year-old adorableness and, there I was, all adorable, so that must've been easy to cast. For no reason known to me now, or possibly even then, I approached the adults one day and told them I did not want the part.

I remember the feeling of disappointment that came from them and, from me, the sadness and confusion. I remember how I did it and walked back to my seat and sort of sunk down in my chair. I cannot say today why I did that and I doubt that I could've said then either.

Eight years ago, I was back in that school. It's a behemoth of a building just blocks away from where I live. On this day, I walked into a stairwell and was overwhelmed by a sudden feeling that brought me to tears which poured out of my ugly, sobbing face. I don't know what the feeling was or why I had it and this tale will not dive into speculation.

I can't say if that staircase had anything to do with my dropping out of the second-grade show. I feel like I've been sunken down in that chair for thirty-seven years now and I don't know why. I talk about one day getting up from the chair and putting on a show, but who knows what will happen? Even if I never do, there is an ounce of redemption for me when I see my children confidently on stage. It is a complex joy and relief about who they are and what they have and have not been through.

‡‡‡‡‡‡‡‡

In 1993 I found myself in Spain for the first time. Well, I didn't just find myself there. I wasn't lost or anything like that and the trip was planned. One of the other people on the trip was the late Brenda Taub.

Brenda was an alto with a deep, rich singing voice, but while her speaking voice could be deep, it was naturally a bit nasal, maybe half nasal, as if only one side of her sinuses participated in producing the sounds of her words. Late in her life, which only spanned five decades, Brenda became very ill. Her last years were spent surviving. Every time I saw her, at some point, she would pull out a pouch and many small bottles and arrange maybe dozens of pills and capsules, joking that they made up a meal. They were surely enough to be filling and they were, I suppose, keeping her alive.

In Spain, I found that Brenda laughed about her encapsulated meals, but real food would sometimes make her cry. We walked into McDonald's one day (I got gazpacho in a milk carton!) and my friend had me ask, as her interpreter, if the French fries were cooked in lard. I thought this was a ridiculous question. I know not the ways of this establishment, whose ambient smell makes my stomach turn. I was wrong.

One day, Brenda and I went out to lunch. The sun was surely close to the earth on this day and our bodies and feet felt like they belonged to ambitious tourists, only because they did. We needed shade and food and drink and rest.

We sat and studied our menus. When the server arrived, we had a long conversation about ingredients and limitations, which ended in the ordering of a salad for Brenda.

My friend, I remember, was always hot and often sweating. Perhaps it was due to her illness or the treatment of her illness or maybe it was her age. I am well aware, more than twenty years later, that this last one was an apposite possibility. Brenda was just beginning to cool down with the chugging of her room temperature water when our meals arrived.

Brenda tasted her food and soon began to cry. She was a heavy woman and mature, but the image of a small, vulnerable child is the one that stays with me from this day. She was sobbing before she could communicate to me that there was bacon in her salad, bacon and so much disappointment at a few different levels.

Towards the end, I feel like she could only count on her meals in pill form. In the end, she couldn't even count on those.

‡‡‡‡‡‡‡

My daughter just found $10. She is overjoyed. She called her father just to tell him that. "Abuelita, guess what I just found?" She exclaimed to her grandmother, "And I found a dollar on the street the other day!" Her life is so good right now.

You know how that feels. It's about finding the money and it's also about feeling lucky. I know someone who picks up pennies which are heads up. The ones that are tails up, she turns over, leaving them for someone else to claim as lucky.

In February of 2016 the children went geocaching for the first time with their father. He was out of work and I was teaching, so off they went to nearby Van Cortlandt Park for a hike and an adventure.

After placing their own cache, they searched for treasure, following the coordinates given to them online, looking in bushes and overturning stones.

At one point they saw an old, dirty, half-buried drink bottle. They were ready to ignore it, but upon disturbing it a bit, they noticed a distinctive green within.

Geocaching is about the quest. Sometimes participants will leave a piece of candy or a riddle or some other treat. Finding something is always fun, but it's more about the finding than the thing.

On this day, before my family came upon their first cache, they discovered this dirty bottle. When they opened it, they found a roll of dollar bills, all from the 1990s. In total it was about $1,500.

My children continued to seek and hide caches periodically for a couple of years, always looking carefully at trash, just in case. Luckily, they've gotten excited about many little trinkets along the way because their first excursion sure set them up for disappointment evermore. Lucky.

✝✝✝✝✝✝✝

I don't really like to go to concerts unless I'm on the stage. Sitting and watching isn't really my thing. If I'm listening to music, I prefer to sing along or, at least hum. About a year ago, I started plugging into the music on my phone and, based on the looks from passers-by the volume that comes out of my mouth is greater than the one that goes into my ears and the quality of the sound is amazing, but possibly in a negative way. I can't be sure. I'm singing for the feeling I get in my chest, not the feeling strangers get in their eardrums.

My thirteen-year-old daughter is thirteen and, while I'm not sure that has anything to do with this, I wanted to make sure that fact didn't go unnoticed. In just a few weeks, she decided that there were a handful of concerts she had to go to, at least partially due to the influence of her older friend, I'm sure. I will be accompanying a teen trio to one of these concerts before the end of the month. I volunteered to do this because I like Panic! at the Disco and I already sing along to the songs, so I don't have to just sit and listen. As a matter of fact, I will probably be doing more and better singing along and dancing than most of the other audience members, all half my age, at most. I never really try to embarrass my daughter, but I'm thinking there's a bit of inevitability ripening around that.

Now about my son. He's eleven and a strict rule-follower. Because I am a lover of language, I don't use vulgarities. Curses as adjectives don't make sense to me. I'm not judging really, but my son is, I'm sure. He has probably made-up rules about cursing and, when he hears it, his neck and jaw lock and his gaze focuses directly ahead of him as if he is trying to leap into the future and shut down his senses simultaneously. This is not an exaggeration and it's a little weird. Of course, he was the one to report to his father that so many of the songs in Panic! at the Disco's new album were about alcohol. It doesn't surprise me that his favorite song by them is *High Hopes*, about succeeding in achieving one's dreams. You know, by following rules and not cursing and stuff.

I sent my daughter a message the other day complaining about one of the lyrics. In comparing it to a silver lining, "Only gold is hard enough," doesn't make any sense. Gold is very soft. That's why it's mixed with other metals. She responded, "It's 'only gold is hot enough.'" Oh. Ok. I'll accept that. Even if it doesn't mean anything, at least it isn't scientifically inaccurate. I'm always happy to learn and teach correct lyrics. Like when I told my husband, who knows every word of every Beatles song that, "What would you say if I sang out of tune?" actually means something, unlike his version, "What would you say if I sang out a tune?" (I don't know. Maybe you would tell me to be quiet. Especially if you were walking down the street, hearing more of my singing than I could.)

Yesterday, my daughter and I were sitting on the bed and I was singing one of the songs that we will surely hear (and sing along to) at the concert. Keep in mind that I will be singing "heck" or just pausing for some of the words in many of these songs. The singer had a very religious upbringing, which is reflected in a number of ways in his songs, including his use of, uhm, language. I sang, "Roll me like a blunt 'cause I wanna go home." My daughter embarrassedly giggled and erroneously corrected me, "It's 'row me like a boat!'" I laughed in her face. This time, I knew I was right and then I had to ask, "Do you know what a blunt is?" So glad my son wasn't part of that conversation!

‡‡‡‡‡‡‡

My life changed last week. It was probably shortened as well, but the little time I have left will smell so sweet, not like a perimenopausal armpit. That was not a simile. I'm really talking about my perimenopausal armpits, mostly my left one.

I started using antiperspirant for the first time, either in my life or in decades–not sure. 98% of my FaceBook friends are childbirth professionals I've never met and half of you are going to judge me because poison and stifling my natural processes and clogging pours. I know all about that. I'm a witch. I heal people with the earth. I know. My perimenopause wanted poison on my freaking armpits, OK?

I've made various kinds of deodorants and I've tried crystals and powder and all sorts of things. I've asked friends who said things worked, adding that they had to wash and reapply midday. Uhm. Then they don't work, like my rain jacket, whose lining sticks to my wet skin in large and small chunks every time I take it off.

I tried men's deodorants and they said, "Haha, little girl. We have the same ingredients as women's deodorants, except without the flowery scents." I like to wear men's scents, maybe because I'm never going to actually smell a man near me because they don't want to be close to my stinky armpits.

I know that there are parts of the world where body odor is embraced as natural and commonplace. That's fine for others. I won't mind smelling your armpits nearly as much as I mind smelling mine. Really!

Last week I got antiperspirant and I now understand why people use it! I got antiperspirant and a new rain jacket and my future, albeit truncated by my unhealthy choice, feels dry under my jacket and under my arms.

‡‡‡‡‡‡‡

When he was younger, my son was a great lover and sometime master of puzzles, including mazes. As a responsible purveyor of the best kind of humor, known to many as corniness, I of course, always told him his work was "amazing."

I shared my great interest in labyrinths with my children and they were clear on the difference between the two, which I unwillingly demonstrated by getting lost in corn mazes on at least two occasions, while providing ample nutrition for the mosquitoes. A labyrinth would never do this to me. Furthermore, it might help me find a peaceful state and forget about the mosquitoes if there were any around.

Last week I rubbed elbows with almost 200 colleagues. The rubbing of the elbows was figurative, of course, but one evening, it felt to me as if there was actual rubbing of nerves happening. Not that anyone was getting on my nerves. All of my interactions were positive. I just needed to be alone for a little while in order to prevent the disquieting from becoming a greater share of the entirety of my feelings.

After a cocktail reception, during which I strategically accepted small bites to stack the odds against later hunger, I declined invitations to dine in groups and headed back to my room.

To my delight, I found on my path a solitary labyrinth. Despite my admiration of them, I had never walked along or even come across a walkable labyrinth myself. I took off my shoes and followed the path. It led me just to where I needed to go and I didn't get lost. With my head down, I repeated something I can't remember, but I'm sure it was perfect at the time.

Before sleep, I cried passionately because that's how I do. It felt so good. While this tale may be close to nothing for you, to me, it was amazing!

‡‡‡‡‡‡‡

Years ago, I remember explaining to someone how my cousin was marrying my other cousin. They weren't related to each other. Neither of them was even related to me. Also, I explained that one of my favorite uncles isn't actually my uncle.

I don't know why so many people have become like adopted family when I definitely have enough family of my own. I'm not even going to talk about my father's dozens of siblings. Let's just stick to my mother's side.

Over the weekend, we had relatives visiting from Switzerland, Panamá, and Boston. While telling my children how we were all related, I found myself getting sucked into what sounded like an Abbott and Costello skit.

These three and the other one all have the same mother, this one, and they have the same father and he's also my mother's father. This one has the same mother as my mother but a different father. My uncle from last week has the same mother as my mother and a different father and a different father from this one and those. Luckily, we only had a handful of guests.

The last time I saw my father, he told me he had eighteen children. He told me this while we were out and about with a little boy he had adopted. I don't know what it is. Maybe we all just like to explain family ties at get-togethers. It's certainly interesting conversation.

‡‡‡‡‡‡‡

My children spent five nights at a sleep away camp last week. They slept away from home for almost a week, my poor little babies. They were all by themselves with the four dozen other lone children and a bunch of counselors and other people to take care of them. Very scary, at least for me.

My daughter went last year and she's a pro at independence. She's ready for college abroad somewhere. She's thirteen. My son, however, had never even had a sleepover with another child at their house. Also, he's a sensitive boy who tries to crawl back in my womb regularly. I was far away, with the Catskill Mountains between us and there was no communication in or out. My son wasn't able to call for womb service!

I was nervous for a few reasons. One of them was that I had once gone to sleep away camp myself as a child. I had boarded a bus that took me to a faraway land, possibly even a whole hour away. I stayed there for an afternoon and an entire night and came back the next day. It's possible that the interminable affair lasted all of twenty-four hours.

Diana, from downstairs, was very pushy. I say that because she wanted to do things her way all of the time. That's the only reason. Yes, you're right in remembering that she always wanted me to go into the bathroom with her when she used the toilet. She's also the person who had me sign up for that stupid, waste-of-time pageant and the one who convinced me, someone who didn't like dolls, that I had to beg my mother for a Cabbage Patch Doll for my birthday. I kind of felt bad when I got one because it was a doll and make-believe games were out of my comfort zone and no fun at all, which I realized upon unboxing the fake human in the bathroom at some predawn hour after my mother noticed that I was awake and decided to give me my birthday gift early, so I sat on the toilet lid with the light on in there so I wouldn't disturb the others who were asleep because we all shared a room, and I looked at the birth certificate and I dressed the artificial baby and I was pretty much done playing at that point, forever, with that stupid thing. Yes, that Diana. She was a few years older than I was so, when she talked my mother into letting me go to summer camp with her, I ended up, at the age of seven, spending my summer with preteens and teens. It was a not great experience. Let's go on to a new paragraph now and see if I can bring us back to the point, or even a point.

Part of this not-for-seven-year-olds camp involvement was a night away somewhere with tents and sleeping on the ground and sun and mosquitoes and stuff. Playing with dolls is beginning to sound appealing. I was a mature, five-and-a-half-foot-tall seven-year-old, so the people in charge didn't notice that I really didn't belong. Diana was supposedly taking care of me. That was a great idea.

All I remember about the day we arrived was the smell of urine in the tents. Also, hot heat coming from the everywhere. I either slept or didn't sleep and then it was morning. Morning felt a little disgusting because the everywhere heat was still in place and showers were not part of the programming. I take a shower every morning even if I've taken one the night before unless, apparently, I am suffering through a camping trip.

After getting dressed, a few of us went for a walk. That was cool because there was a bridge made out of modern non-wilderness stuff and there were other signs of civilization. There was also a small body of water and a whale. I will never forget that. That was the best part of, not just this camping trip, but the whole stupid summer camp. Well, I don't know how to say this. It was not a whale exactly, or at all even, but the idea that it might be was very real and amazing. It was some pipe spurting water from a nearby building. I'm not sure I walked away entirely convinced, though.

Walked away we did and back to the campsite. Back to the campsite where responsible adults were to be responsible for us, the minors. We arrived and found that they had made pancakes for breakfast. They had made pancakes and the pancakes had been eaten and the pancakes were all gone. I eat even more than I shower, yet there I was, unbathed and hungry, having very much not fun with children I couldn't relate to and only the memory of a fake whale to sustain me until I got home. I can't remember. Maybe they fed us something else, but we definitely didn't get pancakes.

Nonetheless, I sent my children off to camp last week. They showered and ate and played and came home singing songs. Taking care of people is harder than taking care of dolls. It's also immeasurably more fun.

‡‡‡‡‡‡‡

When I met my husband and he was first getting to know my family, he kept telling me that I should write a book. Who would want to read about my family? Stupid little stories, say once a week, might be especially ridiculous.

I remember one time in particular. I'm going to say it was the summer of 1981 and that my mother had heard Queen's *Another One Bites the Dust* "ten thousand pairs of times" by then. This may sound like an exaggeration, but it's a direct quote from my mother, which she has probably uttered ten thousand pairs of times. We were in my aunt's backyard in Far Rockaway. My mother was cutting someone's hair. One of the many roaming children tripped and fell and my mother said, "Another one bites the dust."

I don't know why I've never forgotten this or why I told my husband about it, but in response, he urged me to write a book. I wondered how I could share the story of another one bites the dust. It's kind of boring.

I remember this today because, recently, I had my own biting of the dust experience quite against my will as my canine nephew tried to make me one with the earth.

My sister's dog is of the large variety. I don't know what kind of dog he is, maybe a boxer-pony mix, but like a fat, clumsy pony. We have a special relationship. I would say it's a love-hate thing, but neither of us feels so strongly in either direction. He has ruined more than one beautiful article of clothing of mine, so maybe we can say it's a tolerate-slobberate relationship.

On a disgustingly hot and humid day, I was daintily sitting in a fabric folding chair. It was one of those aluminum-framed chairs that surprise us when they are able to greet a new season. I don't know what events the devil had whipped up in order to make me end up with Baxter's leash in my hand, but there I was with it in my dominant hand and a glass (plastic cup, whatever) of Pêche Lambic in the other one, because my priorities weren't quite right apparently.

There I sat, barely not melting, when another dog dared approach our vicinity. Before I could, well anything really because it only took a second and how many things could I possibly do in that time, but maybe start to think that I might know what was going on, Baxter had dragged me off of my perch and face down onto the ground. Luckily, the gods of prim had spread out a picnic blanket before me to make the ordeal less messy and perhaps less painful.

I was stunned in my prone position and someone wrangled the leash from me in time before Baxter managed to topple all in his way as he torpedoed towards another dog so that he could smell his butt or something.

It was hilarious. There was no blood or dirt, which certainly helped, and the other picnickers pointed out repeatedly and amazedly how my cup had remained upright in my hand throughout. That helped too.

If the thin ground cover hadn't been there, I would've surely bitten the dust. I thought immediately of that childhood scene, but I didn't mention it because I knew my mother wouldn't remember and, is it even funny?

My mother says corny stuff all of the time. I guess I haven't fallen far from the tree, and it happens to be a cornstalk onto which I cling with a mighty grip. I often have to tell people that something I've said is a joke. Then they laugh at me, not the joke. The goal is the laughter, people. We make people laugh and it's ok if it's at us. I just keep telling myself that.

‡‡‡‡‡‡‡

My tiny little baby daughter just had two days of orientation for (gulp) high school. Yeah, I don't know how that happened. Not only is she going to high school, but she's always been homeschooled, so I'm basically losing her forever, sending her out to be eaten alive, to be eaten by wolves, to walk like an Egyptian and all that jazz.

Thirty-one years ago, I went to my own high school orientation. I missed a day of it because I went on a trip to Canada, and every homeschooler will tell you that travel is more important than school. (My daughter is going to a specialized high school and I'm concerned about the workload. I was talking to her about it recently in public and, at one point I said, "We'll see how it goes. You can always drop out." I'm betting that the incredulous eavesdropper has never heard of homeschooling.) I had also done a summer program at the school during the, you know, summer, so I was all caught up with the ins and outs. No senior was going to sell me a pass to the nonexistent pool on the roof!

I was ready for high school. That's not even true. I wouldn't know until four years later that high school wasn't really for me. I thought I was ready because I had updated my wardrobe. I can't remember the clothes, but I remember the shoes. I had gotten a pair of black lace-up boots, the laces of which would never be tied. In the weeks prior, I had gone to that bizarre store. What was it called? Oh yes, Bazaar. It was full of all sorts of unnecessary things and a bunch of colorful, plastic junk. I exchanged a little cash for multicolored paperclips and tiny plastic clothespins, also in a variety of colors. In preparation for my look-how-cool-I-am debut at high school, I had put some paperclips on the laces of the right boot and the clothespins on the laces of the left boot. I omitted any red ones of course, as I would still do today, because eight-year-old me decided that red is the devil's color and that feeling has never really gone away.

Then there was the other pair of shoes. I don't remember them exactly. Maybe they had a wedge heel. They were definitely black because, when I was nine, my mother told me that black matches with everything, so most of my shoes are still black today. None of those black shoes match with red, however, because of the whole Satan's color issue.

High school was a fifteen- or twenty-minute walk from my house. On my one day of orientation, I wore this second pair of shoes. It was a beautiful day, too warm for the boots. Before I reached the school building, my feet already hurt. Then I walked around some more inside. Eventually, I had to return home. Twenty minutes of walking may not seem like 100 miles to you, but on that day, it sure seemed like that to me. The route to and from school was pretty desolate. If I had come across another person, I might have asked them to carry me. Instead, I took off my shoes and hobbled with my bare feet on the ground. When I removed my shoes, the heels of my feet looked like they were inside out. Luckily, the Canadian weather was going to me warm and I could wear mules for the next few days.

I ended up wearing those shoes quite a bit that year, probably anytime I wasn't wearing my amazingly-adorned boots. They never hurt me again, though, because I wore socks. If nothing else, in high school I learned that socks can make a difference. I hope my daughter's lessons aren't as hard to learn.

‡‡‡‡‡‡‡

I met my father when I was eight and saw him again when I was twenty-six. Growing up, I had only stories about him. My family liked to point out how much I looked like him and how ugly this made me. Let's assume it was a family joke. He's Italian and the rest of my family is not, so they liked to joke about my differences, like my big nose and my father's name, which I wasn't even given, so ha ha ha. The laugh may not be on them, but it's not on me either because I have the non-Italian name of my mother. OK? When I was eight, my father wanted to give me his name and I was like, "How do you even spell that, and why would I want to double the syllables in my name, and have you noticed the alliteration I've got going on?" It didn't happen.

When I was a child, my mother shared her reality with me. I knew my father to be a drunk and a womanizer and all the things that someone might say about the man who left her with a newborn and never looked back. I knew he had lots of other children and I used to jokingly say I might end up marrying one because we wouldn't know we were siblings. That was weird.

I am writing this tale during the 2020 pandemic. I'm pretty sure you know what I'm talking about no matter when you come across these words. I reached out to a couple of my sisters in Colombia to see how things are going. One is doing super well as she seems to always be doing, the other is doing equally poorly, again as seems to be her custom. These observations are based on complexities that may be partially fabricated by my own upbringing. I can't pretend to know the real reasons behind these circumstances, but the children who grew up under my father's roof, I think had it harder than the rest of us. Luckily, most of us grew up largely fatherless. I didn't set out to make this an anti-myfather account. I am not pulled strongly in that direction ever. It's just what's coming out. Sorry, my father.

Finally, here I am at the crux of the tale! When talking to the sister who is doing less well, she shared with me that she is self-quarantined in a town where the people are very poor. She initially went there to flee an abusive partner and, when she found herself with a cold, she realized she could not go home, where she lives with our father, because, as she put it, that would be deadly for him. She said that, because of his lung problems, getting a cold would be fatal, and so she was keeping her distance until she was better. I'm not sure if she was thinking about the dangers of COVID-19 for people with lung issues or if the severity of his malady does, in fact, make it so dangerous for him to get a cold. No matter.

Twenty years ago, I sat with my father and told him that I had thought he was a smoker. I knew he used to be because I heard more than once about the time he was smoking in the closed room with me and got angry at my mother when she tried to open a window. The story goes that he told her I would end up being a smoker too so it didn't matter. On that day in Colombia, my father told me that he had smoked for many years. He said he stopped from one day to the next. His friend was a doctor who had given him a chest x-ray. My father looked at the image and his friend pointed out a small black area on one of his lungs. "Do you see this?" he asked. My father, concerned, asked if that was a damaged portion of lung. His friend responded that the small, dark patch was, in fact, the only healthy lung tissue he had left.

That's the story he told me twenty years ago. It's surely a good thing he stopped smoking when he did. While I often think about visiting some of my siblings, I never give much thought to seeing my father again. After talking to my sister the other day, I want to. I hope I get a chance to do it, that I can see him again through my own eyes and not through the stories and that he can see me as myself, the daughter who never smoked or became the things he predicted for me as a newborn. As I write this, for the first time I wonder if thinking those things about me made it easier for him to walk away.

‡‡‡‡‡‡‡

I like to say that I am somewhat stitious rather than superstitious, focusing my belief in things magical only on a smattering of positive ones. So now I'm going to tell you about a waterbug. Those of you who know the creature I mean, likely because you're from New York City, may wonder how me telling you about a waterbug might be at all positive. For the others of you who might think I'm referring to another insect, I will explain forthwith.

The New York waterbug is a big, chubby cockroach, at least an inch long. As if that wasn't bad enough, it flies. I am going to conjecture that most people, upon seeing one of these insects in their home, would react with a combination of fear and disgust. I don't know how to describe my response, really, but there is at least a soupçon of denial therein. If I ignore it, I don't have to deal with it and it can go on living in the hidden parts from whence it came, along with myriad other things we shouldn't really talk about, especially since I said I was going to share something positive, and now look, I'm thinking about creepy unmentionable crawlies living among us, uck.

Well, just the other night, I was sitting on my bed, likely making believe I was working, while really mostly being distracted, when my inattentiveness was yanked to, well, attention by the small, yet altogether too-big bug crawling on the floor away from the very bed on which I sat. Thank goodness it was crawling in that direction rather than towards me, lest I be forced by my own squeamishness to sleep on the couch for the night.

I have not killed a regular roach in decades. There is no way I was going to attempt to kill, or even trap, this steroidal, evolutionarily survivingest roach I had before me. I am trying, but can't even imagine myself attempting such a feat in my bedroom against this flying invader. Flying, remember? It's a big freaking flying roach. I watched it make its way towards a pile of out-of-place items on the floor, near the wall and decided that I was going to let it disappear, mostly by me not looking in that direction again.

I should clarify that, even though a waterbug siting is not completely extraordinary, it is relatively rare to see one inside my apartment. Two hands are too many to count the number of these winged cucarachas I have had the misfortune of seeing within my quarters in my lifetime. On this night, I was willing, if not happy, to allow us to coexist, imagining that it might go back to some crevice where it would live alone because there were no other such creatures anywhere nearby. Please just let me have this fantasy.

Of course, I worried that it might crawl on me or fly around or crawl around or that I might just see it again. I wanted none of these, but I figured I'd just ignore the problem. Worrying certainly wasn't going to help, and I wasn't willing to actually take any action, so the only thing left was to go to sleep and wish for the best. In the morning, as I got ready to go out, I only glanced in the direction of my crawly complication, making it less likely that I would see it, hoping that our paths would never again cross.

My hope was not fulfilled, but here alas is the good part. Upon returning from my Pilates class and/or errands and/or tackling the great demands of the morning, but probably just Pilates class and maybe I got a pastry too, I found on the very welcoming mat outside my door, an upturned, lifeless waterbug. Was this my, yes at this point we can call him "friend" from the previous night? I certainly claimed it as such. I did more than that. Do I recall I got a little emotional at the sight? Ok, yes. Let's say I did. Here's why.

I went to bed with this thing in my room. It wasn't really threatening, but my avoidance made it a bigger issue than it could've been. I didn't just ignore it as if it didn't bother me. I ignored it because it was too much for me to take care of. The next day, there was my problem, placed on my doorstep, clearly defeated. I gingerly pushed it off the mat with my foot because, even dead, I could hardly stand to deal with it. I went ahead and decided that the world was telling me that things are being handled. It was not enough for me never to see the bug again. There was the evidence of the issue, all resolved, by not me.

And no, it is not possible that this was a different waterbug from a different apartment or from outside or anywhere else because this is my story and I am a positive thinker, thank you very much!

‡‡‡‡‡‡‡

For years, my daughter begged to get a dog. Her father left the decision to me and my ruling was always no. I forbade the repeated requests for stretches at a time, always knowing that my response would be the same whenever the topic was allowed to come up again. I was logical, of course, citing the facts that we lived in an apartment and that my cleaning standards were different than those of the other residents of said apartment, so I would always end up cleaning up after the dog or after whomever thought they had cleaned up after the dog.

Then, one day, I moved out of the apartment, leaving the other residents behind, along with the freedom to get a dog. I knew they wouldn't abide by my preference for a Great Dane or other such monstrously-sized phenomenon, but I strongly hinted against any small variety of yappy, useless fur creature. A few months later, my children had acquired the perfect pup. They drove down to his farm home and chose him over his siblings because he was the quiet one. He sure fooled them!

Our black and white, luxuriously long-haired Border Collie, a herding dog, soon began to keep us in place as we made our way down the hallway while he also made his way into our hearts. Loki is a soul mate of mine. I love him and am also happy to be responsible for him only part-time. I do miss him, though, when he's not around.

It turns out that Border Collies are barkers. If you were to knock on our door, or even a nearby neighbor's door, you would surely feel terror from the protective volubility emanating from sweet Loki. However, he is not so much saying, "Stay away from my people! I will rip you to shreds if you dare enter," as, "Grandma, there is someone here. Protect me." The meaning of his barks is not writ large, but once I open the door he's quiet and nonthreatening, even walking in the opposite direction, so that's evidence enough for me.

Not only is he non-threatening, he's also a scaredy-dog, frightened by many things, some more than others. When he was a puppy, someone was letting him lick a spoon (certainly not I!) and it fell to the floor. Since then, he's been afraid of spoons because they might fall (and explode?). Same thing with treats. He used to take them between his teeth from my hand, but one day, gravity foiled the smooth transition of the bone and it landed on the floor, sending him cowardly scurrying away. Now I have to put the treat directly on the floor for him.

This irrational fear is the reason Loki, while loving walks and even getting very excited for them, seems to be traumatized by his harness and leash comically avoids letting them touch him e v e r y t i m e we try to put it on him. He'll back away and raise a paw out of the harness if we don't hold it in place before he's all buckled in. Once it snaps in place, he's happy and fine.

I figure that at some point in Loki's past, the heavy handle of the retractable leash crashed to the floor. I don't know what he thinks it means when things fall, but it's clearly devastating. Recently, after our usual frustrating prewalk charade I chided mostly the air rather than lovely little Loki. Then I turned to him and explained that we can't live in the past, letting our fears have such a tight hold on us. Just because a bad thing happened to us, it doesn't mean it will keep happening. I asked him why he couldn't just move beyond this illogical fear.

I quickly shut myself up, though, as I wondered if that could be good advice for me? Does the universe think about me the way I think about Loki and his fears? It's easier for me to believe that he is being irrational even though I do practically the same thing. As the years pass, I wonder if one of us will get better. Both of us improving would have a positive impact on my life, one substantially more than the other. I mean, it would make getting out of the house with him a great deal less tedious!

Part II

About a month after I wrote this tale, I took a trip to a surfing town in Mexico. One day, I was left alone on a boat for a few hours. From this boat, I could see whales and dolphins. Eventually, I decided to go in the water, holding onto the ladder, as I had fearfully done thirteen months prior in Colombia. It was a warm day and I wanted to be in the water even though I don't really swim. The ladder kept me safe, but then, I decided to go away from the boat, as if I wasn't going to drown. I didn't know how far away the ground was. I certainly couldn't touch it, yet there I was, not drowning. I was floating there, kind of swimming, for hours with no one around close by. A little later, under a caring companion's kind tutelage, I snorkeled. I did these new scary things, me. The next day, I sat on the beach shaking my head "no" at the parade of vendors. I did not want a pareo or a t-shirt or hat, candy, a necklace, oysters, shrimp, or freshly cut fruit. I laughed at the guy who was selling zero-calorie, low-fat doughnuts. They were regular doughnuts. The one thing I bought on the beach was a colorful new collar for Loki. When I put it around his neck, it is mostly buried within his fur. The colors are vibrant, but it doesn't matter to me that they don't show much. What matters is that, when I put the collar around Loki's neck, he acts as if he isn't scared at all. Maybe any new collar would've had the same effect. Maybe I brought back some of the magic I got in Mexico and it changed both of our lives.

‡‡‡‡‡‡‡

In 2019 internet access in private homes in Cuba was legalized, though users would still need a permit and money to take advantage of this luxury. Most still go without service at home unless they live close enough to a hotel or park where there is WiFi. In November of 2020 I sat in a small park in Havana, one of the fewer than 1000 hotspots throughout the largest of the Caribbean Islands. Luckily it was the middle of a weekday, so I didn't have to compete with hordes of users for the already slow service.

It was there that I decided to call my mother, lest she continue to worry (surely) about her baby. Me, I am the baby. Yes, I was 47. I probably told her about the hyperbolic heat and how my Cuban friends were happy to see me again, and then my mother started talking about all her normal things as if I was calling from around the corner. She seems to have taken up a hobby decades ago and is now apparently training for the Olympic competition that might one day exist for complaining. She is quite often gripey at this point in her life. I listened for a little while as she complained about my sister and commiserated by stating one of her familiar idioms saying, "Si, Mami, conozco el almendrol." This meant that I knew how my sister was, that I understood her pain. Literally, I was saying that I know the almond tree. Thusly I ended the conversation.

On my way out of the park, towards the small ice cream shop, where I should have opted for a frozen dessert rather than that mediocre pastry, I saw a lush tree that had littered the ground with plump, green pods. I had asked locals about different plants many times on my trips to Cuba because I couldn't easily look them up on my smartphone as I might have elsewhere. This tree was beautiful with vibrant leaves sprouting in profusion and it was generous with its fruit. I had never seen it before. I did not know it. I asked my friend for its name and he simply said, "That's an almond tree." Maybe I owed my sister an apology.

‡‡‡‡‡‡‡

Have you ever walked on the beach looking for treasure? Most of the beach time in my life has been spent with family, so the treasure was all around me. One summer was a little different. My cousins, my only friends, left me. Still my experiences managed to revolve around them. They went to visit relatives in Panama. They came back with joyful stories, but it doesn't hurt to think that they just didn't want to make me feel bad because they were surely miserably missing me.

It turns out that I had some stories of my own. While my cousins were away, their family acquired a new house. I got to go see the house and stay over while they frolicked on far away beaches without me. I got to meet some of the neighbor children. There happened to be a girl my cousin's age, another girl my other cousin's age, and one my age. They were all very nice, and I remember only Maeve's name because I had thought it was "May" and, never having heard that common Irish name before, learned a long time later what it actually was. (Incidentally, my aunt once greeted Mrs. O'Connor as Mrs. Wiggins (a character on the Carol Burnett show, which I fondly remember us watching as a family) just because she mixed it up one day. Also, my grandmother said something about "the Jewish family next door" once—yes, the O'Connors.) Anyway, I met three girls that summer. When the cousins came back from Panama, a bunch of us went to the airport as we were apt to do in those days, and I told them all about our new friends.

What I remember most was telling them that the girl who was my age was either not so nice or not so smart or some other negative thing. I did this because I didn't want to be replaced by this girl. I was young and dumb because, obviously, cousins can never be replaced!

‡‡‡‡‡‡‡

We didn't drink soda when I was growing up. We drank juice and sometimes milk with Ovaltine malt powder. We didn't buy into the dairy industry's push to drink milk, but let me tell you who did buy into what. In the 80s, cranberry juice started to become really popular. Also, macadamia nuts, but I don't have a story about them. I don't have a story about cranberry juice either, but never you mind those details and just read on. I think that the sugar producers were the ones behind the cranberry boon because, have you tasted cranberry juice? Unless you are doubled over with a UTI, you're likely not reaching for it at snack time. Cranberry juice cocktail is what actually became popular.

Another, similar-looking juice started to gain attention in the early 2000s. A particularly influential friend at the time got my mother to hold forth on the importance of drinking pomegranate juice. She knew that drinking the juice had many advantages and repeated that the juice itself was "power." I imagined our friend's expressive face recommending this juice passionately and also had an inkling that his interest was mostly in the virility-related benefits.

I like pomegranate juice. I know it has antioxidants, and vitamins, and power, and I love the fact that it doesn't need a bunch of sweetener or other juices to make it palatable. I do have a little problem with its modern popularity, however.

When I was eight or nine years old, so before even the cranberry juice explosion, I was at home watching television while plucking arils from their pithy home, when I got a fabulous idea. Children and their ideas! Little life experience or smarts even—how good could this idea possibly have been? During a commercial break, I went to the kitchen to call my mother from our yellow wall phone. The handset's spiraled cord was long enough to give one privacy while standing outside of the kitchen, but I didn't need privacy because I had a great idea that had to be shared. Also, I was home alone or maybe with my sleeping sister, so unaccompanied either way.

I excitedly called my mother at work and told her that we should make pomegranate juice. She communicated somehow that it was not a great idea, that it would be too much work. I was very disappointed, even if I hadn't been thinking about the money-making possibilities of my proposition. The color of pomegranate arils is rich due to their liquid treasure. We were rich in our own way, but alas, it wouldn't be because we made and sold pomegranate juice.

‡‡‡‡‡‡‡

You know how the New York Times shares descriptions of how people spend their Sundays? Here's how I do not ever spend any day of the week, except for this one day.

For a Sunday in August, I had booked a facial at the spa at an unusually late hour for me. I had done a prenatal visit for a colleague in stupid Staten Island, so I treated myself afterwards. It was an overcast weekend in late August and that day the temperature peaked at a pleasant 72° as I walked the eight lonely city blocks to the King Cole Bar at the St. Regis Hotel after my spa visit. My husband had introduced me to this bar many years before. He knew it because of the Maxfield Parrish mural on prominent display there. We had gone in once as if it was a museum, but didn't feel comfortable enough to sit at the bar and have a drink. My divorce had been final for less than two months at this point and I was going to make myself comfortable with a drink at this very bar before I headed home. My martini was a bargain, even with my generous tip, at just over 3% of the cost of their most expensive offering, some cognac I may never taste.

Before my drink was done, I had started to talk to two women at the bar. One of them was visiting New York. When she stood up, she had a Rimowa suitcase at the end of one hand and a crutch under her opposite arm to help her walk on an orthotically-booted foot. A yoga pose in her Los Angeles home had foiled her equilibrium and left her in need of the frumpy accessory for a while. The box with wheels and a handle had cost her over $1000 and there was something wrong with it. It made sense for her to want to have it repaired, but it was just after 5 p.m. on a Sunday, so no matter how long she chanted at the five roads intersection trying to summon a demon so that she could sell her soul to make it happen, it would have to wait because the Rimowa store around the corner, on Madison, was closed.

They were planning to go downtown to Balthazar for a meal and invited me to join them. In many countries, an invitation implies treating the invitee. That isn't usually the case in the US, so while I thought about whether or not I should go, they begged and convinced me that we would have a great time because, while I'm not sure how great I am as a friend, I'm a pretty amazing stranger. They were a boisterous, flirtatious pair and my divorced self had nothing exciting to do for the foreseeable future, so off I went with them.

In about fifteen minutes, the taxi got us down to the SoHo restaurant. One of my new friends asked if we could be seated and we were disappointed to hear that the wait for a table would be more than an hour. I surprised myself as I asked the maître d', "Even for us?" and I surprised the ladies when, buoyed by my ebullient smile, he suggested we have a drink at the bar as we wait for the next available table.

The party vibe continued at the bar though our stay there was brief. Before we were escorted to our table, we had made some more friends who suggested we join them after dinner for drinks at Raoul's. This suggestion was made by handsome men and more like the aforementioned international type of invitation, so it seemed like a good idea to me.

At the table, we looked at the menu. I hadn't been to Balthazar in many years and, even then, it had only been for dessert and champagne. We weren't going to have a full dinner and, because I tend to allow myself to be pushed over, I, who don't usually like beef, agreed to share a mound of it in the raw. No regrets. Let me tell you—I love Balthazar's steak tartare!

Before I dug into the yummy deliciousness, one of my new friends, the local one, casually said she was going to make a call to order some cocaine. It was as if she had said she was ordering ice cream and would I like some, except a little different because instead of saying "ice cream" she said "cocaine." She was having cocaine delivered to the door of the restaurant. No, I did not want any. I am not like ice, which, in its quest for equilibrium, loses itself. I have no trouble not going along with whatever is going wherever. I simply declined. Agreeing to the meat had been enough of a stretch.

When the delivery arrived, my tablemates took turns going downstairs to the restroom as I stayed behind, eating and drinking, and talking to not-yet-friends at other tables. Eventually we were done there and, as we split the bill, my desire to pay in cash caused visible annoyance. I reluctantly handed over my bank card, quickly calculating in my head that there was indeed enough money for my galivanting à la Français.

As we wrapped things up, the booted Californian reveler, asked if we were going to Raoul's. Her friend said she was headed home. I looked at my calendar and noticed that I was never again planning to have another day like this one, so off I went with my hobbley friend, a few blocks away to Raoul's.

What, I wondered, was going on with the festive atmosphere everywhere on this summer Sunday. I wondered as I allowed my drink to be paid for and told the story of meeting my good friend the lame luggage-toter only hours prior. At this point, I managed to be only on my third drink of the day, but it was time to go. The west coast crutch lady, in the least stable version of herself yet, managed to get herself into a taxi, and I waited by the door for a car that seemed to be coming from very far away.

There was a couple seated at the bar near the door. The young lady told me I looked familiar and I joked that she had probably seen me on TV. I've been on TV before, but I am recognizable to no one because of it. It didn't take her long to realize that she had indeed seen me on the screen. She was studying at Columbia University where I had recently been featured in a documentary about homebirths by a journalism student. We laughed as I told her that it was a good thing I hadn't been doing anything embarrassing. On this atypical Sunday, I had been my typical self, and I dare say, there's nothing shameful in that.

‡‡‡‡‡‡

Many thanks to all of you who read my tales
in the beginning, and in the middle and end too.
Those of you who nudged me on Tuesdays when I
hadn't yet posted got this book published.

‡‡‡‡‡‡

www.ingramcontent.com/pod-product-compliance
Lightning Source LLC
Chambersburg PA
CBHW020442130626
46549CB00001B/258